Shadow Echo Me

Shadow Echo Me

The Life and Times of
Captain Thomas Wiggin
1601–1666

THE MAKING OF AMERICAN VALUES

Joyce Elaine Wiggin-Robbins

Library of Congress Control Number:		2016904515
ISBN:	Hardcover	978-1-5144-7698-7
	Softcover	978-1-5144-7697-0
	eBook	978-1-5144-7696-3

Print information available on the last page.

Rev. date: 03/28/2016

To order additional copies of this book, contact:
Xlibris
1-888-795-4274
www.Xlibris.com
Orders@Xlibris.com
734177

CONTENTS

Dedications

To the memory of my parents
Arthur J. Wiggin and Vera K. Babb

The love of my children
Arthur Ralph Mullis
Katherine Lee (Mullis) Van Leuven

The future of my grandchildren
Kailey Ryan (Van Leuven) Tanner
Krystin Rae (Van Leuven) Miner

And the generations to come, beginning with
Madisyn Elise Tanner
Savannah Krystin Tanner
Charlotte Sterling Tanner

The Wiggin Memorial Stone[1]—as it's affectionately known in Stratham, New Hampshire—is found in the family burial plot at Sandy Point and was placed there by a descendant in the early twentieth century, probably before 1920. The dates indicate the years Captain Thomas Wiggin was a resident on the Squamscott[2] Patent, Dover, until 1638, and then on Squamscott to his death in 1666. His death date is off by a year—an innocent mistake by the engraver. The stone does not signify the location of his grave.

The settlement of Squamscott was founded in 1638 and was incorporated as a formal township named Stratham in 1716. It celebrates its 300th anniversary in 2016.

---

1 Stratham Heritage Commission, Wallace Stewart photo, used by permission

2 Squamscott is a name with variant spellings. Early on it was Quamscott and Captain Wiggin called his house Quamscott House. So watch for the variant and know it's one and the same.

Acknowledgments

Without one ancestor who came before us—who walked in the *shadows*, listened to the *echoes*, and became the *me* they were meant to be—there would be no *us*. (J. Robbins)

We are not islands unto ourselves, and this book would never have come to be without the generosity of so many people. Some of these people I have worked with for years, and they have never let me down.

Shadow began as a result of over forty years of research and wondering what to do with all the data. In the beginning, computers were in their fledgling stages and were not a very safe place to store data, so the file cabinets and bookshelves grew to unbelievable sizes. By 1990, my children installed a computer in my home as a way to fight my boredom of being housebound and caring for aging parents. My daughter remarked to her "Papaw" (my husband, Robby), "There, Papaw, you'll never have to buy her another thing. She has it all." After two decades, he's still laughing about that one as I begin to wear out my fifth computer. At one point, before tabs, I had four of them humming all at once.

My admiration, love, and gratitude go to so many:

- William (Robby) Thomas Robbins, my husband, without whose support I would never have started this project.
- My son, Arthur R. Mullis, has been my traveling partner and photographer in England and America as he continues to win awards for his eye through the camera lens.
- My daughter, Katherine L. Van Leuven, my editor and formatting authority who also designed the cover for this book. She deserves more credit than I can give here. Katherine has a degree in mass communications/advertising and is a real bonus for any writer.
- Peter Ernest Wiggin of Stratham, New Hampshire. *Shadow* is also the result of encouragement by Peter to record all my research, including what we call "my Devine interventions" along that research trail.

Peter—who is the same age as my son, Arthur—has been my right hand as we became genealogy detectives bouncing off brick walls, digging up bones, and developing a personal history for Captain Wiggin built on solid evidence. Peter was always ready with his camera, as a tour guide, with arranging for a riverboat (piloted by his brother Bruce) for a day on the river, advice, and so much more.

- Bill Wiggin (William David Wiggin, son of Sir Jerry Wiggin), member of Parliament, London, who so graciously gave of his time whenever I needed it. In 2007, when I fell in Westminster Palace, shattering my left arm, Bill sat with me and my son, Arthur, in the hospital. Our visit was cut short, but the friendship has endured. Bill has become a cousin in many ways.
- Carlos Wiggen, Switzerland, e-mailed his way right into my life. Carlos is an author of some renown in Europe who has done a lot of research on the surname *Wiggen* (and variants), and he so graciously shared his manuscript findings and translations with me. To this day, we remain fast friends.
- My unending thanks go to Rev. Dr. Anthony V. Upton and his wife, Dr. Penny Upton, of Warwickshire for their time and efforts with my search of the English clergy databases. Accomplished writers, lecturers, and researchers in their own right, both have been so helpful with the religious records that were foreign to my American brain. Dr. Penny Upton has contributed to this work through her thesis on the fabric of Warwickshire churches. The mystery of Captain Wiggin's father, Vicar William Wigan, was unraveled due in part to the assistance of this husband-and-wife team.
- To Wendy Goldman-Rohm, a teacher with a New York Times Best-Selling background who taught me the value of a matrix with a "hook." Wendy (Rohm Literary Agency) has spent a lot of agonizing hours online with me, teaching me to channel my characters' conversations based on historical fact—to breathe life into them. Don't ever let anyone tell you putting conversation into the mouths of seventeenth-century people is easy. Watch for a sequel to this book titled *Shadow Echo Me: The Man in the Scarlet Suit.*
- My professional researcher, Mike Day (Mayday Genealogy, Twickenham, England), has been so accurate in finding original documents in London. One of Mike's finds opened a whole new knowledge base on who my ancestor was.
- To all those individual researchers who have contributed to my knowledge and notes, I was so blessed to have you even if for a short time.

- My father, Arthur J. Wiggin (1912–2005), who set me off on this journey in 1990 with a handwritten genealogy and notes on our ancestors, was a giant in my life. Even death, at age 93 in 2005, did not take him from me. Today, he's still pointing the way.
- My mother, Vera K. Babb Wiggin (1915–1991), never knew about this work as her progression into the depths of dementia robbed her of cognizance. She became one of the main characters in *Shadow Echo Me: The Man in the Scarlet Suit* as we struggled to cope with her daily needs as well as her decline.
- My two granddaughters, who have grown into such lovely young ladies, were so loved by my parents. When she could not understand anything else, Mother always related to her two young great-granddaughters. Kailey earned her degree in education, has married, and has three daughters of her own. Krystin, the younger granddaughter, was a history major in college. She has earned her masters degree and has recently married. I have no doubt that Krystin will become the next historian of this family.

It is for the children that I undertook this work. I loved my grandparents with all my being, and I wanted the children to remember not only their Papaw and me, but my parents as well. One ancestor just led to another.

My thanks to archivists all over England, some of whom still live in my computer:

- Margaret, Archivists Bristol Record Office
  Bristol, Gloucestershire, England
- Patrick Denney, Secretary, Society Merchant Ventures
  Bristol, Gloucestershire, England
- Eve McLaughlin, Author of the McLaughlin Guides for Family Historians
  Secretary, Bucks Genealogical Society, England
- Naomi Herbert, Librarian's Assistant
  St. John's College, Cambridge, England
- Mithra Tonking, Lichfield Diocesan Archivists, England
- Mark Twissell, City Services
  St. Mary's Guildhall, Coventry, United Kingdom
- Robin Whittaker, Archives Manager and Diocesan Archivists
  Worcestershire Record Office, England
- Nick Fry, Record Office, Archives and Local Studies, United Kingdom
- Paul Newman, Senior Archivists, Cheshire Record Office
- Di Cooper, Archivists Lichfield Cathedral

And to the private researchers who have given me so much of their time:

- Louise Bouchard, a cousin whose generosity goes beyond description and whose encouragements with this book are unsurpassed. Her expertise with reading Old English was to be called upon many times. Her trips to the Massachusetts archives were endless, and I owe her so much.
- Linda Scriven, whose home we invaded for editing sessions and a bottle of wine. You are a tolerant lady who has taught me a lot on our trips to Salt Lake City to do research. Thanks for being my traveling companion for so many years.
- Debbie Wilson, a cousin who has become like a sister to me and whose friendship shall last a lifetime. She's ten times over a Wiggin.
- Judy Lester, for her expertise on her hometown of London, England.
- Ann Allen, a private Gibbs researcher.
- Jimmy Scammon of Stratham, New Hampshire, private researcher and historian.
- The Stratham New Hampshire Historical Society members who have given me their ears and eyes for so long; you are cherished.
- To my cousins (Linda Hoban, Elaine Chase, Sharon Morrill, Brian Wiggin) and my aunts (Frances Hackett and Marion David) who shared information whenever I asked for it. I'm blessed by you.

Introduction

My involvement with Joyce's quest began over a decade ago, when we crossed paths in a world as new to us then as New England was to Thomas Wiggin in 1630. We crossed paths digitally in a cyberspace world of which without we would have transitioned from this earthly realm never having known each other. When we first met Joyce, she was living in Florida, busy with the care of her aging parents, and I was in New Hampshire busy with work and raising a daughter.

In the beginning, our orbits brought us in close proximity many times, but we never chanced upon each other. It wasn't until a friend and client of mine happened to notice a posting on the Internet and mentioned it to me, and I looked into it, that I sent off a brief e-mail introducing myself and my interest. Her response was immediate and is as fresh in my mind today as it was then. "Peter," she said, "I've always known you were out there but just didn't know how to reach you." It was then, at that moment, that the cyber-affair began in our quest to more clearly understand this ancestor of ours and the life and times in which he lived. Captain Thomas Wiggin would become the basis of this extended family relationship that would bring two "geno-orphans" back together after almost four hundred years. It can truly be said of us that it was the enigma of a man, Captain Thomas Wiggin, which brought us together.

Throughout this odyssey of ours, we have ping-ponged countless ideas, thoughts, feelings, and facts off each other. Joyce's being those of a tenacious, professional genealogical researcher and mine being those of an avocational historian with a passion for anything seventeenth century. The commonalities we share were immediately recognized in this four-hundred-year-old blood-tie relationship and extreme passion for history. In our quest to explore, discover, and define just exactly who this enigma named Thomas Wiggin was, we would discover who we were.

Joyce's visit to New Hampshire in 2012 was as carefully and meticulously planned by her as the research that she has done. During her visit, we were fortunate to be able to spend a day on the very body of water that Captain Thomas would have sailed, the bays and Piscataqua River. With my brother Bruce piloting his twenty-four-foot Eastern, we spent an entire day retracing

Thomas Wiggin's trips on this water highway. Bruce's boat is comparable in size to one the Captain would have used to navigate the lengthy, shallow inland waterways reaching the site of Quamscott House, the location of Captain Thomas's first recorded "farm" and "dwelling house."

This daylong trip from Portsmouth (the lower plantation) up to today's Dover and Stratham (the upper plantation) allowed us the luxury of experiencing firsthand the size, scope, length, and breadth of the geography that surrounded Thomas Wiggin in the seventeenth century. Little of the geography has changed since then, although the shoreline is now dotted with many more dwelling houses, and bridges link many of the opposite shores. But other than that, it remains almost identical.

Perhaps the greatest benefit realized through these forthcoming books is that any individual with unbridled focused passion, which allows them to think outside the box, and a network of others in place to collaborate with, can result in a work which becomes not only a benchmark but a stepping-off point for further study.

It is my sincere hope that the creation of *Shadow Echo Me: The Life and Times of Captain Thomas Wiggin, 1601–1666,* will inspire others. It has been an honor for me as an avocational historian to have been a participant in this process—a unique process resulting in what I consider to be one of, if not the most focused, well-researched topic of our time.

Hopefully, others—through their mere passion of the subject and utilization of today's technological resources—may find the courage to put either their thoughts into words or collaborate with others who do. The ability now to reside in the comfort of one's home and reach out—not only across an eastern seaboard, but across the globe in search of information which substantiates formerly vague facts—is an infectious incentive for the nonprofessional. Once begun, it becomes infinitely easier for an author to make the time to do even more. The reinforcement of these remote creative passions can only be a benefit to any profession or study.

No longer is written history or any other subject relegated to only those with lengthy professional credentials, those who win, those who survive, or those who rule the day. Through tenacious research made easier by utilizing today's technologies, which is everywhere at our fingertips, spurred on by a passion for a subject, great works can be created. Works that will cause others to think more openly about established norms.

Regards,
Peter E. Wiggin
Stratham, NH
March 2015

*The following two maps are the works of Peter Wiggin, who has so graciously given them for insertion in this book to help the reader pinpoint where the early grants were located.

Hilton 1629[3]

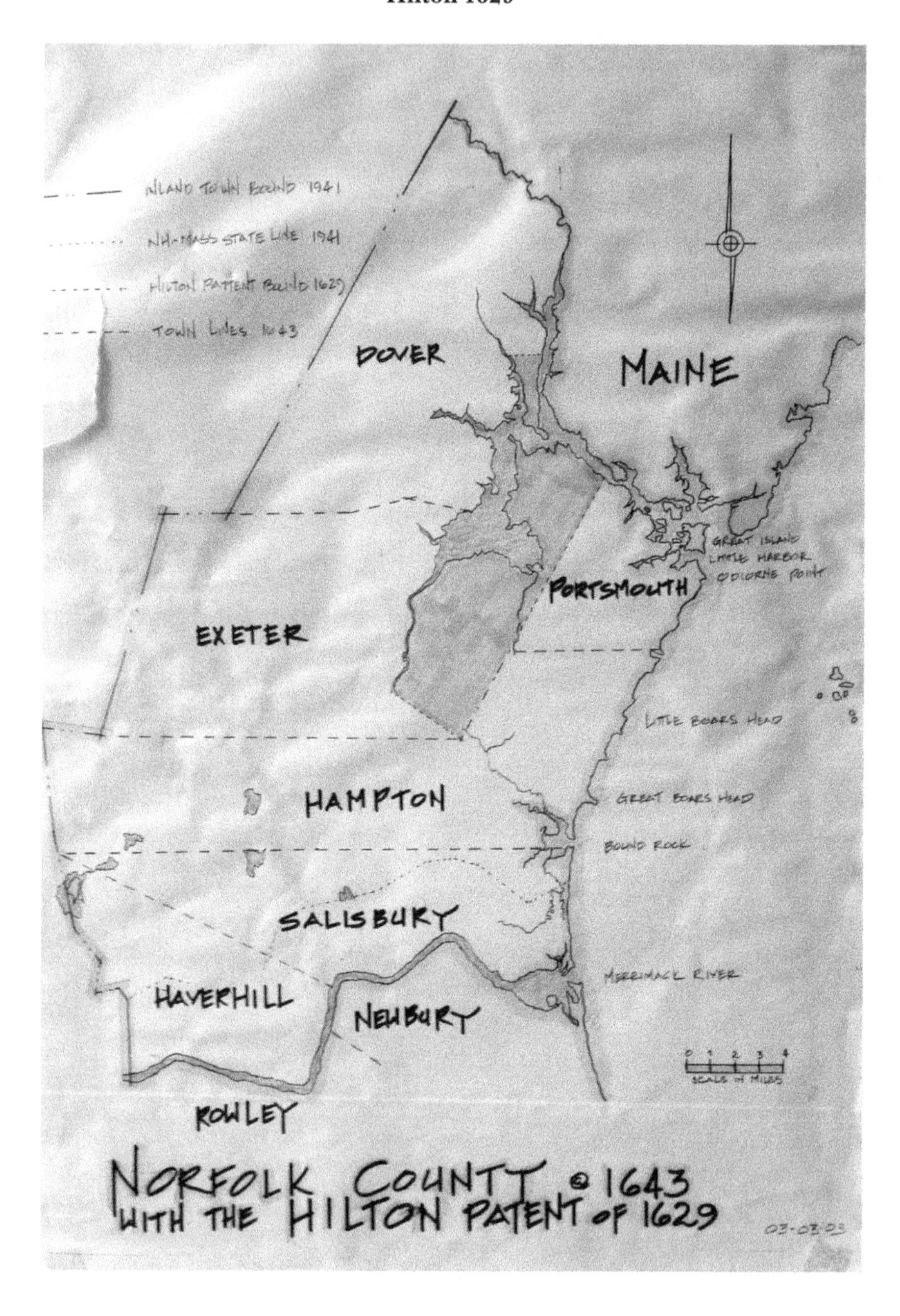

---

[3] 1629 Dover Map drawn by Peter Wiggin of Stratham, NH

Wiggin Plantation[4]

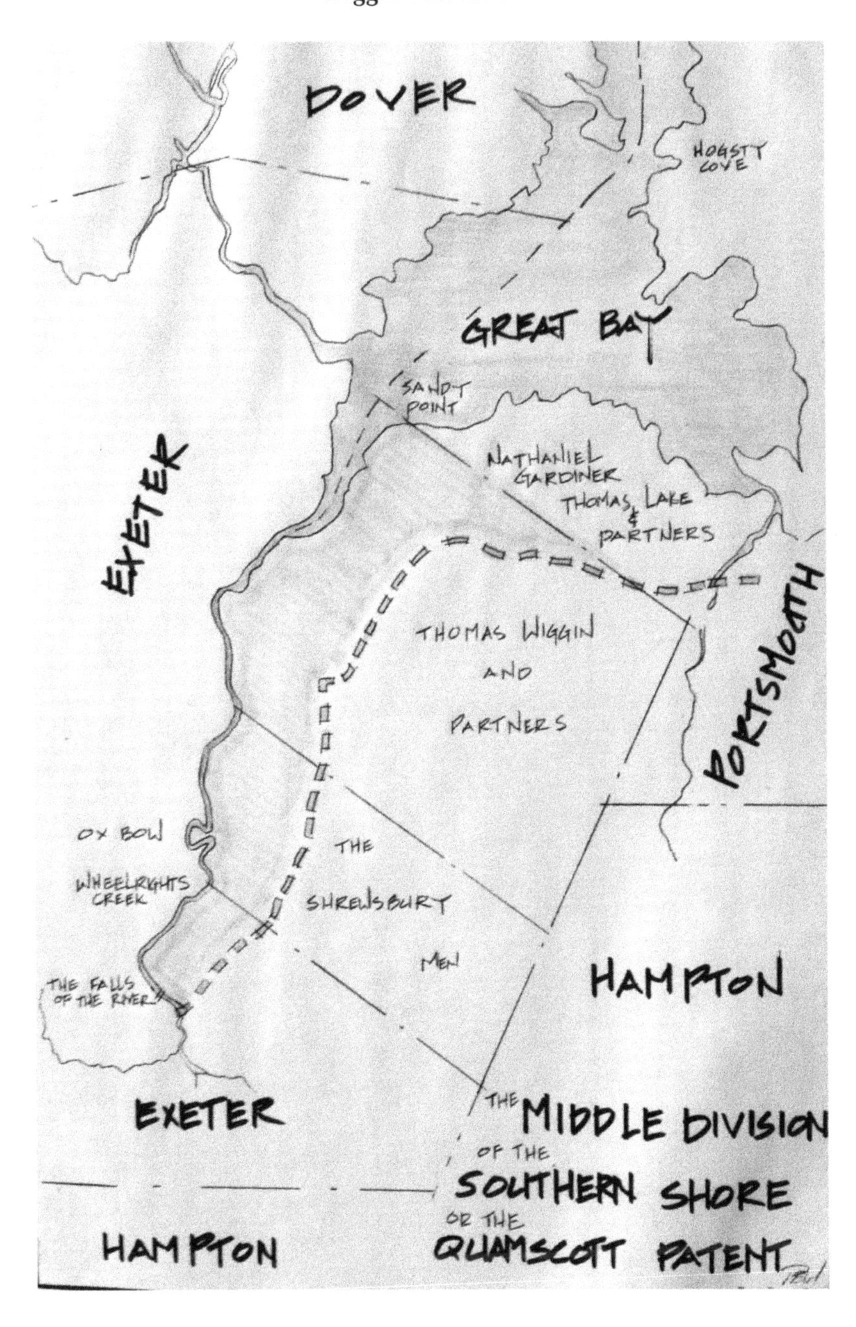

4 Wiggin Plantation, Squamscott, Map drawn by Peter Wiggin of Stratham, NH

First Planting of New Hampshire Piscataqua Patents[5]

It is not my intent here to champion anyone's cause in determining the boundaries of these controversial patents/grants nor the date of those grants. John S. Jenness[6] took the controversy a step further towards understanding the patents by drawing and coloring these two maps. Because I had such a time finding them I want to preserve them by including them in this book. For the new student of Wiggin genealogy, the Bloody Point land was claimed by Hilton settlers early on and became contested as not being a part of the original Hilton Grant. The incident at Bloody Point between Captain Thomas Wiggin and Captain Walter Neale was over who had title to that land. These two maps are an attempt by Jenness to point out the locations of the various grants. A student of the early grants, patents or plantations would do well to study the Avalon Project archives.[7]

The following two maps are referred to in numerous documents. It took a decade to find the maps themselves. The maps are in color so for purposes of this book, which is printed in black and white, I have labeled each section so I can identify them for readers.

---

5 Town charters granted within the present limits of New Hampshire, Vol XXV. Town Charters, Volume II; New Hampshire, Governor and Council; Concord: Edward N. Pearson, public printer, 1895 with John Jenness, 1827-1879, Notes on the first planting of New Hampshire and on the Piscataqua patents. Contributors: Batchellor, Albert Stillman, 1850-1913; John Scribner Jenness, 1827-1879; Massachusetts; Published by Edward W. Pearson, Public Printer in 1895. The two maps are found in the Appendix section.

6 John Scribner Jenness, b. 1827, d. 1879; Son of Richard Jenness and Caroline Jenness.; Lived in Rockingham County, New Hampshire his whole life and is buried in Portsmouth, New Hampshire.

7 Yale Law School, Lillian Goldman Law Library, The Avalon Project, Documents in Law, History and Diplomacy, 127 Wall Stree, New Haven, CT 06511. Avalon.Law.yale.edu.

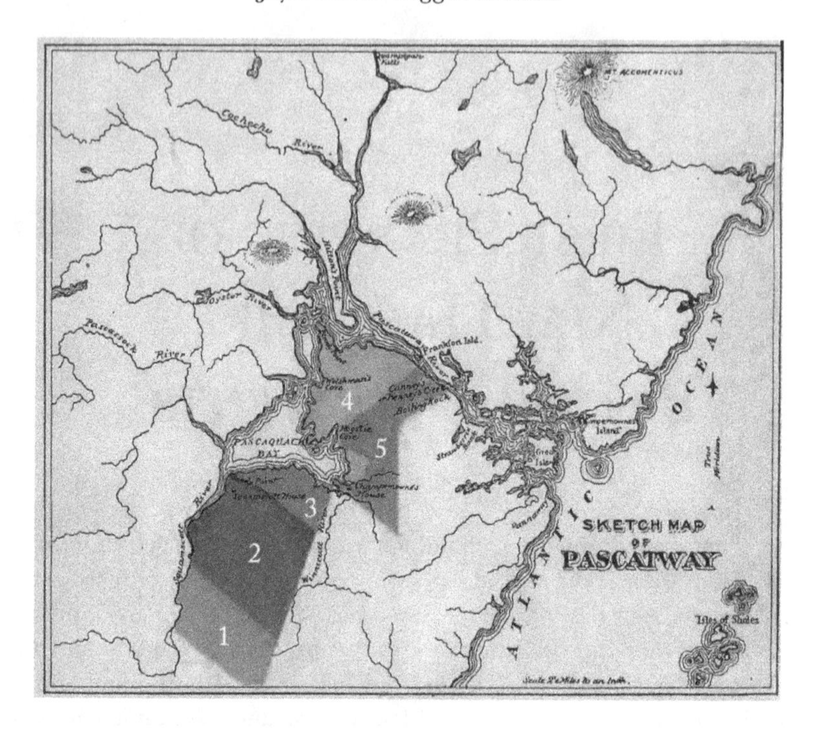

Sections comprising the Squamscott Patent[8]

Key to original colors:

1. Yellow: The Shrewsbury Men
2. Blue: Known as the 'second division' to Captain Thomas Wiggin and partners
3. and 5 Green: 'third division' Grant to Gardiner, Lake and partners
4. Red: Known as 'first division' Granted to Dover and confirmed to that township in 1641 by law of the Massachusetts General Court when the Hilton Patent was put under their jurisdiction

[8] As described in the Report of Committee on Partition, May 22, 2656, Provincial and State Papers, Volume 25, p.707

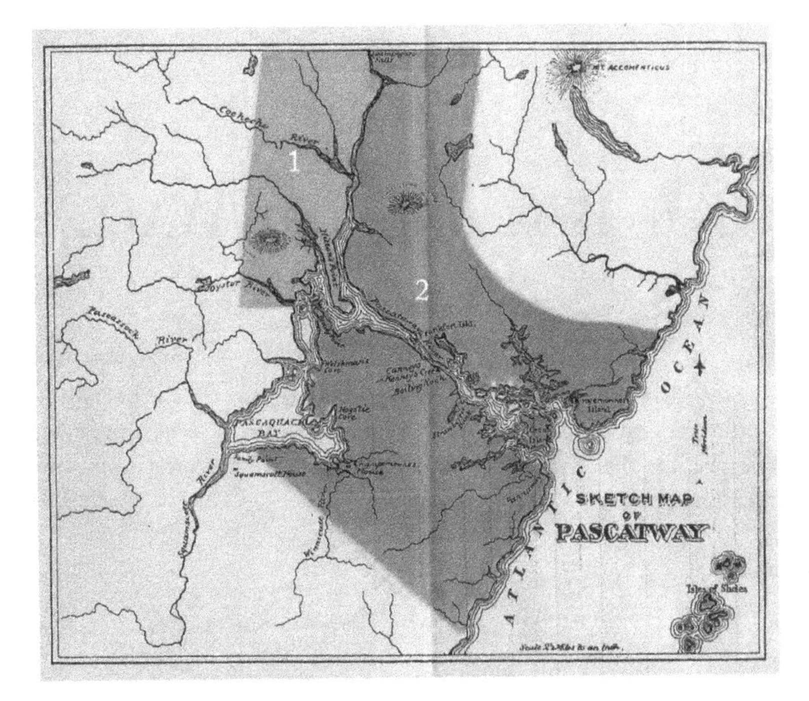

Section comprising the Piscataway Patent[9]

The Piscataway Patent is shown in Green. "Granted on 3 November 1631 to Sr. Firrdinado Gorges & Captain Mason & Others." This grant "on a comparison of Hilton's Patent with it shows that there is not the slightest conflict between them. The Piscataway Grant expressly mentions and locates the Hilton Plantation and carefully excludes it from the conveyance."[10] Jenness maintains the settlers of Hilton's Patent usurped the land, across the water from Dover Point, known as Bloody Point. He says they needed pasture and this section of land fit the bill. He says, "We may be morally certain that these patents did not conflict at all with each other…"

Key to original colors:

1. Red: Hilton's Patent dated 1629,
2. Green: Piscataqua Patent. To Gorges and Mason (and others) dated 1631

---

9 As described in the Provincial papers, Documents and Records Relating to the Province of New Hampshire, Vol 25, Library of New Hampshire, Albert Stillman Batchellor, Editor; Concord 1895; the Appendix page 687.

10 Jenness' explanation in the Appendix, page 679, of the book as described in note 4.

The Box and The Wall

You will see me writing about "the box," and I want to get across to you one huge step forward in your research. Get out of those boxes, especially where dates and names are concerned. Accept that as you go back in time, just from one generation to the next, names and dates will change. Vowels come and go, pronunciations change with regional dialects, and dates are easily confused.

Calendars

- 45 BC: Julius Caesar reformed the Roman calendar. He introduced a leap year every four years.
- 1582: The Gregorian (Pope Gregory XIII) calendar took effect and is used worldwide today. It too has a leap year every four years for adjustment purposes.
- From 1087 to 1155, the English year began on 1 January.
- From 1155 to 1751, the English year began on 25 March.
- From 1752 to present, it began on 1 January.

Dates are not nearly as confusing as vowels. Vowels are subject to area dialect, education of the scribe, and a host of other reasons. This is why we find the name *Wiggin* spelled in so many different ways. I can't count the number of times I've heard, "Oh, but our surname didn't have an 's' on it." If someone can't accept that final "s" as being a mobile version of the surname, how are you going to explain the vowels bouncing all over the place? I stopped counting after logging twenty-seven variations of the surname *Wiggin*. You will find a will in the seventeenth century spelled differently by the scribe than by the person signing it. A good example is Vicar William Wiggin's will, which is filed in the probate records as "Wigan" even though he signed it "Wiggin." The same goes for his wife, Elen Sambrooke Wiggin, whose name goes through so many changes, it's hard to follow. She is found as "Helen," "Ellen," and "Elen," while *Sambrooke* is listed as "Sambroke" and "Sambrook." She signs her will as *Ellen Wiggen*.

Another box to jump right out of is the family stories and legends. I'm fairly confident in assuming you have all heard the old family story of two brothers who came over to America, one going north and one south, and not liking each other very much, the southern brother put an "s" on his name. You will find this legend in nearly every surname you research. Keep in mind that in decades past, hundreds of years past, there was no TV or movies and storytelling was a form of entertainment. Those stories persist even down to today. Laugh at those stories and then throw them away. You will deny yourself a lot of correct data on your ancestor by latching onto these stories.

Next, watch out for the box labeled "birth dates," "marriage dates," "death dates," and so forth. That one will trap you in the worst way possible. Accept that most dates are given by someone other than the person they relate to. Allow that it may be way off. Death dates and records are given by anyone from a neighbor, a preacher, the local sheriff, or a surviving family member no matter how distant. The same goes for old census reports. The census taker might have gotten his data from a neighbor, clerk of the court, sheriff, postmaster, or who knows.

One of the things I found I had to stick to was accumulating at least three different sources on any date to just begin to trust it. Christening dates don't hint at a birth date; maybe he was an adult before he was christened. Birth dates and christening dates are seldom the same. Remember too that a date on a will signifies nothing other than the person was alive on that date. Even a probate date does not signify the death date. Sometimes you have to make an educated guess or use the "about" or "between" variable.

Names often take such unrelated forms that we find them difficult to follow. As an example, the place Captain Thomas Wiggin chose to settle in was called Quamskooke by the native Indians, and the Captain called it Quamscott. Andrew, his son, called it Squamscott. Place names were an evolution based on dialect, just like surnames.

Walls are not nearly as difficult to scale as that box is to climb out of. Most walls will crumble with time. You will create more walls by being in a box than you ever dreamed of. Once you find out how to avoid boxes, then walls will never rear their ugly heights.

If you read something that's hard to grasp, perhaps a theory you've never considered before, throw aside your mental block regarding it and keep reading. Give a new idea time to ferment and see how well it sets after time.

I hope I have listed all the variables for you, but if you should know of one I didn't list, go with it too.

PREFACE

WHO HE WAS

I have a little shadow that goes in and out with me,
And what can be the use of him is more than I can see.
He is very, very like me from the heels up to the head,
And I see him jump before me when I jump into my bed.
—Robert Lewis Stevenson

People moving into New England in the seventeenth century were representatives of a restless nature that would go on until the American Revolution. There is nothing mysterious about these immigrants. New England was not a place to find refuge from a secret past, nor did they; if they had a troubled past in England, it soon caught up to them in New England.

Dream ships sailed into a prosperous future on a handful of promises that, for many, would never come true. Everyone was welcomed somewhere in New England, and there were soon no strangers among them.

Money was important as a measure of wealth, along with breeding, but land was even more important in New England. There was so much of it to be taken and tamed. With the Native American population decimated by acquired European diseases the English had little resistance to claiming whatever land they wanted.

Many of New England's settlers go unaccounted for prior to their arrival on these shores just because they were men doing their chosen jobs and not rocking any boat. They do not appear in court cases, government records, and in most cases, don't even appear in deeds of land transfers in England. Even church records of births, marriages, and deaths may not provide answers because of the commonality of given names and surnames. Sixteenth- and seventeenth-century English families were not very original when it came to naming their issue, using the same naming pattern for generations down every branch of the tree.

The vast majority of people calling themselves researchers today simply look on the computer to see what someone else has found. Thus, erroneous data goes around and around, likely never corrected without herculean effort. As an example, you will find Captain/Governor Thomas Wiggin, described as a "sea captain" and as "a common folk, farmer, Puritan, and so forth" without any source references simply to make a story fit. I call it "cutting off the toes to make a shoe fit."

Shadow Echo Me began as a result of decades of research and wondering what to do with all the data I had accumulated. In the beginning, computers were in their fledgling stages and not a very safe place to store data, so the file cabinets and bookshelves grew to unbelievable sizes. By the early 1990s, my children installed a computer in my home as a way to fight my boredom of being housebound while caring for aging parents[11]. Before the invention of additional screen tabs allowing more than one page on a computer screen, I'd have four computers humming all at the same time.

Shadow is also the result of encouragement by Peter Wiggin of Stratham, New Hampshire, to record all my research, including what we call "my Devine interventions." Peter—who is the same age as my son, Arthur—has been my right hand as we became genealogy detectives bouncing off brick walls, digging up bones, and developing a personal history for Captain Wiggin built on solid evidence.

So why did it take me over thirty years to be comfortable enough with my research to declare which of the dozens of men named Thomas Wiggin was Captain Thomas Wiggin of New Hampshire? I found 154 men with that name, all over England, covering a twenty-year period of birth dates. Systematically I worked through every single man named Thomas Wiggin to narrow down the possibilities.

Talk about herculean tasks. Every single Thomas Wiggin had to eliminate himself with ongoing church records of birth, death, and marriage; the ones left after that had to be researched in records of apprenticeship, education, occupation, family wills, and so much more for elimination.

The Thomases left on the short list were then researched according to pedigrees, opportunity, and criteria supporting all the known actions of Captain Thomas Wiggin after 1627.

I used a technique called regression analysis (often used in the accounting world to format budgets) as the criteria for my research. Take a sourced fact and

---

11 My next book, Shadow Echo Me, The Man in the Scarlet Suit, covers the struggles of caring for aging parents and dementia of any sort. The book has an alternating matrix so Captain Wiggin has a chapter, then a chapter in my home so that in the end you will see that the centuries may come and go but people don't change that much.

find all the variables that change or modify that fact. Most of the facts would self-destruct, and what I was left with began to form a pattern.

What a dream it would have been if I could say he was Thomas Wiggin of London, born 1592. However, that Thomas never left London. He also didn't possess the credentials or knowledge to carry out the activities in New England that we find Captain Thomas Wiggin performing with ease. It was a wonderful and interesting journey, tracking this London clan back to their roots in Lancashire. He was but one Thomas I did the same thing with, traveling back in time.

There were two more men named Thomas Wiggin born in 1592: one in Oxfordshire and one in Durham. Neither of those two left their homes either and were traced in church records showing birth, marriage, and death records during the time the Captain was in New England. These three were the only Thomas Wiggins born in England in 1592.[12]

After eliminating Thomas of London, I was left with Thomas of Warwickshire, Northamptonshire, and a couple of other counties. I was not comfortable with Thomas of Warwickshire for a good ten years, until I had so many documents substantiating a preponderance of the evidence, making him a sound choice. Still, I continued to collect records, just waiting for those puzzle pieces to fall into place. My final lock-in pieces came during a trip to London in 2007. Securing copies of the two 1632 letters attributed to his pen, with hours of research at the English National Archives in Kew, including sessions with their resident archivists.

Thomas Wiggin was born in Bishop's Itchington, Warwickshire, in 1601 to William Wigan/Wiggin and Ann Gybbes. Ann was an heiress in her own right, born into a prominent Warwickshire family. William Wiggin[13] (and he signs his will with that spelling) was a vicar and a clerk in Warwickshire churches following his assignment as vicar in a church supported by Sir Christopher Wray, chief justice of England. Wray was Wiggin's patron at his ordination in Cheshire.

Thomas had a sad and probably restless childhood with the death of his mother, Ann Gybbes Wiggin, soon after the birth of her last child (a son in 1603) when Thomas was only two years old. Due to overwhelming evidence, I believe Thomas was apprenticed to his grandfather Thomas Gybbes/Gibbs, for whom he was named.

In support of Thomas Wiggin's birthright, I will present pedigrees showing his birth connections along with supporting associations and activities,

---

12 A birth date estimated from his second marriage intention record of 1633 submitted by a bondsman of London, England.

13 To further complicate my research, the Thomas of London had a father named William too.

especially in London during his apprenticeship years. His London years support his connection to the Whiting family, the lords and ladies of shipping and commodities, where he gained knowledge of the New World.

Thomas Wiggin's steady nature, innate sense of timing, and knowledge of commerce, surveying, networking, and farming will serve him well. Thomas is a strong and just man and will be highly honored by those around him as he helps to build the foundation of a new nation.

The adulthood and character of his two sons is also a testament to the Captain's own character. It gives us a peek behind the walls of a home life that no record could ever portray. A sense of propriety, truth, and trust that he handed down to his two sons were parts of his character too.

Captain Wiggin's influence on New Hampshire's early history and its ongoing path to independent statehood in a new nation was readily absorbed and held to a high standard for decades to come. While his birth remained shrouded in mystery, his life in New Hampshire did not.

Why He Came

By the early seventeenth century, Europe[14] has become destabilized on several fronts, but the most devastating to its society was the Protestant Reformation. Up until this time, there was no religious freedom anywhere in the world, and there wasn't going to be religious freedom in early New England either. King Henry VIII's separation from the Catholic Church and creation of the Church of England did little to change people's behavior. Even though church attendance was required by law, in New England[15] as well as Old England, the records are full of charges against citizens who did not attend church.[16] Some were even burned at the stake as heretics in England for not adhering to the edicts of the church. The whole religious upheaval by Henry VIII was never meant to release his subjects from church control, but the movement of reform and separation from the church had begun. The rise of the Puritan movement—those who wanted change within the church—would create a whole new society and add purpose to a migration that had already begun for economic reasons.

Puritanism was a huge risk—a risk in ways modern man cannot even fathom. Puritanism would topple a king and test the very values of English society as a whole.

For centuries, the populations of Europe were controlled by the Catholic Church in every single matter of their lives. These were basically uneducated peasant people who were not stupid, just not formally educated or "thinkers." They were followers for good reason. If things went wrong in their world (crops failed, loved ones died), then it was God's will and did not result from anything

---

14 While a lot of reading went into the research of European and English history, my favorite authority has become the work of Anthony F. Upton, "Europe 1600–1789," which he wrote while an emeritus professor of modern history at the University of St. Andrews, Scotland, 2001; ISBN 0 340 66337 5 (bb); Oxford University Press Inc. NY, NY.

15 Court records are full of early New England men who were working on Sunday, "tipping" (drinking), or just not attending church. It was a serious offense to skip church three Sundays in a row.

16 *Book of Martyrs*, shocking records of the trials of "heretics," written by John Foxx (1517–1587).

they themselves had done. By not making decisions, or being freethinkers, they were able to place the blame on the Catholic Church, or God, for any disasters that befell them. It was never their fault crops failed or someone died; it was the will of God. Life was much simpler that way. These seventeenth-century people are not to be blamed for their way of life. They were ruled by an elite class who controlled them through the use of religion.[17]

Religion and marriage were ties that bound European nations together and identified them as the core of Christendom. Royalty married royalty, which strengthened ties between nations. Even while England warred with Spain and France, King James was seeking a wife for his son amongst their royal families. Not until 1648 would Europe move toward a diversity of religions that would become irreversible.[18] Until the continent of Europe became stable, England wouldn't be either.

Great Britain would eventually lead the way into a capitalistic-generated world economy so powerful it would sustain losing the American colonies. But losing those colonies would be for the same economic reasons the English settlers came to America in the first place. Some things just never change, because from century to century, people do not change enough.

The impetus to move into a capitalistic society was a combination of internal strife leading to civil war in England; heavy taxation of its people to pay for conflicts with Europe; a population of people struggling to survive; crop failures, due in part to the Little Ice Age; and plagues. Merchant earning power had dropped substantially by 1645 with little means for a recovery. History has taught us that when heads of state put all their attention into their military efforts, the general population cannot sustain the supportive load. Great Britain's entire history, even before Roman occupation, was one of conflict with its neighbors. Conflict for the sake of greed, especially by heads of state, cannot sustain itself. The general population will not support it unless basic human needs are being met. It all seems to be a never-ending circle of events.

England's economy in the early seventeenth century was struggling. Ports on the western coast saw their commercial markets in Europe disappear due to military conflicts and were relying on being used as ports for staging the royal fleets for attacks on Spanish and French shipping, military conflicts with Spain in Ireland, or these were being used to send out fleets to the fishing banks of North America. All other trade had dried up. The economy of both Barnstaple (Devon) and Bristol (Gloucester) were plummeting to the point

---

17 *Leviathan or The Matter, Forme and Power of a Common Wealth Ecclesiasticall and Civil* by Thomas Hobbes, 1651, revised and reprinted in 1904. Cambridge University Press, England; available on Google digital books. If you wish to study the church, then this is an excellent resource.

18 The Peace accords of 1648 in Westphalia, Germany.

they could not meet the royal demands for ships, men, and ordnance for its wars, or even find the funds to repair docks and port fixtures. Bristol at one time had rivaled London in commercial port activity, but by the late sixteenth century, the foreign trade had shifted to Eastern European countries and the Port of London. Even the Welsh and Midland's woolen trades had shifted from Bristol to London.

This sort of economy has a rolling effect. Oddly enough, birth rates go up, so marriage ages drop. I suspect parents needed to "relocate" their children as soon as they were old enough because they could not feed them. In Europe, food prices in the early seventeenth century were rising as much as 15 percent a year. Because of crop failures, more people were moving to cities. They were seeking employment but found death by disease. Plagues and other illnesses were taking as much as one-third of the population in a single year.

When basic needs are not being met, people become despondent, and the first thing that comes to mind is "flight." To get away from this, people have to turn their backs and start over. However, the Great Migration of 1630–1640 would be shut down by a king who suddenly realized he was losing his tax base with the migration and pending emigrations of the landed gentry of England. After 1640, for the most part, English subjects were going to remain in England.

Life, Liberty, and The Pursuit of Happiness

Thomas Wiggin was growing up in a world of rules governing his every move. In order to work, he needed an apprenticeship. He was not allowed to marry while in apprenticeship. He would be allowed to work only under the rules of his guild after apprenticeship. Sons might inherit a small amount from their father, unless he was the eldest son, who inherited the lion's share.

There was no such thing as equality, excepting in the class you were born to. If Thomas wanted to advance himself, he had to do it through service to the Crown and recognition by the titled class. England was a class society. It was, in fact, a collection of classes, each governed by separate rules, which all acknowledged a sovereign power. As an example, one of Thomas Wiggin's employers in 1633 was Lord Saye and Sele[19] of Broughton Castle, Oxfordshire. The lord was one of the acknowledged leaders of the Puritan movement and a strong leader in the Midlands during the English Revolution of the mid-1600s. He functioned under a set of rules very different than those affecting Thomas Wiggin's life; and yet, as his employer, the lord held sway over Thomas, which created almost a double set of rules for Thomas to adhere to. He had to fulfill the lord's desires but remain inside his own class rules. Servants who fell into a class below Thomas Wiggin's status had yet another set of rules while serving a man who was bound to his own rules; it was the "trickle-down effect" of the seventeenth century. The poor servant at the bottom of the pile had no freedoms at all, and yet he too acknowledges sovereign powers. Each class, while living within the confines of their particular set of rules, was bound to the other classes for the common good. As Dr. Anthony Upton stated, "chains of patronage, emanating in the last instance from the ruler himself"[20] was the glue that held it all together. Beginning with the ruler, each subsequent class had something the class below it wanted. The sovereign ruler wanted the support

[19] Don't get confused over this title. Saye and Sele is one man from the Fiennes surname. You will read more of him as you progress through this manuscript.

[20] Stated in a letter from Dr. Upton to the author.

of all the classes beneath him, freedom from invasion, and the guardianship of Christianity or Catholicism.

Is it really any different today? We still function on self-imposed rules that make our world run smoothly. We acknowledge the power of our political leaders and our bosses. In a manner of speaking, we place ourselves in a "class" that has its own rules. The difference is we have the freedom of choosing what sort of world we want to live in and what kind of society we are comfortable functioning in, and we accept those rules. We can even change our class, several times. We vote for our political leaders, and if we get it wrong, we get a second chance. We don't have to lop off their heads to create a new society!

In England, the Crown had the power to appoint the county sheriff, the tax collectors, and a variety of other peacekeepers. However, in order to exercise some control, the Crown always put the local landed gentry in these offices because of the respect they held within their counties. Most of these appointed offices were unpaid, and some were held for life. The landed gentry had more monetary worth than the king or queen, and that fact—combined with their status of respect among their county residents—protected them from a lot of harassment by the Crown.

Landholders also included the Church of England. The Church was a huge landlord in the rural counties. The power held by the Church of England often rivaled that of the Crown itself. The Church of England administered what we now call "entitlements" (the equal to today's Medicaid) and care for the poor.

In order to understand why Thomas Wiggin's father was at the two smaller parish churches in Warwickshire, we have to understand the prevailing traditions. Non-inheriting sons often found themselves in the clergy, and sons who were fortunate enough to attend university often ended up in the clergy or were at least ordained. There were other ways to enter the clergy. One Wiggin priest has a record that says he was "brought up in the schools," and yet another says he was "instituted in the church, ordained deacon"—which means he was tied to the church as a gravedigger, carpenter, and so forth, until he was thirty-two years of age and was not allowed to marry. So the church had a hierarchy that rivaled the civilian hierarchy, and obviously, the largest parishes were going to be assigned to those clergy who came from powerful families.

In Summary: Reformation was taking place long before Thomas Wiggin was born, but it was in full swing by the time he was of age. The Puritan movement was not confined to the British Isles; it encompassed all of Europe and Scandinavia. One effect the movement did have on history was a Catholic restructuring and the establishment of the Jesuit Order by the pope. The Jesuits took over education and the re-education of the Catholic population with marked success outside England. However, in England, the Puritan movement would topple a crown by putting so much pressure on King Charles, eroding away the royal powers, and finally taking the country into civil war. Religion and war was once again going hand in hand to topple a king.

The question still remains. Why did Thomas Wiggin leave England? He became the overloaded bearer of too much of life's burdens. Death had ruled his life, apprenticeship had stifled him, and opportunities had dried up. Wiggin was more than ready when he was in the right place at the right time to become an employee of the ranking classes in a place wide open for opportunity and wealth without the birthright to it: New England.

The shadows of his life echo down through the decades, and it's time for all to understand where Captain Wiggin's knowledge came from, where his heart was created, and why he deserves his place in history.

Respectfully,
Joyce Elaine Wiggin-Robbins
2015

Author's Introduction Section I

You can't possibly know a person without some sort of visual image of them and without knowing something of their character. We have some information to build on regarding Thomas Wiggin from records of his actions between 1627 and 1666. He's been described by researchers (remember, they didn't know him either) as staunch, dedicated, loyal, and a no-nonsense sort of person—all this from interpreting his actions regarding the Massachusetts Bay Colony, law on the Piscataqua, and his personal contacts and religion. Nowhere will you find a description of a physical nature regarding eyes, hair, height, and so forth.

Let's disregard, for the time being, the interpretations of those early researchers and go for one of our own. We know him today far better than any of them did, and with all the information at hand, plus what I'm going to give you in the two sections of this book, you should have a far better grasp of who he was. We will breathe life into him and make him a part of history as a human being and not just a record someone else has compiled. We may not have records of "he said, she said," but actions speak louder than words, I believe the old saying goes.

In this first section, I present the pedigrees of his family and his contacts. Each one is important in Wiggin's life as they build his values, education, and even his physical picture. It is from them he learns the lessons in life that will serve him well.

I will address the conventions of dress—costuming if you will—in Section II. Every item worn had a significance and a purpose. Each item told a story of who the person was and from where they came. Dress is far too important to ignore.

So enjoy reading while you learn who Thomas Wiggin's family and connections were.

Family Group Sheet Bishop's Itchington, Warwickshire, England

William Wiggin, born about 1553 and died between 1617 and 1620
Married 21 August 1590
Ann Gybbes, born 18 April 1575 and died about 1603

Issue: (b = born)

1. Katherine Wigan, b. 18 July 1591
2. John Wigan, b. 14 February 1592
3. Edward Wigan, b. 1 February 1594
4. Hannibal Wiggin, b. 15 January 1596
5. William Wiggin Jr., b. 18 February 1598
6. Thomas Wiggin, b. 20 September 1601
7. Rychard Wiggin, b. 1 March 1603

I present to you above the basics of Captain Thomas Wiggin's birth family. It will be greatly expanded in the chapters to come.

Wiggin Family Bible[21]

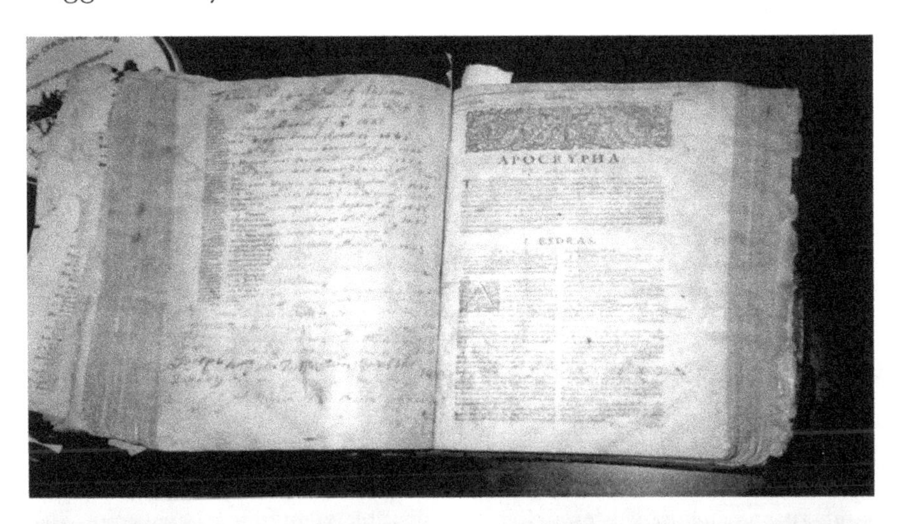

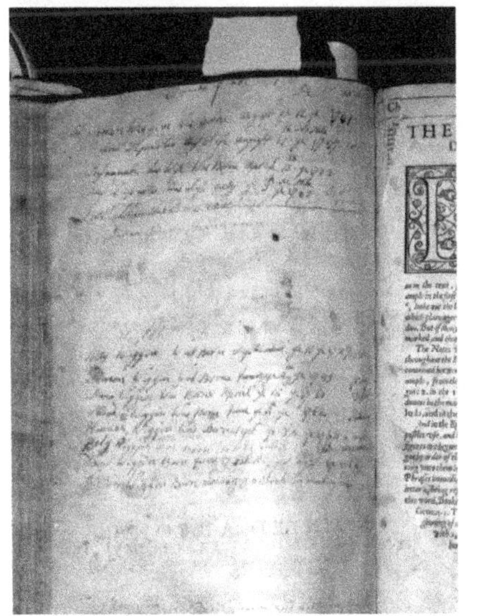

[21] Photos by Peter Wiggin and used with permission

Wiggin Bible[22]

It is not the intention of this manuscript to discuss the virtues or otherwise of religions, especially of Puritanical religion. It was a fact of the time, and the effects of it upon the New Hampshire Wiggin clan were enormous. The first generation of families in New England were stemming from Church of England stock: Pilgrims, Puritans, Catholic, and Quaker . . . perhaps more.

Deposited at the Mormon Repository in Salt Lake, Utah, I found a handwritten genealogy referencing a family Bible belonging to the Captain as *having been preserved.*[23] There was no mention of where this book was.

When I learned about this book, I was keenly interested to see it. Some clue as to the origins of Captain Thomas Wiggin should have been found in it. There are none. The book, first off, isn't a Bible; it's a prayer book. Still, it's very antiquity ought to have rendered some clues as to who he was if he had ever owned it. I do not believe he ever did. It does appear to have come into the possession of someone in the third generation who began recapturing the family history.

Following two years of unending research down each branch of the Wiggin tree from Andrew, son of Captain Thomas Wiggin, I finally found the person who had possession of this book. What a lovely family they are. They are now down to one family heir, and I've urged them to donate the book to the Wiggin Library in Stratham, New Hampshire. Meanwhile, they have sworn my cousin Peter Wiggin of Stratham and me to silence as to its whereabouts. We are the only two people who have viewed this book in decades. The owner is elderly and does not want people knocking on the door to have a peek at it. We were allowed to photograph this book, and while it is not a Bible, as reported, it is historically very interesting and with a lot of handwritten notations in it. Someone about the third or fourth generation down from Andrew has inserted a short pedigree.

There is no history recorded in this book, and it does appear from the handwritings to be the work of several different generations. The handwriting

22 "All photos for this chapter are the work of Peter Wiggin of Stratham.

23 New England Families, Genealogical and Memorial by William Richard Cutter, PG 69.

also indicates that someone in about the third or fourth generation started the recordings and didn't elucidate on either Andrew or his father, Thomas Wiggin.

Written on a page preceding the Apocrypha, penned in ink, is "Thomas Wiggin, son of Andrew Wiggin & Hannah his wife." The page is missing about one-fourth of the total area, but what remains is as follows: (Names in parentheses are mine.)

> Thomas Wiggin son of Andrew Wiggin & Hannah his wife:
> (torn) Borne March 28th, 1661 (Thomas)
> (torn)ison Wiggin borne April 17th, 1664 (Simon)
> (torn)nah Wiggin was borne August 10 1666 (Hannah)
> (torn)—Wiggin was borne March 22nd 1667 (Mary)
> (torn) —Wiggin was borne January 6th 1671 (Andrew, Jr.)
> (torn)reet Wiggin was borne September 4th 1674 (Bradstreet)
> (torn) Wiggin was borne 24 March 1677 (Mary)
> (torn)gin was borne September 14th 1678 (Abigail)
> (torn)gin was borne October (or November) 14th 1680 (Dorothy)
> (torn)in was borne January 6th 1683 (Sarah)
> (torn)in borne March 11 1682/3 (Jonathan)

I have added the names in parenthesis for your reference. All the above is in the same handwriting.

On the same page is a listing of descendants starting from the1730s in at least two different handwritings. It appears to be a list of the issue of Simon Wiggin Jr., Lt., b. 12 April 1701, and his wife, Susanna Sherburn. There are two handwritings and the ink has faded, but the names can still be read with the exception of the first two or three entries, where the page has been torn off.

> "Children"
> (torn) borne 4 September 1731 (Betty)
> (torn) born 4 March 1734 (Sarah)
> Susannah born 18 April 1738
> Henry born 8 May 1740
> Thomas born 11 September 1742
> Mary born 19 July 1744
> Joseph born 28 April 1748 (different handwriting)

Below this entry in the original handwriting appears "Joseph Wiggin borne April 28, 1748." *Joseph* is spelled in the old-fashioned way, using *f* for the *s*'s. Sandwiched in between the two entries appears a series of dash marks across the page, followed by the date 1741.

On the blank page prior to "The Printer to the Diligent Reader" appears the following: "Simon Wiggin born August 12, 1701, and departed this life on 11 August 1757. Johannah his wife was borne March 13, 1703 and departed this life July 9, 1763."

In a different handwriting, underneath this entry appears: "Levi Wiggin was born ——" followed by a series of numbers that look like 01 08 ——. Below that, it reads "Simon Wiggin was my ——. (This word could be "Uncle.")

Following that is about a quarter of a page of writings that have faded over the years into unreadable entries. I could only make out the word "Simon."

On the bottom of this page, penned in ink, is the following:

Betty Wiggin born September 10 '57
Simon Wiggin born January 21 '59
Anna Wiggin born April 15 '60
Sarah Wiggin born 321 June '62
Hannah Wiggin born 24 (?) '64
Betty Wiggin born— '66
David Wiggin born June 17 at night '69
John Wiggin born Monday at 9 o'clock (the rest is unreadable)

This list appears to be the issue of Simon Wiggin (1731–1823) and Hannah Marble (1735–1811) as shown in the Wiggin Manuscript (Arthur C. Wiggin, "Wiggin Genealogy," A combination of manuscripts in NH Historical Society).

On the inside cover, and also in the back inside cover, are scribed a lot of signatures of members of the family. Most of them are but faint shadows of the original hand that scribed them. Here's a list of those I could make out:

Arthur C. Wiggin
Charles E. Wiggin
David Wiggin
Simon Wiggin
Henry Taylor Wiggin
Samuel Wiggin
Barker Wiggin

Some names occur more than once.

Mayhem and Intrigue[24]

The fireplace incident, as it's called, took place outside of the dates of my writing for this manuscript, so I will not expound on it with the exception of trying to put this record straight. It is a good example of how the early incidents in the life of the Wiggin men got so scrambled due to naming practices. All too often, dates are ignored and the facts attributed to a name alone.

The fireplace incident has been wrongly recorded by historians and needs to be corrected. It's a colorful tale and often repeated, and yet it points out the problem with giving boy-babies the same name for generations and down every limb of the tree.

The incident in the fireplace intrigued me so much, I sought out the original reports amongst the Provincial Papers of New Hampshire and found them recorded as such:

> 1685 New Hampshire: R. Chamberlain, Justice Peace, makes an order to have Anthony Nutter, of Welshman's Cover, yeoman, to answer for his abetting and aiding *Thomas Wiggin, of Swampscott, yeoman,*[25] in assaulting and wounding Walter Barefoot and Robert Mason.
>
> Coll. N. H. Hist. Soc.,[26] 2 p. 197: a report by Walter Barefoot, Esq., Deputy Governor of the Province made an oath to the effect that "Thomas Wiggins and Anthony Nutter, yeoman" were the two men involved in throwing both Barefoot and "Robert Mason, Esq., proprietor of the Province" into the fireplace over a disagreement regarding Mason's claim to

[24] There is a wonderful drawing rendition of the Fireplace Incident, but as I could never find out who had rights to it, I did not use it. I wrote the publishers who claimed to know nothing about the drawing and didn't have computer information on it.

[25] Note here he is not called "Captain" and is called "yeoman."

[26] Documents and Records Relating to the Province of New Hampshire, 1623-1686, Vol 1; Nathaniel Bouton, D.D., Sec. of the N.H. Historical Society, Concord, pub. George E. Jenks, State Printer, 1867.

> the settlements of New Hampshire via inheritance from his grandfather. Walter Barefoot had suffered two broken ribs and a lost tooth as a result.
>
> Coll. N. H. Hist. Soc., 2, p. 198: Two witnesses, Joan Carter and Wilmot Martin also name the men as Thomas Wiggins, Captain Barefoot, Mr. Mason and Anthony Nutter.
>
> Coll. N. H. Hist. Soc., 2, p. 198: Prudence Gatch made oath to the same names, Thomas Wiggins and Anthony Nutter.
>
> Coll. N. H. Hist. Soc., 2, p. 197: Walter Barefoot, Esq., Deputy Governor of the Province Nutter, yeoman" and he describes the confrontation. Coll. N. H. Hist. Soc., 2, p 195: Robert of New Hampshire also says that "on 30th December last (1685), Thomas Wiggins and John Mason, Esq., proprietor of the Province of New Hampshire" also names "Thomas Wiggins and Anthony Nutter, yeoman".
>
> Joseph Ryan, Attorney General confirms the charges in a statement that follows the last entry. He says, "...therefore pray judgment in behalf of his Majesty", but does not state what that judgment was to be.

Historians have taken these records and run with them. You find so often the claim it was Captain Thomas Wiggin who committed this act. Please note the dates of 1684–85. The Captain died in 1666.

At least one report says it was "Captain Thomas Wiggin, son of the Captain Thomas who came here in 1633" who committed this act. That confuses the reader even more as Thomas Wiggin Jr. (1640–1700) was never called Captain. I don't believe it was Thomas Junior, and here is why. When Walter Barefoote died, he made Thomas Wiggin Jr. and his wife, Sara Barefoote Wiggin, his main heirs. He always seemed to have good relations with them, and if he had suffered so much damage at the hands of his brother-in-law, I doubt seriously Barefoote would have made him an heir.

There are records of Andrew having altercations with John Tufton-Mason, and he even threw Mason into a ditch and took away his pistol and some papers. In 1668, Robert Tufton-Mason took Andrew to court for robbery and for "biting him in the face for pretense of love."

Robert Tufton-Mason was married to Catherine, daughter of Thomas Wiggin Jr. and Sara Barefoote Wiggin. They had three issue: (1) John Tufton, b. 1698 and died 1718 in the Caribbean; (2) Katherine Tufton, b. 1691 and died 1691; (3) Elizabeth Tufton, b. 1695 and died 1767 in Greenland, New Hampshire. Catherine Wiggin was married twice more: to Captain Simon

Wiggin and to Thomas Martin. She had three children with Captain Simon Wiggin: Hannah, b. abt. 1697; Deborah, b. 4 July 1698; and Simon, b. 1701 and died 1757.

Based on this knowledge, I put to you that the offending Thomas Wiggin was Andrew's eldest son, grandson of Captain Thomas Wiggin. This Thomas Wiggin was born 1661 and died 1693; he married Martha Denison and had a daughter, Hannah.

Thomas Wiggin, son of Andrew Wiggin (and Hannah Bradstreet), grandson of Captain Thomas Wiggin, throws both Walter Barefoote and Robert Tufton-Mason into a fireplace after they attempt to forcefully evict him from the Barefoote home.

So the relationship in this incident is correctly stated as:

Walter Barefoote (brother of)

Sara Barefoote who m. Thomas Wiggin Jr. (son of Captain T. Wiggin)

/

Catherine Wiggin (their daughter)

/

Married: Robert Tufton-Mason

Is it any wonder historians had problems keeping these men named *Thomas* straight!

Andrew Wiggin m. Hannah Bradstreet

/

Thomas Wiggin (their firstborn son)

/

Threw Robert Tufton-Mason and Walter Barefoote into the fireplace

Warwickshire County Map[27]

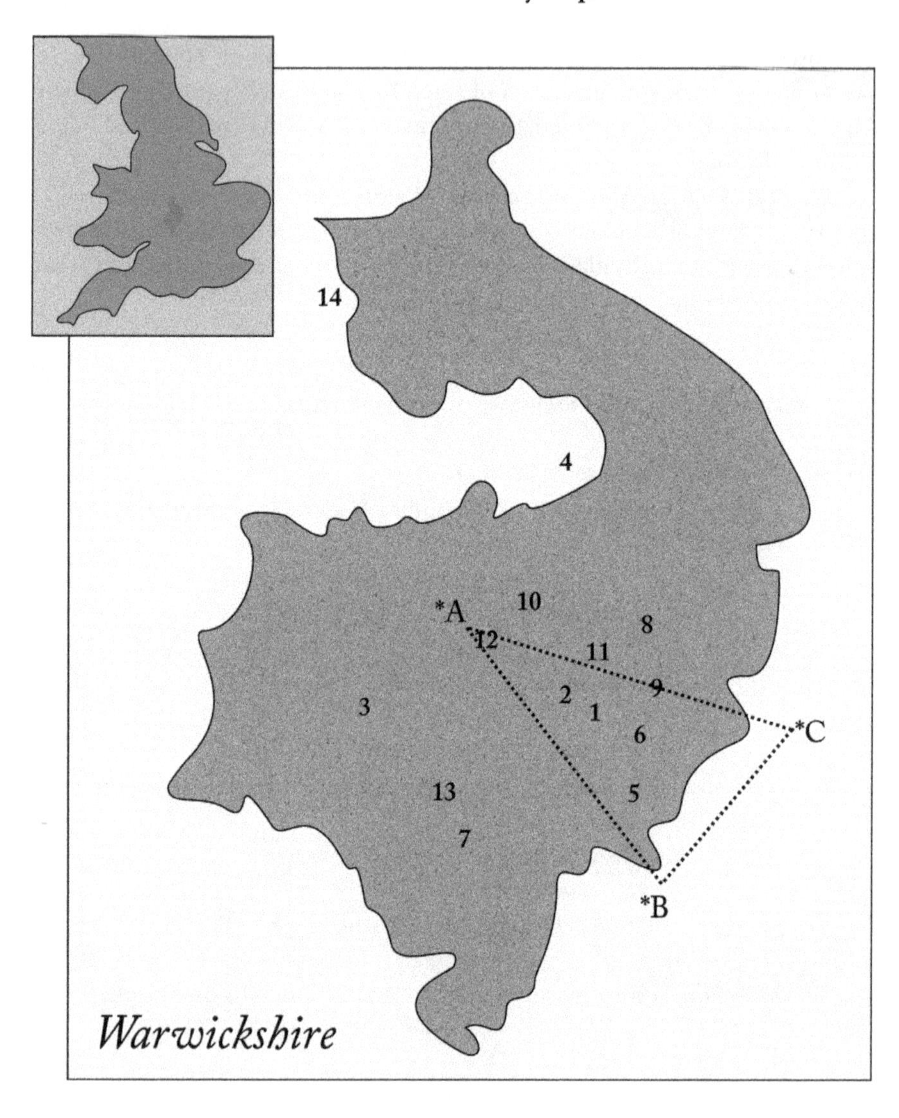

27 Compiled by Joyce Elaine Wiggin-Robbins

WARWICKSHIRE, ENGLAND

Key to map:

1. Bishop's Itchington: Birthplace of Captain Thomas Wiggin.
2. Chesterton: 4th generation Butler Wiggin/Kingston Farm now Wiggin family seat.
3. Coughton: Home of Edward Wigan, brother of Captain Wiggin.
4. Coventry: Home of Ellen Sambrooke, 2nd wife of Vicar William Wiggin, stepmother of Captain Thomas Wiggin.
5. Fenny Compton: George Wyllis/Willis; immigrated to New England.
6. Hodnell, Old Hodnell, Wills Pasture, and Watergall: Margaret Wilkes Dymock and Thomas Gybbes lands, 2nd wife of Thomas Gybbes/Gibbs.
7. Honington: Seat of the Gybbes/Gibbs family.
8. Long Itchington: Vicar William Wiggin was affiliated with this church.
9. Ladbroke: Gen. 4, Butler Wiggin m. Mary Ladbroke; lived on Kingston Farm and London.
10. Lillington: Anne Gybbes's marriage to Vicar Wiggin, recorded in this church 1590; Vicar William was a clerk in this church; burial of Thomas Gybbes 1631 and likely wife, Margaret Wilkes.
11. Offchurch: Burial church of Vicar William Wiggin as per his will.
12. Warwick Castle: See Puritan Triangle definitions.
13. Wellesbourne Mountford: Lands owned by Gen. 3: William Wiggin.
14. Wiggin's Hill: "The farm of Wicga's People" with seventeenth-century buildings dates back to the Domesday Book[28].

THE PURITAN TRIANGLE[29]

A. Warwick Castle, Warwickshire: Home of 2nd Baron Brooke (Robert Greville, 1608–1643), heir to his uncle 1st Baron Brooke (Faulke Greville)
B. Broughton Castle, Oxfordshire: Home of 1st Viscount William Fiennes (1582–1662)
C. Fawsley Hall, Northamptonshire: Home of Sir Richard Knightley (1533–1613)

---

[28] Domesday Book, the first survey of Great Britian, dated 1086, ordered by King William the Conqueror so that he might know what his new kingdom consisted of regarding men and their armaments, property, family titles, etc.

[29] I will write about "The Puritan Triangle" (as I call it) later in this manuscript.

St. Gregory's in Winter, Offchurch, Warwickshire, England[30]

[30] Photo supplied by Brian Green, Feldon Group, Warwickshire, England, and used with permission.

Warwickshire[31]

OFFCHURCH

Offchurch is a very ancient place occupied since the time of King Offa of the Mercians. The name signifies "burgus or curia, a court where a senate is held." Located five miles northeast of Warwick is a very elegant parsonage-type house that once belonged to the church. The Bury and the church were not united during Captain Wiggin's time due to a split in the Knightley family over religion.

The above record is a conundrum in as much as the Knightly family of Offchurch was Catholic, and the Offchurch church was Church of England. However, the Knightleys of Northamptonshire were Church of England and the patrons of this church. There was a split in the family over this issue of churches.

KNIGHTLEY

The Knightley family of Northampton held some forty-one manors in the central midlands and, excepting for the branch at Offchurch, were staunch Puritan and supporters of Cromwell.

Offchurch was the home of the catholic branch of the Knightley clan. The main Knightley clan was in Northamptonshire and was Puritan. The Offchurch Knightleys were royalists and occupied Offchurch Bury, an estate near the church where Vicar William Wiggin is buried. Sir Edmund Knightley and Lady Ursula,[32] his wife, acquired the estate through inheritance from the Alcocke family with contingent remainder to his brother Sir Valentine Knightley.[33] In 1542, Sir Valentine acquired the property and left it to his son Edward, who

[31] Photos for this chapter supplied by Brian Green of the Feldon Group, Warwickshire, England.

[32] L. and P. Hen.VIII, xvii, 285(6). In 1537, George Alysbury had written to Cromwell, asking him "to have me in remembrance to the king about the manor of Offchurch" (ibid xii(2) 437).

[33] Feet of F. Warw.East. 3 Eliz; British History Online

was dealing with the manor in 1585 and again in 1604. The Offchurch branch remained Catholic, and the manor was taken into Crown hands for at least twenty-one years. The direct male line died out in 1688 with the death of Sir John Knightley, and the estate fell to his wife's grandson by her first husband, providing he took the surname Knightley.[34] The Wightwick-Knightleys held the manor into the nineteenth century.[35]

Sir Edward Coke's mother was Winifred Knightley. Winifred married Robert Coke in 1543, and they lived in Norfolk, England. One of the letters Captain Thomas Wiggin wrote from Bristol, England, in 1632 was to Sir Edward Coke.

Andrew Knightley was born 1586 in Offchurch, Warwickshire, England, and died 1660 in Offchurch. He was the son of Edward and Elizabeth Lenthall Knightley of Northamptonshire and Offchurch, Warwickshire. Andrew never married and had no issue. I often wondered if Captain Wiggin named his first son Andrew due to a friendship with Andrew Knightley, but discounted it after I compiled the Captain's London records. I think it more likely he had a good relationship with Andrew Cator of whom you will read later.

BISHOP'S ITCHINGTON

The Itchingtons are a little tricky to follow. Originally, there was an Upper Itchington and a Lower Itchington. In 1547, Lower Itchington was depopulated by Thomas Fisher, the owner, who died in 1577. It is now known as Bishop's Itchington.

Saint Michael's, the parish church, was rebuilt in 1872. A restoration project was completed in 2011 by the Feldon Group.[36]

Bishop's refers to the bishops of Lichfield, who had the church as early as 1152.

Itchington means a "town on the Itchen"—a river that runs north through the village.

This town is the town of record for the Wiggin family. The births of all the vicar's children are found in the parish church records. Vicar William Wiggin remembers the poor of the parish in his will. I never found a record indication Vicar William Wiggin officiated at this church.

GYBBES/GIBBES/GIBBS in CUBBINGTON

I submit here just a few records to show the proliferation of the Gybbes clan in Warwickshire. They cover nearly the entire county, and Vicar William Wiggin and wife, Ann Gybbes, didn't have to reach out far to find help when needed.

---

[34] Dugdale, 361

[35] British History Online has a concise history of the Knightley family.

[36] An affiliation of churches in the area

Cubbington is located just north-northwest of Offchurch and north-northeast of Warwick:

> Contents:
> Conveyance dated 26 May 2-3 Philip & Mary (1556) by Richard Orlache of Long Itchington, husbandman, to Nicholas Gybbes of Cobbington, husbandman, of a messuage[37] and quarterne of land.
> Seal a black letter T.
> Cubbington DR 18/10/14/2*1556*
>
> Contents:
> Feoffment dated 26 May 1556 by Richard Orlache to Nicholas Gybbes. Seal as last.
> Cubbington DR 18/10/14/3*1571*
>
> Contents:
> Release dated 17 Sept. 1571 by Anne daughter: & heir of Richard Orlache to Robert Gybbes, of a messuage & close in Cobbington.
> Seal T. D.
> Cubbington DR 18/10/14/4*1580*
>
> Contents:
> Release dated 8 Oct. 22 Elizabeth 1580, by John Niccols of Lillington and Anne his wife, relict of Robert Gybbes, to John Butler of the Cubbington husbandaman[38], of their claims
> Cubbington DR 18/10/14/6*1580*
>
> Contents:
> Feoffment dated 8 Oct. 1580 Nicholas Gybbes to John Butler. of a messuage and quarterne of land in Cubbington.
> Cubbington DR 18/10/14/8*1580*

These are but a few of such records on the Gybbeses. It is through old deed records like those above that you find your genealogy. Deeds and clerical records are, by far, the best sources. Note below another connection between the Gybbeses and Sir Robert Rich. I did a lot of research to find out if Captain

---

37 A dwelling house with outbuildings and land assigned to its use

38 A person who cultivates the land

Thomas Wiggin could have done an apprenticeship under Sir Robert Rich on board a ship. Such records just don't exist. However, keep in mind that it was a possibility.

> HUNNINGHAM/HUNNINGTON MANOR: (Sir) William Newport Hatton inherited the property of his mother's brother, Sir Christopher Hatton, and took the name of Hatton; (fn. 71) he died in 1596, and in 1611, his daughter and heir, Frances, and her husband, Sir Robert Rich (afterwards Earl of Warwick), sold the manor to Thomas Gibbes.[39]

KINGS FARM

Just west of Bishop's Itchington is an area known as Kings Farm. It was called Kington in the Domesday Book. On the outskirts of the farm is Pittern Hill, where a motte-and-bailey castle called King John's Castle was situated. King John held court there, and the name is now given to the southeast area of Warwickshire and called Kineton Hundred.

Looking north from the farm road between the barn and the manor house is a view of Chesterton Windmill. It stands out in the sunlight, and in the distance beyond that is St. Mary's Church, located in Warwick. Just left of the church is Warwick Castle. Chesterton Windmill is one of Warwickshire's most noted landmarks. It stood for over 350 years as sentinel to the farmers of this area. The Roman Fosse Way runs close by. The mill, built in 1632, was not there during Thomas Wiggin's youth, but he would have seen this new curiosity on his 1632–33 visits home. No doubt, it would influence what he did back in New England.

The property was held last by Butler Wiggin's son upon the death of Butler (great-grandson of Vicar William Wiggin), who sold it. It has now come back into the hands of the Wiggin clan and considered their "home seat." Bill Wiggin, MP, London, is of this family. Butler held it with a couple of other investors, including the then owners of Warwick Castle.

WASHINGTON AND GOODYEAR
Redway Range, Warwickshire

Of interest to the historian, both the Washington and the Goodyear clans were represented in Bishop's Itchington. They both had extensive landholdings in the county, and both also had homes in London.

---

[39] Source: http://www.british-history.ac.uk/

Walter Washington of Radway, Bishop's Itchington, Warwickshire: His wife, Alice (Lighte) Washington, was administrator of his will in 23 April 1597.[40] They had a son named John and a daughter, Katherine.

Walter's sister was Anne, and a commission was issued to her on 18 September 1646 to administer the goods of Walter Washington.[41]

The 1545 letters dated 13 April to Francis Goodere of London, gent., and his heirs granted both Radway Grange and the Manor of Baginton, along with monastic property in Warwick with a demesnes[42] and an abbey.[43] Radway holds fame as the site of the Battle of Edgehill, the first fierce battle of the English Civil War, 23 October 1642.

Henry VIII granted Radway lands to the Coke family following the dissolution of the monasteries.

BISHOP'S ITCHINGTON POOL

When Edward VI died, the Duke of Northumberland desired to place his daughter, Lady Jane Gray, on the throne. He had a servant hide a large sum of money in the Bishop's Itchington pool. After the decapitation murder of his master, the duke and the servant were tortured in an attempt to recover those funds. It isn't known if he finally gave up the hiding place, or if he later used it for his own good.[44] It is said the boys of Bishop's Itchington grew up diving in that pool seeking the treasure! Thomas Wiggin and his brothers could well have been part of that group of boys.

FENNY COMPTON

Fenny Compton is covered in so many other places, I won't repeat it here. Suffice to say, it was on Bishop's Itchington's doorstep and an important connection to the Wiggin clan going back centuries to Oliver Wiggin, priest. Look for more on Oliver in the chapter dealing with the clergy of England. You will find the spelling as "Fennycompton" in ancient records.

---

40 Cobham, 31 (P.C.C.)

41 Admon. Act Book (P.C.C.)

42 *Demesne* means "land belonging to and adjoining the manor house or an estate occupied or controlled by the owner and worked for the exclusive use of the owner."

43 Recorded by Dugdale.

44 New Guide.An Historical and Descriptive Account of Warwick, William Field, Antiquarian books, 1816, p 101.

WIGGIN OF WARWICKSHIRE
Manor of Shrewley[45]

Shrewley is located on the M40 north by northwest of Warwick.

> *Shrewley* was held before the Conquest by Toli. In 1086, it formed part of the estate of Hugh de Grentemaisnil, and it passed with the rest of his lands to Robert, Earl of Leicester. Shortly after the Conquest, the earl appears to have granted Shrewley to Ernald de Bosco, who gave land there to the nuns of Pinley, and the grant was confirmed by the earl.
>
> Apparently, the manor of Shrewley afterward came by some means into the hands of the king, and it appears to have been part of the fee of which Henry I enfeoffed[46] Wigan, his marshal. Wigan seems to have forfeited it, but it was restored to his son Ralph, who held it by the service of Marshalsey. Ralph paid relief for his estates during the years 1163–1165. The nuns of Wroxall held part of the serjeanty in 1198, and in 1206, Ralph lost a suit against the Abbot of Reading for common rights in Shrewley. He died about 1215 when his widow, Aubrey, received it. It appears that Henry was acting as warden of Ivo, son of William Wigan, though he made gifts of land at Shrewley both to the nuns at Pinley and at Wroxall, and he held Shrewley until his death in 1235. In July of the same year, Ivo apparently came of age, and the king took his homage for William Wigan's land in Warwickshire. Ivo, who took the name "de Shrewley," was dead by 1242, when his cousin Peter, son of Thurstan brother of William Wigan, obtained seisin of all Ivo's lands in Warwickshire, on payment of 40 marks. There was, however, considerable doubt as to whether Peter was the true heir, for by an inquisition, it was found that Peter was 25 years old before Thurstan married his mother, and that Thurstan and William had a sister, Lucy, who had a son named Ralph. Ralph's son Godfrey claimed Ivo's estates, and the jurors left it to the king's discernment to decide who the true heir was. In the event, Ivo's land was

---

[45] http://www.british-history.ac.uk/vch/warks/vol3/pp115-120; from: 'Parishes: Hatton', A History of the County of Warwick: Volume 3: Barlichway hundred (1945), pp. 115-120.

[46] To give land for their pledged service

divided between them in 1242—two carucates in Shrewley and Wileby falling to Peter's share and other land in Wileby to Godfrey's. Peter had already, in 1237, given to William de Lucy a carucate in Shrewley, which became a separate manor. There is no further reference to Peter in connexion with Shrewley, and by 1251–1252, the serjeanty had passed to John de Shrewley. It had become much subdivided, and the part held by John in demesne was only one virgate of land, the rest being held under him by the Lucys and the nuns of Pinley and Wroxall. Fulk de Lucy tried to set up a view of frank pledge and to put up gallows at Shrewley, infringing John's prerogatives as lord of the manor. In 1284, Fulk was forbidden to exercise these rights. John died before 1302, when his daughter Maud was lady of Shrewley. Helisence, widow of John, had dower in the manor but was dead before 1309 when Maud, then widow of Walter de Culy or Curly, sold the manor to Sir John de Dufford. Sir John sold it in 1312 to Philip, son of Philip de Gayton; but this was done without the King's licence, and Philip had to pay a fine of 10 marks for pardon. Philip died at his manor of La Grave in January 1316, and his brother Theobald, who was his heir, died a few days after. Philip's heirs were his sisters Juliana, wife of Thomas Murdac, and Scholastica, then widow of Godfrey de Meaux. Though Theobald had never had seisin of the land, a third of the manor was assigned to his widow, Margery, who was in October 1316 wife of Henry de Valence. Half the manor was assigned to Scholastica, and the remainder to Juliana, dower in his land. His successor was William, son of Wigan, who was dead in 1221, when the land in Shrewley was delivered to his nephew Master Henry de Waltham.

The surname *Wiggin* is as entrenched in Warwickshire as in any other county, and the older the record, the more the detail, as is the general rule in England. As you can see by the above record, lands passed from father to son (if there was one) or from uncle to nephew. It stayed in the family surname one way or another and occasionally passed through a female marriage to another surname. Non-inheriting sons often took up land close to the father's holdings.

CHESTERTON WINDMILL

Chesterton Windmill is noted as one of Warwickshire's most noted landmarks. It has stood for 350 years as sentimental to the farmers of this area.

The Roman Fosse Way[47] is close by. The mill was built around 1632 and so was not there during Captain Thomas Wiggin's youth.

In 1667, Benedict Arnold built a similar structure in Newport, Rhode Island, in the United States. It is very similar to the Chesterton mill. However, it was built after a similar structure blew down in 1675, and there are some who say this town dates back to the Viking (pre-Columbian) era. The Arnold family came to Rhode Island in 1635, where he became governor in 1663.

WARWICK CASTLE

In 2007, the largest English entertainment company, named Merlin Entertainment, bought Warwick Castle from Madame Tussauds, who had owned it from 1978. Said to be one of England's largest tourist draws, it stands as sentimental of an era where castles were havens for the powerful ruling gentry. The castle can be seen from the hills of Bishop's Itchington, and Thomas Wiggin would have stood and stared at it, perhaps dreaming up stories in his young child-mind with no hint that its owners would one day play such a large part in his life. The castle was granted to Sir Faulke Greville[48] in 1604 by King James I. Greville converted this stone edifice into a country home, and it continued in the family, which became the Earls of Warwick beginning in 1759. The castle was in poor condition when Sir Greville came into possession, and he spent a great deal of money restoring it. He was stabbed to death within the castle walls by a disgruntled servant.

His tomb was inscribed with the epitaph he had composed:

Folk Grevill
Servant to Queene Elizabeth
Conceller to King James
and Frend to Sir Philip Sidney.
Trophaeum Peccat

Did Captain Thomas Wiggin ever grace the wall of Warwick Castle? Probably not, but its occupants certainly graced his life and ambitions.

---

47 One of the main Roman roads in Britain linking Exeter in SW England to Lincoln in the East Midlands. So it cut diagonally from the SW to the NE of the lower half of the British Isles.

48 The Lord Brooke, 1st Baron Brooke, 1554-1628, biographer of Sir Philip Sidney, the poet.

Connections

Sons of Ministers

When Thomas Wiggin returned to New Hampshire in 1633 (with second wife Catherine Whiting), he brought with him a minister. Thomas is not unique when it comes to ties to religion. David Thomson, "The Father of New Hampshire," was the son of a minister, and so was Samuel Maverick. Thomas knew both of them (or at least he knew of David Thomson). All three men held strong beliefs in law and order and possessed a strong thread of moral fiber in them. There were powerful men in England who were eager to supply the colonists with ministers; among them was his Lordship, the Earl of Arundel.[49] David Thomson, thought by many to be an agent of Gorges and Mason,[50] was in fact an agent for the Council for New England. Even the hotheaded Miles Standish respected Thomson for his moral values. Samuel Maverick married Thomson's widow, Amias, who—through David's death—had become an heiress to David's Scottish holdings.

Soon after David Thomson's death, Maverick's request to the Duke of Arundel for additional settlers was achieved with "sundry ships" arriving in 1629, especially for the settlement of Naumkeag (now Salem, Massachusetts). John Winthrop's fleet would arrive a year later.

Samuel Maverick was well known to Thomas Wiggin through his political leanings, as Maverick was not secretive about them. Maverick and his wife, Amias, were exiled to Maine and the control of Gorges because of his strong support of a petition presented to the General Court in May of 1646, which declared that "the Colony had no settled form of government according to the laws of England." Because of Maverick's views on this subject, he was fined and even jailed briefly. Samuel and his wife remained in Maine until after the

49 Earl of Arundel is the oldest extant earldom and peerage of England, from 1176 to the present day. In Wiggin's day, it was Thomas Howard and his son Henry.

50 Charles Dean, "Notes on the Indenture of David Thomson," pub. Mass Hist. Soc, May 1876; and "David Thomson, The Scottish Founder of New Hampshire," Part 3, 2000, pg. 1, Genevieve Cora Fraser.

(English) Reformation, when he was made a Royal Commissioner by King Charles II[51] and returned to Massachusetts on behalf of the Crown's interests. They settled in what is now Manhattan, in a house given to him by James,[52] Duke of York, who became King James II.

Next to marriage connections producing blood relationships, there are tight friendships that survive from generation to generation. Many of them are occupational relationships and/or religious in nature. All had as strong a tie as a wedding ring.

Every one of the connections is important. Thomas is rubbing elbows with a lot of men interested in the New England settlements. He will get information from each of them.

NUTTER, KING, AND HILDERSHAM[53]

Lincoln Record Society,[54] Arthur Hildersham, Andrew King, and Anthony Nutter are connected with the diocese of Lincoln. This was the diocese of Vicar William Wiggin when he served William Wray, Chief Justice of England.[55] Nutter, King, and Hildersham appeared first before the ecclesiastical commission and, since they refused to answer upon the oath ex officio, they were committed to prison. On 13 May 1592, they appeared in the Star Chamber. At length, it was found that no illegal practices could be proved against them, and they were released on their promise of good behavior. King was, in 1595, a schoolmaster at Chesham Woburn in Buckinghamshire; he was preacher there in 1605. Nutter held the rectory of Fenny Drayton in Leicestershire from 1582 to 1604/1605.

---

[51] Reigned 30 Jan 1649 to 3 Sep 1651

[52] Second surviving son of Charles I, King of England. Born 1633; died 1701. King of England from 1685. Last Roman Catholic monarch of the British Isles. Succeeded his brother, Charles II, to the throne.

[53] A General Martyrologie, containing a Collection of all the greatest persecutions which have befallen the Church of Christ From the Creation to our present Time., Whereunto are added, The lives of sundry Modern Divines, Famous in their Generations for Learning and Piety, and most of them great Sufferers in the Cause of Christ. By Sa. Clarke, Pastor of Bennet Fink London (London, Printed by A.M. for Thomas Underhill and John Rothwell in St. Paul's Churchyard, near the Little North-door. MDCLI, quarto, 24+520+4).

[54] Vol 23; AAB-9192; pub 191 in University of Toronto-Robarts Library; Episcopal Visitation, AD 1591; Proceedings against the Puritans, AD 1590–1592. In 1590, the government proceeded against some of the puritan leaders on the charge of holding unlawful assemblies, subscribing to the Book of Discipline, and attempting to establish a Presbyterian system. The most prominent of these men were Thomas Cartwright and Edmund Snape. Three others: *Arthur Hildersham, Andrew King, and Anthony Nutter of the Lincoln diocese.*

[55] See chapter on the vicar's life.

Hildersham, in 1593, became vicar of Ashby de la Zouch in the same county. All three can be found in the list of nonconforming clergymen as follows:[56]

Anthony Nutter is the uncle of the Anthony Nutter who became the friend of Thomas Wiggin, son of Andrew (son of Captain Thomas Wiggin), and is the one involved in the incident at Walter Barefoot's home when Thomas Wiggin threw John Mason and Walter Barefoot into the fireplace.[57]

Andrew King[58] stayed in trouble as a nonconforming vicar and went to prison at one time. In 1605, he is shown as schoolmaster at Chesham and Chesham Woburn. In 1605, he was admonished to conform; he appeared and alleged "Mr. Bowl, fellow of Trinity college, Cambridge, provoked him to dispute." Again, in 1605, he was summoned but failed to appear and was excommunicated until he corresponded to relate he was in prison in London. "He was one of the militant spirits of Puritanism," and as early as 1573, he was in Star Chamber before the High Commission.

Arthur Hildersham's[59] (1594–1674) grandmother was Margaret Pole/Poole, 8th Countess of Salisbury, the last of the Plantagenet dynasty, which accounts for the story that Elizabeth I called him "cousin Hildersham."[60] Arthur married Ann Barfoot,[61] but I've been unable to find out who she was. Arthur Appears in the Lincoln Records again in April 24, 1605: ". . . vicar of Ashby de la Zouch, co. Leicester, for many years one of the leading Puritans, after several times refusing to conform, was deprived. He too appealed to the court of Arches, but apparently did not prosecute his appeal. In the previous December, he had refused to confer with the bishop and Dr. Mountacute, saying that he (and others) would not come "to be borne downe with countenance and with scoffs." (pg lxxiii; Introduction)

---

[56] Ibid.

[57] Be aware here how confusing this incident becomes if you rely on names alone. It is not Captain Thomas Wiggin (who is deceased when this incident takes place), but his grandson Thomas (son of Andrew); nor is it John Mason, the patentee of New Hampshire, but his grandson in this incident. John Tufton-Mason (here) marries Thomas Junior's daughter, Katherine Wiggin, and Thomas Junior is married to Sara Barefoot, sister to Walter.

[58] I have not been able to connect Andrew Kinge to Margaret Kinge, 1486–1559, wife of Robert Gybbes. But the surname is strong in Warwickshire, and there was surely a connection through occupation to Vicar William Wiggin.

[59] Samuel Clarke in *The Lives of Sundry Modern English Divines* (1651)

[60] Queen Elizabeth called him "cousin" as he descended of the Plantagenets. http://en.wikipedia.org/wiki/Arthur_Hildersham A Puritan and pupil of Thomas Cartwright, "father of Presbyterian" church of England.

The Presbyterian Review, Volume 9; edited by Charles Augustus Briggs, Archibald Alexander Hodge, Francis Landrey Patton, Benjamin Breckinridge Warfield; 1888, Scribner's Sons, NY, NY.

[61] "Barfoot" is the ancient spelling; she likely is related to Sarah and Walter Barfoot.

In a memorandum in the bishop's court book, 24 April 1605 states that 15s 8d each for Mr. Sherewood, Nutter, and Mr. Hidlersham (sic) is to be sent to Mr. Carpenter's "a hosear at the grene man in Cornwall" [perhaps *Cornhill*]. Possibly, this money was intended for their expenses while waiting for the hearing of their appeal, or while they were obeying a citation to appear before the archbishop.

Bradstreet

You will likely take interest in the listing of Simon Bradstreet as a nonconforming vicar of Horbling[62] (1596–1621): a fellow of Emmanuel College; rector of Hinderclay, Co. Suffolk, 15 Dec 1595 to February 1596 and one of the preachers at the king's accession. In 1604, the church wardens of Horbling omit to present him for not wearing the surplice, and they confess that "*he hath not worne the surplus at enyty mesence his coming thither*"; whereupon they are admonished to provide a surplice and tender it to him. Beginning 3 Oct 1604, he appeared before the bishop at Huntingdon for several days, and again in 1605. They were rather easy on Bradstreet because he was so well liked, but in 1607, he "*does not wholly conform himself to the orders and ceremonies appointed in the prayer book and canons, and in the cross and surplice.*" In 1611, he again "*is not conformable.*" Bradstreet held the vicarage of Horbling until his death, and was buried there on 9 Feb 1620, although the records show, at various times, there are other vicars in attendance and Bradstreet is holding a different position.

It doesn't take a lot of imagination to see why the next generations in these families are settling in Colonial America. They have grown up in the religious turmoil about to erupt in England. Watching one's father go to jail for his religious beliefs—beliefs he is staunch in—made lasting impressions on these sons.

> *Petition of Thomas Wiggin & Simon Bradstreet To the Honeed Generall Court now assembled att Boston The humble petition of Thomas Wiggin & Simon Bradstreet Whereas this Court was pleased to graunt to ye petitione 1000 acres of Land &c vpon the greate Ryver of Newichawaunock for the use & benefitt of or mill there It is or humble desire that the Land may lie layde out by Elder Nutter & Thomas Cany in such free place as wee shall make choise of on ths sd Ryver& wee shall pray &c The magis Judge meet to graunt the peticoners Request*

[62] Horbling is a village and civil parish in the South Kesteven district of Lincolnshire, England.

if their bretheren the Depute Consent here to Edward Rawson Secret 27 May 1653.[63]

There are more entries in the Lincoln Record Society books, but for our purposes, this should suffice. I never found anything on Vicar Wiggin, so he must have conformed. He was under the Lincolnshire Diocese while vicar to William Wray, Chief Justice of England, before going to Warwickshire.

LANE CLAN

Lane is covered in other sections, but to keep him in contact with Captain Wiggin, we must also speak of him here:

Ralph Lane,[64] Raleigh's governor in Virginia, first introduced tobacco to England. He had learned to smoke it and taught Raleigh. When the servant of the latter first saw his master enveloped in tobacco smoke, supposing him to be on fire, he dashed a pail of water over him. Raleigh taught Queen Elizabeth I to smoke.[65]

The Lane clan is well entrenched in London, and the records are full of their activities. Captain Sampson Lane of Devonshire is in Strawberry Bank, Piscataqua, New Hampshire, by 1633 and, I suspect, even earlier. Captain Sampson Lane owned the ship *Neptune*. He has a brother in the Caribbean. Sampson and Ambrose Lane are brothers. Ambrose Lane was of Teignmouth, Devonshire, England, and in 1649, he is found in England and has left his brother, Sampson, in charge of his New England estate. His son, Ambrose Junior, is in New England at that time. By 1651, Ambrose Senior is back in New England and has been appointed an associate with Captain Thomas Wiggin

---

63 Documentary History of the State of Maine, Vol VI; pub Brown Thurston Co, 1889; By James P. Baxter, A.M;PG 70-71

64 Ralph Lane, governor of Raleigh's first colony on Roanoke Island, North Carolina, 1585–1586.

65 Sir Walter Raleigh, a favorite of Queen Elizabeth I of England, is credited with having popularized smoking in Britain during the second half of the 16th century. During the 16th and 17th centuries, tobacco was recommended as a cure for coughs, the pain of labor, headaches, rheumatism, inflammations of the nose and air passages, hoarseness, and pains in the stomach, lungs, and breasts as well as for the treatment of gonorrhea, epilepsy, cancer, and plague. However, Queen Elizabeth's successor, James I, tried aggressively to discourage tobacco use. In his now-famous treatise *A Counterblaste to Tobacco* (1604), James described smoking as "a custom loathsome to the eye, hateful to the nose, harmful to the brain, dangerous to the lung, and in the black stinking fume thereof resembling the horrible stygian smoke of the pit that is bottomless." Despite such royal opposition, however, tobacco use continued to spread, and by the mid-17th century tobacco was being cultivated throughout the world. (Source: http://teacher.scholastic.com/scholasticnews/indepth/upfront/grolier/smoking.htm)

"*to keep one court a year at Strawberry Banke.*" Ambrose died on 17 June 1656, and his widow, Olive (executrix of his will), and son, Ambrose Junior, returned to England.

Richard Lane[66] (1596–1657), son of Roger and Beatrix Lane of Herefordshire, England, becomes Thomas Wiggin's close friend during their apprenticeship years in London.[67] Richard's activities are easy to follow as he champions Puritanism,[68] and his mouth gets him in trouble. Eventually, he has to leave London and his wife and small children until things cool down, so he sails to the Caribbean on a voyage of discovery in 1629 while Thomas Wiggin sails to New England.

Richard and Thomas will meet again in Bristol in 1632. Richard Lane is returning from the Caribbean and Thomas Wiggin from Piscataqua, New England, and they spend time together in Bristol. Lane has knowledge of a staple crop, and he wants backing to grow it in New England. Wiggin writes a letter championing Lane, and we will discuss this letter later in detail.

My friend Fred V. Schultz[69] has done a masterful job writing about the Lanes, so I am not going to reiterate here. Suffice to know that Richard Lane and Thomas Wiggin were young friends and associates in London who continued their contact into the 1630s.

A word about the crop madder. Madder, grown in the west of England, was used to make red dye for royal clothing. The dye is made from the roots of the plant and is very unstable in both color and endurance. While giving off hues of red, it never gave a scarlet red.

The Lanes of the Caribbean (the same Lanes who had a madder farm in the west of England) discovered the bark of a tree on the islands rendered a red dye, and they wanted to send it to England for processing. The English madder trade strongly protested and worked to ban its importation. The Lanes found a market for it in France; so although they were "English governors" in the

---

[66] On 5 April 1671, a marriage license was issued to Captain John Lane (an Uncle of Richard Lane), age about 41, to Elizabeth Saltonstall, a widow, age about 34. She was the widow of Charles Saltonstall. Both husbands were considerably older than she. Both men were wealthy and adventurous mariners. She appears to have prospered through her marriages.

[67] On December 14, 1613, he apprenticed to Nathaniel Thornhill of London.

[68] "A Reminiscence Sung," "Richard Lane seems to have been a man who knew his mind and didn't conceal his views. In 1631, he was subject to a review for unorthodox, nonconformist beliefs—euphemistically speaking, Puritanism."

[69] "A Reminiscence Sung" by Fred V. Schultz. ttp://freepages.family.rootsweb.ancestry.com/~rawl/reminiscence.html. "The Lanes of Herefordshire eventually became known as the Lanes of the Ryelands. Roger Lane was an apothecary in Hereford, England. At that time, one who followed this trade not only made and sold drugs but practiced the healing arts as well. Roger and Beatrix had ten children born in Hereford, and all were christened in St. Peter's Church between January 29, 1590, and January 10, 1602."

Caribbean, they were shipping their new product to England's enemy, France, and pocketing the money.

During this same era, both Europe and Britain were taking an interest in *cochineal.* Cochineal is a bug that uses cacti as a host plant; the dried bodies of the female insect *Coccus cacti* have a scarlet coloring because of an active ingredient known as *carminic acid.* This acid renders a true scarlet coloring that doesn't fade.

Richard Lane, while on his fact-finding trip to the Caribbean in the early 1630s, found a "staple crop". He wanted to grow in New England[70] with the backing of the lords. Nowhere do they tell us what this crop was. One crop I always believed Lane found was the potato, in all its varieties, which was so popular in the Caribbean. The potato was not a popular crop in Europe or England, and when Sir Walter Raleigh introduced it to Queen Elizabeth I and her court, the cooks threw out the potatoes and cooked the vines, nearly killing the entire court. The queen banned any further importation of that vegetable. Richard Lane's *rediscovery* would not have met with approval by the English lords if it was a potato variety.

Lane was told by the lords to take his family's madder plants to the islands and grow it. When that crop failed, he probably found out about cochineal—an insect that, when dried and crushed, produced a very stable scarlet-red dye.

WILLIS

The Willis/Wyllis family of Fenny Compton lived two miles south of Captain Wiggin's birth home. George Willis was a Royalist and a Mason agent in Maine who was driven by an indefinable trait, as he already owned a huge estate in Warwickshire. So why did he choose to migrate? He was not a mariner, nor was he destitute, and he retained ownership of his estates in Warwickshire. George Wyllys settled in Hertford, Connecticut, where he became governor in 1642 and died in 1645, leaving his Fenny Compton estate to his son George.[71] George Willis Sr. retained his shares in the Piscataqua Patent his entire life and was the only one of the original investors to do so.

Fenny Compton was owned by the Wiggin clan prior to the Willis occupation. Oliver Wiggin, a clergyman in the Church of England, held title to Fenny Compton. We read about Oliver in the section dealing with the clergy of England and men named Wiggin.

---

70 See the chapter on the 1632–33 letters by Captain Thomas Wiggin.

71 George Willis Jr., in 1655, conveyed "the manor" to Ambrose Holbech and Nathaniel Ekins. A moiety of the manor, however, was in the possession of Bridget Wyllys in 1674 and was conveyed in 1769 by George and Samuel Wyllys to William Holbech. The manor then descended with that of Farnborough.

PRIDEAUX[72]

John Prideaux m. Ann Shapton

/

William Prideaux 1424–1472 m. Alice Gifford 1445–1512

/

Faulk Prideaux 1471–1531 m. Katherine Poyntz 1467–1487

/

Humphrey Prideaux 1487–1550 m. Widow Jane Fowell Courtenay 1490–1523

Issue:

- Margery 1515–1554: married Robert Gybbes
- William 1518–1564: lived in Cornwall
- Thomas 1522: died a monk in Flanders
- Richard about 1520–1603: heir to his father
- Roger about 1520–1582: of Soldon, Devon, was a sheriff
- Elizabeth 1523–1575: married Robert Drake

NOTES:

- Jane Fowell (1473-1523) was the widow Philip Courtenay[73] with whom she had a daughter, known as the heiress Elizabeth who married William Strode who died 5 May 1578.
- Katherine Ponytz was the daughter of Humphrey and Elizabeth Pollard Ponytz.
- Alice Giffard was the daughter of Stephen Thomas Giffard and Agnes Churchill.
- Elizabeth Pollard was the daughter of Richard Pollard and Tomasin Cruse.

Humphrey Prideaux,[74] born 1487 in Theuborough, Devonshire, England (son of Faulk and Katherine Poyntz Prideaux), and died 8 May 1550; married Jane Fowell b. 1490 in Fowelscombe, Devonshire, England, and d. 31 October 1523; married second Edith Hatch.

---

[72] Genealogical and Heraldic History of The Commoners of Great Britian and Ireland, by John Burke, Esq., Vol 1, London, pub for Henry Colburn, MDCCCXXXIII, pgs 203-205

[73] Philip Courtenay was son of Philip Courtenay of Molland (1432-1489).

[74] Age 44 in 1530. Escheator of Devon 1534. Will dated 4 Jul 1549, probated 10 Jan 1550/1551.

You will find pedigrees on line that claim Edith Hatch was the mother of Humphrey's issue. Such is not the case according to English records. He may have made Edith his second wife following the death of Jane in 1523.
Issue of Humphrey Prideaux and Jane Fowell Courtney Prideaux:

- Margery Prideaux, b. 1512 and d. 1554; first wife of Robert Gybbes of Honington (1528–1586) with issue: Elizabeth, Jane, Anthony (never married), Margaret. (See Gybbes pedigree) Note: Robert Gybbes m. second Catherine Porter (1516–1558) with issue: Ralph, Tristram, Thomas (1552–1631), father of Anne who married Vicar William Wiggin/Wigan, parents of Captain Thomas Wiggin.
- Elizabeth Prideaux (1523-1575), married Robert Drake of Wiscomb (1528-1600), son of John Drake of Ashe and Amy Grenville.

DRAKE

In 1627, Captain Thomas Wiggin called upon John Drake for assistance in securing a *letter of marque and reprisal against the French.* With a marriage tie to the Drakes, he had good reason to think he'd get some help in finding out why his application had not been acted upon. More is written on this incident in the chapter covering 1627.

John Drake m. Agnes Kalloway
/
John Drake 1474–1554 m. Margaret Cole 1476–1554
/
John Drake 1500–1586 m. Amy Grenville 1513–1578
/
Robert Drake 1528–1600 m. Elizabeth Prideaux 1523–1572

ISSUE of Robert Drake and Elizabeth Prideaux:

- Amy 1547
- John 1549
- Humphrey 1551–1604
- Robert 1553
- Henry 1555
- Ursula 1557
- Elizabeth 1558

- Bernard 1559
- Nicholas 1561–1640
- Gertrude 1563
- William 1564–1625

THE FIENNES OF BROUGHTON CASTLE LORD SAYE AND SELE

Richard Fiennes m. Ursula Fermor
/
Richard Fiennes 1557–1613 m. Constance Kingsmil 1562–1587
/
William Fiennes 1582–1662 m. Elizabeth Temple 1574–1648
/
Nathaniel Fiennes 1608–1669 m. Frances Whitehead 1625–1691

ISSUE of Nathaniel Fiennes and Frances Whitehead:

- Mary 1654–1731
- Celia 1662–1741

WILLIAM, LORD SAYE and SELE

William Fiennes, Lord Saye and Sele, Broughton Castle, Banbury, Oxfordshire, employer of Thomas Wiggin for seven years as agent for the Hilton Patents that Fiennes purchased in 1633. With Wiggin's marriage connections to this family, and with the experiences he had accumulated by 1633, Thomas Wiggin was an easy choice as agent.

Knowing the connections below should answer the questions: "Who chose Thomas Wiggin as the overseer of the two lords, Willis and Whiting's purchase of the Hilton Patents in New Hampshire, and who negotiated the sale of those patents to the two lords?" There is nothing stronger in ancient England than marriage connections.

A. *John Temple m. Susan Spencer*

2. Thomas Temple, son of John, had a daughter he named:

3. Elizabeth (granddaughter of John and Susan Spencer Temple) who m. Henry Gibbs

2. Elizabeth, John Temple's daughter, m. Wm. Lord Saye and Sele

B. *Robert Gybbes m. Margaret King*

2. Robert Gybbes's son Thomas had a daughter he named Anne. She married Vicar William Wiggin, and they became parents of Captain Thomas Wiggin, 1601–1666.

2. Robert Gybbes's son Robert Junior* m. Catherine Porter

3. Ralph Gybbes, son of Robert Junior, m. Gertrude

4. Ralph Gybbes had a son named Henry (Ch. 1593)

5. Henry married Elizabeth Temple above

*Robert Gybbes Jr. died a few months after his father, Robert, but before his eldest son, Anthony (by his first wife). Anthony died single, leaving the estate to his half-brother Ralph, father of Henry, who m. Elizabeth Temple.

Robert Gybbes m. Margarete King/
Robert Gybbes 1528–1586 m. Catherine Porter 1516–1558
/
Ralph Gybbes 1555–1613 m. Gertrude Wroughton 1552–1611
/
Henry Gybbes 1593–1668 m. Elizabeth Temple 1590–1667

ISSUE of Henry Gybbes and Elizabeth Temple:

- Hester abt. 1614
- Martha abt. 1618
- Thomas 1621
- Henry 1626
- John 1627
- Ralph 1631–1669
- Robert 1634–1674

PLEASE NOTE: In my genealogy, I use the original spelling of *Gybbes* for simplicity. However, the spelling of *Gibbes* soon became common, and that evolved into *Gibbs.*

Peter Temple m. Millicent Jekyll
/
John Temple 1542–1603 m. Susanna Temple 1547–1606
/
Thomas Temple 1567–1637 m. Esther Sandys 1570–1667
/
Elizabeth Temple 1590–1667 m. Henry Gybbes 1593–1668

JOHN DELBRIDGE[75]

John Delbridge was of Barnstaple, Devonshire, and I debated on inserting his history here or in the Barnstaple section. Since he was a connection for Captain Wiggin, I decided to use him in this chapter. I love the history of this man and was fascinated in reading about his efforts to rid the oceans of pirates preying on merchant ships. It was as if his pleas were falling on deaf ears.

> 1/360/31[76] 1632: This record has no title
>
> *Copy of a letter from John Delbridge to the Mayor of Barnstaple detailing the grievous injuries done to English commerce by Turkish piracy, and recommending that the merchants of the kingdom should combine and urge His Majesty to take adequate measures to protect the foreign trade of the nation from maritime robbers.*
>
> 5 December 1621,[77] Parliament speech: . . . noting that the West Country was now oppressed not only by impositions but also by Turkish and *French pirates.*

The above further cements the problems with piracy stretching from England to the fishing banks of America. It also points out another reason Captain Thomas Wigan (sic) wanted a letter of marque and reprisal against the French.

John was also invested in the Virginia and the East India companies and the Somers Island Company. And in 1621, in consortium with Sir Edwin Sandys and John Ferrar, he financed a voyage to New England, where he had also applied for a license to participate in the Cape Cod fisheries and was opposed by Sir Ferdinando Gorges, who said Delbridge was trying to breach the New England Company's monopoly there.

What an incredible, colorful life John Delbridge lived. Domiciled in Barnstaple and holding such a variety of offices made him a man to know and to reckon with. John was a freeman, mayor (1615–1635), capital burgess, militia captain, and clerk of the market. Thomas Wiggin would have to go through John Delbridge with any shipping out of the west coast of Devonshire. Thomas

---

[75] Delbridge, John (1564-1639) of Barnstaple and Bishop's Tawton, Devon; Pub The History of Parliament: the House of Commons 1604-1629, ed. Andrew Thrush and John P. Ferris, 2010; Cambridge Univ Press

[76] PRO, Kew, Richmond, England

[77] Delbridge, John (1564–1639) of Barnstaple and Bishop's Tawton, Devon; Pub *The History of Parliament: The House of Commons* 1604-1629, ed. Andrew Thrush and John P. Ferris, 2010; Cambridge University Press

is found in Barnstaple with Delbridge in 1632, seeking title to a patent in New England. As a Parliamentarian from Bristol, John championed the cause of dealing with pirates and taxation. He opposed the Ship's Tax and tax on tobacco coming in from Virginia.

John was more concerned with profits than people. His whole life was spent dealing with tobacco imports from Virginia and fish from New England. In his lifetime, he saw Barnstaple go from a thriving merchant port only to dry up as it was taken over by the military for staging and the loss of any European ports for ships on the west coast. All they had open to them was the Caribbean and America, and that was a costly venture.

> 1624: 23 Feb[78] . . . he resumed his attack on the New England Company's patent, reporting that in the past year Barnstaple sailors had been forced to pay the Company £200 for licenses to fish off the American coast. Appointed on 15 Mar. as a port town burgess to the committee for the bill for freer fishing in America...

> 1625: 10 August[79] . . . heretofore we had hopes and expectations where with to please the country, though we gave away the money. Now there are nothing but discouragements: pardons to Jesuits, the news from [La] Rochelle . . . the interruption of the fishing trade, the losses by pirates. So that, whereas we returned the last time with fasting and prayer, now we may return with sackcloth and ashes.

So again, in 1625, Delbridge seems to be very concerned with the merchandising and that fishing fleets are being sacked by pirates. Nothing seems to have been done to rid the west coast of pirates. Delbridge is also deeply involved with the debates on war in the Palatine.

> 1626:[80] 28 February . . . He was considerably blunter during a debate six days later about the Navy's failings. Condemning

---

[78] Delbridge, John (1564–1639) of Barnstaple and Bishop's Tawton, Devon; Pub *The History of Parliament: The House of Commons 1604-1629*, ed. Andrew Thrush and John P. Ferris, 2010; Cambridge University Press

[79] Ibid.

[80] Ibid.

the ease with which Sallee[81] pirates and Dunkirk[82] privateers were plundering English merchant shipping; On 22 Mar. Delbridge headed the list of Members added to the select committee set up to investigate the Navy's defects. He was also appointed to consider Digges' proposal for a joint-stock company to fund a naval war against Spain, and apparently recommended that this organization should be free from interference by all other trading companies

1627:[83] During the debate on 22 April on the bill to allow marriage at any time of year, he explained that he wished to make life easier for sailors who had problems organizing their weddings during their brief sojourns ashore.

1630:[84] He travelled to London again in April 1633 on the corporation's behalf, to appeal for action against the pirates who preyed on the Newfoundland fishing fleets, William Laud describing him on this occasion as "a great Parliament man."

Delbridge's adult life was spent initially in the cloth trade with access to European ports. As those ports dried up and the cloth industry turned to London, Delbridge turned to America and dealt mostly in fish and tobacco.

John Delbridge died in 1639. The above records give a very detailed picture of shipping activity on the west coast of England. Pirates were a problem his entire life and not much was being done about it. However, they weren't all French, so that alone would not give reason for Captain Thomas Wiggin to apply for his letter of marque against the French. John also opposed the Massachusetts Bay Colony founders/company that Thomas Wiggin came to embrace.

I would have liked to have been a mouse in the room to hear the conversation between John Delbridge and Captain Thomas Wiggin in 1632, when they met to secure patents in New England. Wiggin championed the cause of the Massachusetts Bay Colony, and Delbridge opposed it.

---

81 Barbary pirates, mostly Muslims expelled from Spain and European renegades operating out of the port of Salli (Rabat) in Morocco; also known as Salle Rovers.

82 Also known as Dunkirkers, commerce raiders in service to the Spanish Monarchy. They operated out of ports on the Flemish coast of Nieuwpoort and Ostend and Dunkirk. Although focused mainly on the Dutch shipping, they roamed all the way down into the Mediterranean.

83 Ibid.

84 Ibid.

BONITHON/BONYTHON

Captain/Sir Richard Bonython was born 1580 in St. Columb Major, Cornwall, England, and died about 1652 in Saco, York, Maine. Richard married Lucretia Leigh, born 1565 in Cornwall, and she died 1614 in Breage, Cornwall, England. Issue: Susannah, Gracia, Elizabeth, Lucretia, and John.

There is an important connection here, and we must go back one more generation to make the connection with Richard of Saco's father.

John Bonython married Eleanor Myllayton of Cornwall. Her father was Job Myllayton, who was governor of St. Michael's Mount (Cornwall) in 1547 in place of Humphrey Arundell, who had been executed. John and Eleanor had issue:

1. Reskymer, their son and heir; had a son Thomas (heir), who was a lifetime captain in the Holland Regiment. The Bonython genealogy states that being a captain in "the Low Countries consumed his patrimony."
2. *Richard*, the emigrant to Maine; comptroller of Stannaries of Cornwall and Devonshire 1603 and 1604. Baptized St. Columb Major on 3 April 1580.
3. Edmond.
4. William, Captain of Mawyr[85] Castle, Cornwall.
5. John, Captain of Pendennis Castle, Falmouth.
6. Elizabeth, m. Henry Pomeroy, mayor of Tregone, 16 April 1600.
7. Anne m. Walter Roscarrock, 1606.
8. Eleanor, m. Richard Leigh, gentleman, 9 November 1601. (St. Columb Major Registers: Richard Leigh was the son of William Leigh and Mary Pomeroy, daughter of Andrew Pomeroy of Newton Ferrers, Devonshire.)

Richard Bonython was one of the founding members of the New World colony in New England and had connections to Leonard Pomeroy of Plymouth in Devon, who had married Richard's sister Elizabeth Bonython. Richard and his family went to Saco, Maine, in 1631, with a patent dated 12 February 1629–1630.

John Bevill was sheriff of Cornwal in 1558, married Elizabeth Milliton at Killigarth before 1544:

---

[85] St. Mawes Castle, Cornwall; An excellent reference for the Bonithon, Pomeroy and Bevil lines can be found at https://sites.google.com/site/pomeroytwigs2/the-manor-of-collaton-in-newton-ferrers, Titled "Collaton Manor in Newton Ferrers", by unknown. I found this source to be very accurate while never finding the name of the site's owner.

ISSUE of John and Elizabeth Bevill (Note the wedding ring connections):

1. 1544 Elizabeth married Henry Meggs
2. 1546 Agnes married Walter Kendall
3. 1548 William Bevill married Jane Arundell
4. 1550 Joan married Humphrey Prideaux
5. 1591 Peter Bevill married Grace Viel 9 September 1591. Their daughter Elizabeth married Barnard Greville, whose son was Bevil Grenville, a military hero
6. 1552 Mary married William Pomeroy, son of Andrew Pomeroy and Anne (Matthews) Pomeroy
7. 1556 Phillip Bevill
8. John (born in unknown) married Joan Killowe.

St. Mawes Castle, Cornwall, and Pendennis Castle, Falmouth, controlled shipping along the southern coast of England. St. Mawes was built as a coastal artillery fortress by Henry VIII, the most highly decorated of a string of such forts built between 1539 and 1545 as defense against both French and Spanish invasions. It is decorated with carvings in praise of Henry VIII.

Summary: Richard Bonython lived across the Piscataqua from Dover, New Hampshire. And when his daughter married Richard Cumming, Captain Wiggin sold them land to live on. When Captain Wiggin was approaching his final years, Mr. Cumming was late for jury duty because he was "helping his worship to the ordinary." "Ordinary" refers to a lawful meeting usually held in the local tavern, or *ordinary*.

As you can see by the pedigrees, these families intermarried for generations. It was a way of keeping the power and the wealth to themselves. The first couple of generations in New England practiced the same ritual, but after a couple of planned marriage generations, they were mostly all equal in wealth and/or position within the community. Marriage rituals took on a far different meaning.

If Captain Thomas Wiggin sailed a ship along the southern coastline of England, he was well acquainted with the castles governed by the Bonythons.

POMEROY

In 1620, three merchants—Abraham Colmer, Nicholas Sherwill, and Leonard Pomeroy—were the underwriters of David Thomson's plantation on the Piscataqua River. Each man was given one-third interest in one-fourth of the plantation as payment for their assistance. In other words, each merchant owned 1/12 of the plantation to Thomson's 3/4. The three men owned the ship *Providence*, which brought the Hilton settlers to the Piscataqua.

David Thomson is said to be the first white settler on the river. Included in the list of settlers are William Hilton and Edward Hilton, though they did not come together. There is some conjecture as to whether the Hiltons are brothers or cousins, and a good case is given for their having been cousins. Whichever, it does not change our story either way. The Hilton plantation consisted of 6,000 acres.

Leonard had no children, and his four nephews became his heirs in 1628: William, Abraham, John, and Thomas.

HILTON

While the Hiltons remained business partners and friends of Thomas Wiggin, there was neither a wedding-ring nor a pedigree connection. The Hilton ancestry is well covered in other sources, so I'm not going to reprint it here. Suffice to say, I never found any prior connection between either of the Hiltons and Thomas Wiggin before 1629.

Edward Hilton came over in 1623 in the ship *Providence of Plymouth* and later began a settlement at Dover Point. This ship was owned by Colmer and Sherwill as well as Leonard Pomeroy. William Hilton, Edward's brother, arrived at the Plymouth plantation two years earlier in 1621 and later joined his brother in establishing a fishing business at Dover.

PURITAN TRIANGLE

I would be remiss if I did not point out what I call the Puritan triangle. Captain Thomas Wiggin was born in the center of that triangle of leading Puritans. To the east of Bishop's Itchington is the seat of the Knightley family in Northamptonshire; to the south is Banbury, Oxfordshire, home of Lord Saye and Sele; to the west/northwest is Warwick Castle, home of Lord Brooke. There was no great distance between them, and all three were within five miles of Bishop's Itchington.

FAWSLEY HALL[86]

Sir Richard Knightley[87] (1533–1615) of Fawsley Hall, Northamptonshire, knighted in 1565; member of Parliament from 1584 to 1598; High Sheriff of the county from 1568 to 1582. He was commanded by Queen Elizabeth I to be present when Mary, Queen of Scots, was beheaded in Northamptonshire.

---

86 Fawsley is now a privately owned hotel and spa.

87 First marriage to Mary Fermor

A man named John Penry (a Welshman) had a printing press he moved from place to place, and sometime between 1588 and March of 1589, Penry installed his press at Fawsley Hall, where he produced his second attack, through a pamphlet printing, against the Church of England. Penry's pamphlets attacked the episcopacy of the church, but he maintained the Puritan doctrines.

Sir Richard printed the "Marprelate Tracts" at his own expense. In 1589, he was fined 2,000 British pounds sterling and dismissed from the lieutenancy of the county and the magistracy. In 1605, he was again fined 10,000 BPS.

The Marprelate Controversy was a war fought through pamphlet printing between Puritan adherents and the Church of England. The article writer for the Puritan side had the pseudonym Martin Marprelate, thus the label of the controversy.

Sir Knightley held meetings in his home for the leading Puritans before the English Civil War.

Andrew Knightley of Offchurch Bury (1588–1660) belonged to the branch of the family who adhered to the Roman Catholic faith. Thus a breach between the two branches existed. Andrew married Elizabeth Lenthal; they had no children.

WARWICK CASTLE[88]

Robert Greville, 2nd Baron Brooke (1608–1643),[89] was adopted by his unmarried uncle, Fulke Greville, 1st Baron Brooke, and was his heir. Widely educated while attending both Leiden and Paris universities, he was also extensively traveled. Baron Brooke married Catherine Russell.[90] He was a critic of King Charles and ally of Lord Saye and Sele of Broughton Castle, and together, they promoted Providence Island in the West Indies and Saybrooke in Connecticut and employed Captain Thomas Wiggin in 1632 as their agent on the Piscataqua River.

In 1641, Brooke wrote *A Discourse opening the nature of that Episcopacie which is exercised in England*, aimed at the political power of the bishops. In the same year, his philosophical work *The Nature of Truth* was published. In this work, he refuses

---

[88] *Warwick Castle, the East Front from the Outer Court* (1752), painted by Canaletto, Birmingham Museum and Art Gallery, Birmingham. It is little altered today. Original uploader was Gillian Tipson at en.wikipedia.

[89] English Civil War Roundhead General; commanded Parliament forces in Warwickshire and Staffordshire and was looked on by many as the Earl of Essex's eventual successor. In 1642, he gained the victory of Kineton. He took Stratford-upon-Avon in February 1643 and was killed by sniper fire shortly after besieging Litchfield Cathedral on 2 March.

[90] d. 1 December 1676; daughter of Francis Russell, 4th Earl of BedfordPC(1593 – 9 May 1641) a Royalists.

to distinguish between philosophy and theology. "What is true philosophy but divinity?" he asks. "And if it be not true, it is not philosophy." (Source: *Wikipedia*)

BANBURY CASTLE[91]

William Fiennes, Saye and Sele[92] 1st Viscount (1582–1662), was educated at New College, Oxfordshire. In 1633, Saye purchased Dover Plantation from the Bristol Merchants.[93]

Nicknamed "Old Subtlety" for his devious political maneuvering, he descended from a long line of titled aristocracy. He advocated establishing a government in America, which would include the titled aristocracy.

Fiennes opposed King Charles, but didn't advocate his beheading. After that event, he spent years on the Isle of Lundy, until after the Cromwellian era; but once the Crown was restored, he returned to London, where he was made Lord Privy Seal (1660).

Fiennes married Elizabeth, the daughter of John Temple, Esq., of Stowe and had issue: James, Nathaniel, John, Richard, and five daughters.

In 1631, he employed Captain Thomas Wiggin as agent to his interests in New Hampshire.

Nathaniel Fiennes, second son of Lord Saye and Sele, educated at Winchester and New Colleges of Oxfordshire, like his father was a devout Puritan. He married Elizabeth Eliot, the daughter of Parliamentarian Sir John Eliot,[94] who died a prisoner in the Tower of London in 1632. He left a son who became the 3rd Viscount.

Nathaniel—a member of Parliament for Banbury—was an outspoken critic of episcopacy, fought against the Royalists, was commissioned a colonel in the Earl of Essex's army, fought at Powick Bridge and Edgehill, and was governor of Bristol until he surrendered it to Prince Rupert's forces in 1645. Before retiring in 1659, Nathaniel held several offices: as a member of Parliament for Oxford, Council of State, Commissioner of the Great Seal in 1655, held a seat in the new Upper House and was a supporter of Richard Cromwell as successor of Oliver Cromwell.

---

91 For an excellent book on the history of the Fiennes and related familes, read *Mad Dogs and Englishmen* by Sir Ranulph Fiennes, pub. Windsor, large type edition available; ISBN-13 978-1408486075.

92 See chapter titled "Pedigrees."

93 The Bristol Merchants were the Wright Brothers.

94 Vice Admiral of Devon; confined to the Tower of London several times; twice confined to Marshalsea Prison; died of consumption on 27 November 1632 and was buried at St. Peter's Ad Vincula Church within the Tower.

Chapter Summary

Captain Thomas Wiggin had some very valuable marriage ties, which included the Raleighs, Drakes, Temples, Saye and Sele/Fiennes, and a host of others through the Gybbeses. His connections through the Bonythons, Pomeroys, and Lanes were just the tip of the iceberg from his years in London. Captain Wiggin had the backing and admiration he needed to impress enough people to make a colony in New England thrive. He did not come here as an isolated, unknown man; he was not plucked off the deck of a ship to govern a colony; he was not an adventurer just seeking land opportunity. He was a well-placed man in the right places at the right times, and he built on his associations through marriage and networking.

Wiggin's world functioned on prestigious arranged marriages and social networking, as well as religion and occupational choices. He was choosing well.

THE NARROWS OF LITTLE BAY AND GREAT BAY[95]

[95] Photo by Joyce Elaine Wiggin-Robbins

Early Associates on the Piscataqua 1627–32

As a note here, Thomas Wiggin is called just that in most historical records pre-1632. The "captain" rank seems to have come about while he was in Bristol-London in 1632/33. If he was a sea captain, there is no evidence other than a verbal request in 1627 to Sir John Drake of Barnstaple, Devonshire, as to the disposition of a request for a letter of marque by a man Drake called "Captain Thomas Wigan."[96] Following the resale of the "Bristol" (Dover, New Hampshire) patent to the lords in 1632, his name is seldom, if ever, found without the rank of "captain." We will go into this subject more, but this will suffice, for now, as an explanation as to why I use the rank of captain sometimes and not at others.

In order to understand what happened between the years 1628 and 1632 that set Thomas Wiggin's plans for his future in motion, we have to know whom he was dealing with. While researching Wiggin's roots, I found it very frustrating trying to keep all these associates sorted out, so I created a short bio for each of them. I also found it necessary to know who these men were and especially where they came from, in order to weave an association with each of them to Thomas Wiggin in England, if one existed, pre-1629. Here, in no particular order, are the characters in his life at that time, especially those he found himself living with on the Piscataqua River pre-1633:[97]

1. Sir Ferdinando Gorges: b. abt. 1565, Ashton Phillips, Somerset, and d. 1647. Influenced by Sir Walter Raleigh. Formed the Plymouth Company, which became the London Company in 1606. Responsible for the erection of Fort

[96] This topic will be covered in detail in another chapter

[97] The Piscataqua River would become the dividing line between the states of Maine and New Hampshire; was a dividing line between the Royalist and Puritan factions; was the life-line of commerce in early history of upper New England.

George on the Kennebec in 1607. In 1614, Gorges engaged Captain John Smith; sent out Richard Vines in 1616, who encamped on the Saco River that winter; 1619 sent out Dermer for a second voyage. Formed a new company in 1620 named "Council at Plymouth, in the County of Devon, for planting, ruling, ordering, and governing of New England in America," which made the foundation grants in New England, and this corporation consisted of forty patentees. Styled "Father of Colonization in America." Two grants with John Mason in the district called *Laconia* and attempted settlements; had negotiated a patent from the Council for New England for all the land between the Merrimack and Kennebec Rivers in 1622, which included the land at Hilton Point. In 1629, Captain Mason and Sir F. Gorges divided their jointly held patents between themselves, with Ferdinando Gorges taking the land now known as Maine and John Mason the land now known as New Hampshire. Gorges never set foot in New England, but in 1605, he sponsored George Weymouth's visit to the Kennebec River area. In 1607, he was a shareholder in the Plymouth Company and helped found the Popham Colony, Maine. Captain Christopher Levett,[98] another early explorer, was on the Maine coast as early as 1623[99] and was a Gorges agent as well as being a member of the Council for New England. Gorges died in financial ruin.

2. Thomas Weston:[100] b. 1584 in Rugeley, Staffordshire, and d. bef. November 1647 in Bristol, England. Weston was a London merchant and ironmonger by trade. He was associated with the Plymouth Council for New England, which had financed the failed Popham Colony in Maine. Weston was seeking young, able-bodied men for his settlement in Massachusetts, even young men who had been in trouble and wanted to get away. More than one researcher has suggested our Thomas Wiggin was involved, or a part of, this first movement into Massachusetts in 1622. The dates are right to have made it a possibility. Thomas Wiggin would have been twenty-one years old in 1622 and finished with his apprenticeship.[101] Adhering to this scenario, though, makes the dates very

---

98 Vexed and Troubled Englishmen, 1590-1642, Carl Bridenbaugh, NY, Oxford Press, 1968; pg 51-52

99 A Voyage into New England, London 1628, p5; Christopher Levett

100 *Vexed and Troubled Englishmen,* 1590–1642, Carl Bridenbaugh, NY, Oxford Press, 1968; pp. 398–99; "Thomas Weston, one of the lesser mercantile figures of London" was associated with "transporting emigrants across the Atlantic as cargo."

101 Apprenticeships were served from age 14 to 21 (normally) and cost about thirty English pounds, but also came with certain entitlements upon completion, such as a suit of clothes and/or remuneration. A young man could also earn money on the side with the approval of his "master" while in apprenticeship. In Wiggin's day, apprenticeships were required in order to work in a chosen occupation.

tight and a near impossibility when you do a chronological listing of his life. Personally, I do not believe he was a part of the Weston movement.

3. Abraham Shurt was an agent for Aldridge and Elbridge,[102] merchants of Bristol. He gives his age as "four score" in a deposition in 1626 (b. abt. 1580). He was still living in 1662, age 80. He seems to have been a controversial character, but had good relations with the natives.

4. There are a handful of pioneers on the river who seem to have no bearing on Captain Wiggin's life . . . such as Edward Ashley. Scores came and left just as quickly. Dozens of ships came and left; and so it went in the early years on the Piscataqua.

5. The Hiltons:[103]

A. Edward[104] was a fish merchant and a member of the Fishmongers' Guild of London.[105] Edward arrived in Portsmouth, New Hampshire, in 1623. In 1623 he and William (there seems to be some division about whether Edward and William were brothers or cousins) began the settlement of Dover, NH (Squamscott Patent:[106] Dover, Durham, Stratham and parts of Newington and Greenland) where he resided until 1671.

B. William arrived in 1621 from Biddick, near Washington, Northumberland, England. The son of Roger Hylton/Hilton, he possessed shipbuilding skills, was a knowledgeable fisherman, a skilled seaman, kinsman of Edwin Sandys, then Governor of the London Company of Virginia. In 1623, his wife and two

---

102 These two men were shipowners and prominent in Bristol politics. We will cover Bristol in detail.

103 In 1623, Anthony Hilton, of the South Shields branch of the Hiltons and a "Master Mariner," was commissioned to take settlers to the Jamestown, Virginia, settlement and to explore the Hudson River. He has no direct bearing on the New England Hiltons.

104 Genealogical and Personal Memoirs, Relating to the Families of Boston and Eastern Massachusetts; William Richard Cutter, A.M., Vol IV, 1908, NY Lewis Historical Pub.Co. pps 1813-1820

105 Discovery of Mr. G. Fothergill as ref. in New Eng. Reg. 1xi; "gives name of Edward Hilton of the fishmongers with the memorandum "newe England" after it in a tax roll of London dated 1641."

106 Possession was given to Captain Thomas Wiggin and others on 7 July 1631; Sup. Ct files: New Eng. Reg. xxiv, 264), part going to Lord Saye and Lord Brooke and to individual settlers and some to New England Gentlemen (Gen. Personal Memoirs Relating to families of Boston, pg. 1,814 . . . see FN #5).

children joined him, and they moved to Hilton Point, on the Piscataqua River, now named Dover, New Hampshire.

6. John Hocking, John Wright, and Thomas Wright were Bristol merchants who owned Hilton's Point for about two years' time . . . John Hocking[107] was killed on the Kennebec River by John Alden's[108] men in 1634 after Hocking had shot to death a man who opposed his trading with the Indians on that river. John Wright was a witness with Thomas Wiggin to the Vines grant in 1630. Governor Winthrop says: "The Lords Saye and Brooke wrote to him and to Mr. Bellingham, that however they might have sent a man-of-war to beat down the house at Kennebec, they desired that 'some of ours (of Boston) might be joined with Captain Wiggin, their Agent at Pascataquack to see justice done."

7. Stephen Reeks,[109] master of the *Swift*, also a witness to the Vine's patent, who was on the Piscataqua in 1628/29 when Thomas Wiggin was there.

8. Captain John Mason was an English sea captain who had served as governor of Newfoundland from 1615–21.[110] His discourses on the codfish was a key to staggering figures of involvement in that industry alone in the early seventeenth century.[111] What an interesting man he was! I wish I had the space here to cover his life in detail; but since we don't, let's concentrate on his connection to Captain Thomas Wiggin. It is entirely possible they had an association prior to 1632. Ironically, their descendants would have a rough relationship, and their grandchildren would marry.

Captain Mason, born in 1586 (Kings Lynn, Norfolk, England), was baptized 11 Dec 1586 in St. Margaret's Church and died in 1635 in Portsmouth, Hampshire, England. Although Mason never set foot in New England, he was appointed first vice-admiral of New England in 1635. He died that same year while preparing for his first voyage to the new colony.

---

107 There was an ongoing dispute over trading rights on the upper-river reaches with the Indians. Neither side would budge in this dispute, so it ended in a shootout with a deliberate murder of Hocking. See *Collections of Maine Historical Society* at Google Books Online.

108 Alden was sent to the Kennebec with a shipload of men on behalf of the Massachusetts Bay Colony to quell the quarrel over trading rights with the Indians. The Maine patentees maintained the Massachusetts Bay Colony under Winthrop had no rights on the river.

109 *The New York Genealogical and Biographical Record, Vol XLVII,* 1916, pg 253; pub NY Genealogical and Biographical Society.

110 John Mason, *A Brief Discourse of the New-found-land,* Edinburgh, 1620.

111 *Vexed and Troubled Englishmen,* 1590-1642; Carl Bridenbaugh, NY Oxford Univ. Press, 1968; pg228: 800 people in Newfoundland, 1635; 26,700 tons of shipping; 10,680 mariners; with 13% profits.

Belknap[112] says Mason was a London merchant in his early years (c. 1606–1620). Mason was a churchman and a Royalist in politics—both traits abhorred by Puritan settlers of New England. This period of Mason's life could have easily put him in contact with our Thomas Wiggin. These are Thomas's apprenticeship years. It would certainly have put him in contact with Hannibal Wiggin, who was employed by Bernard Cator, a wealthy merchant of London. It is worthy of note here though, that the Cator family were Royalists and would eventually lose all their holdings in the English Civil War of the mid-1600s. I have no doubt at all that the Cators and Mason were close associates, as London residents sharing the same political views, if for no other reason than politics. Mason would also have been well acquainted with Thomas Gybbes, grandfather of Thomas and Hannibal Wiggin.

On 9 March 1622 (Council's second grant), Mason received the grant of "Mariana," a grant of land lying between the Naumkeag and the Merrimac Rivers, extending from the seacoast to the heads of both rivers and all the lands within three miles from the shore. On 10 August 1622 (the Council's third grant), Mason and Gorges jointly received the land lying upon the seacoast between the Merrimac and the Kennebec Rivers, extending threescore miles into the country, and all islands within five leagues of the premises (Province of Maine). Thus, Mason was joint proprietor of this territory that was to become New Hampshire even before a single settler had built a dwelling on the Piscataqua River.

In 1625, Mason was involved with the expedition against Cadiz as commissary general under the High Lord Admiral, Duke of Buckingham. In 1626, Mason was the treasurer and paymaster for the armies in the war with France and Spain.

7 November 1629[113] finally saw Mason being relieved of his arduous duties for the Crown, and he was granted the patent of land that he called New Hampshire, out of the affection he held for Hampshire, England.

1632 finds him living on Fenchurch Street, London; elected VP of Council for New England with the Duke of Warwick as president, and committee often meets in his house. The Council disbands in 1635, and Mason receives his patent for *Masonia*.

1634, Mason was appointed captain of the Southsea Castle, an ancient fortress commanding the entrance to the harbor at Portsmouth, England. He

---

[112] Jeremy Belknap, 1744-1798, clergyman and historian; Pub three v. of *History of New Hampshire*, b. Boston, MA, minister in Dover, NH, died in Boston, MA.

[113] 1629 is a very important date for our research into Wiggin as it is when he is documented as being on the shores of the Piscataqua River and signing patents as a witness.

was also to make annual visits to the forts and castles in England and make a report to the government.

1635, Captain Mason dies and leaves his New Hampshire lands to his (only child) daughter, Anne, and her young children, the eldest only seven. He directs that he should be buried in St. Peter's Church, London, a church of royalty, kings, and queens.

> BURIAL PLAQUE:
> TO THE GLORY OF GOD AND IN MEMORY OF CAPTN
> JOHN MASON, CAPTAIN IN THE ROYAL NAVY
> TREASURER OF THE ARMY-CAPTAIN OF SOUTH
> SEA CASTLE-GOVERNOR OF THE COLONY OF
> NEWFOUNDLAND-PATENTEE AND FOUNDER OF
> NEW HAMPSHIRE IN AMERICA-VICE ADMIRAL
> OF NEW ENGLAND-BORN 1586 DIED 1635
> THIS FAITHFUL CHURCHMAN DEVOTED PATRIOT
> AND GALLANT OFFICER OF WHOM ENGLAND AND
> AMERICA WILL EVER BE PROUD
>
> BURIED IN WESTMINSTER ABBEY.

Captain Mason's descendant, Robert Tufton (who took the surname *Mason*), married Catherine, the daughter of Thomas Wiggin Jr. Robert was lost at sea in 1696. He was the father of two children with Catherine, named Elizabeth and John, neither of whom used the surname *Mason*. Elizabeth later married Walter Philbrick, who died in 1732; and then she married Rev. William Allen of Greenland, New Hampshire. Captain Mason has descendants through Catherine's two children with Robert Tufton (Mason): John m. Susanna Moffett of Boston and had three issue. John died in Havana in 1718, and his widow m. (2nd) Thomas Martin.[114]

Robert Tufton Mason has a rich history of altercations with both Andrew and his son Thomas Wiggin. One such altercation took place between Thomas, son of Andrew, and Robert in the home of Walter Barefoote, brother-in-law of his uncle Thomas II. The court records of the time are rich in reports of pushing, shoving, name-calling, and the like, between the three men. Andrew had even pushed Robert into a ditch and relieved him of his pistol, which he was told to return in a court case on the incident. These altercations between

---

114 *Captain John Mason*, by Charles W. Tuttle, edited by John W. Dean, pub. Of Prince Society, by John Wilson & Son, 1887, Boston, pg. 40.

the Wiggin men and Walter Barefoote (who was the brother of Thomas II's wife, Sara Barefoote[115]) and Mason forms a triangle of conflict that reads like a TV miniseries! In spite of these conflicts, Walter Barefoote, upon his death, leaves Thomas II and his wife, Sarah Barefoote, the bulk of his estate.

The striking similarity of Captain John Mason's life and that of Captain Thomas Wiggin's are too close not to be noted. The years of Thomas's apprenticeship, the 1627 letter for a marque against the French, his going to New England in 1629, and more—it all fits nicely with the history of Captain Mason.

9. Captain Walter Neale[116] (b. abt. 1595 and d. aft. 1639) was the son of Captain Walter Neale. He was a soldier under Count Mansfeldt in the French and Spanish wars; 1629 finds him in financial straits. In the spring of 1630, he traveled with Ambrose Gibbons on board the bark *Warwick*[117]to the Piscataqua. Built fortifications on the Piscataqua, granted lands to settlers, and for three years was the chief man on that river. This patent seems to overlap the Squamscott Patent and was undoubtedly the reason Neale and Captain Thomas Wiggin encountered each other at "Bloody Point." This famous encounter came to naught as both men decided to let the patent holders figure it out! I think it highly likely these two men had known each other pre-1629 and weren't about to threaten each other's lives over a land dispute. This incident also points to a possible previous relationship under sail on the French and Spanish coasts.

10. Christopher Levett[118,119] (1586–1630, died at sea) whose letters fell into the hands of Thomas Wiggin and thus disclosed the plans to usurp the power of Winthrop. It was Levett's house at Casco Bay they were all residing in from 1628 to 1630. Born 1586 to an ancient and important family in Yorkshire, he resided in Dorsetshire, was a councilor of New England, captain in the Royal Navy, author, and died in 1630 on board ship.[120] From birth to death, Christopher led a varied, interesting, and well-traveled life; and he typifies the strong character

---

115 The surname variants include Barford in England.

116 *Captain John Mason*, by Charles W. Tuttle, edited by John W. Dean, pub. Of Prince Society by John Wilson & son, 1887; Boston

117 You will find many references to there being a "soldier for discovery" on board the Warwick without an actual name being used. It's Captain Neale they are referring to.

118 Wrote a book titled: *A Voyage into New England, Begun in 1623, and Ended in 1624, Performed by Christopher Levett, His Majesty's Woodward of Somersetshire, and One of the Council of New England.*

119 New England Ancestors, New England Historic Genealogical Society; www.newenglandancestors.org/research/database/great_migration

120 *Christopher Levett of York, The Pioneer Colonist in Casco Bay*, by James Phinney Baxter, printed for the Gorges Society, Portland, Maine, 1893.

and will of the men who were venturing into New England. He was well educated with a financially strong heritage and an insatiable curiosity. Although he was married to the daughter of a Puritan, he himself was a Royalist.

11. Richard Bonython:[121,122] Magistrate and agent of Gorges: b. 1580, Truro, Cornwall; died 1650; married Lucretia Unknown, b. 1631; and his daughter, Elizabeth, m. Richard Cummings. Bonython "traded for a lot across the river" for his newly wed daughter to reside on, and this was apparently close to Sandy Point. Richard Cummings is the man of whom it is said "he was late for court duties because he had to help his worship to the privy." "His Worship" being Captain/Governor Thomas Wiggin in the time just before his death. Bonython was trained to arms and commanded a company during the French wars.[123,124] Richard Bonython was on the Maine coast in 1629, "taking a view" with Thomas Lewis, Walter Neal, John Oldham, George Vaughn, and Richard Vines with others" at the same time Thomas Wiggin was there. William Gibbons was Bonython's "factor" on the Maine coast. The life and movements of Richard Bonython place him squarely in the early life of Thomas Wiggin pre-1633 and, afterward, in New England.

12. George Wyllys[125] (Willis): George is of paramount interest to us. He was born in 1590 at the Manor of Fenny Compton, Warwick, England. His ancestral home is less than five miles from Bishop's Itchington, where Thomas Wiggin was born. George attended several universities in England (though there is no record of a degree earned) and became a Puritan during those years. He became governor of the Colony of Connecticut, 1642, and died in Hartford in 1645. The Wyllys families were landed gentry of considerable wealth.[126,127] George and his family arrived in Hartford in 1638.

---

[121] Together with Thomas Lewis, they were the two original patentees of Saco, the patent dated Feb. 12, 1629-30.

[122] There is a good account of the Bonython family in *The Western Antiquary*, William Henry Kearley Wright, Google book search, online; Plymouth, Latimer & Son, Frankfort Printing 1882; with pedigrees found on pg 211

[123] Note: this could be significant as a Captain Thomas Wigan sought a "letter of marque" against the French in 1627. Could they have been together at some point during this conflict with the French?

[124] Dictionary of National Biography, p 367, Vol V, 1886; Macmillian & Co., NY.

[125] Wyllys's biography can be found in the CT State Library site at: http://www.cslib.org/gov/wyllysg.htm.

[126] National Cyclopedia of American Biography, NY: J.T.White, 1898, s.v. "George Wyllys" (CSL. Call# E176.N27).

[127] Wyllys, George: The Wyllys Papers, Correspondence and Documents chiefly of Descendants of Gov. G. Wyllys of CT, 1590–1796. Hartford: CT Hist. Soc., 1924 (CSL Call# Hist Ref F 91.C7 v.21).

In the fifteenth century, the "messuages, lands, tofts, and tenements in the vill and fields of Fenycompton"[128] were owned by Oliver Wygan, chaplain, through his wife, Margaret Tubbe Wygan, whose father, Robert Tubbe, had owned them. The deeds of the area show Oliver to be the son of Edward Wygan. By 1525, Oliver is deceased. To wit: "Quitclaim, with warranty, and for a certain quittance, by Edward Wygan, Professor of sacred theology the kinsman (consanguineous) and heir of Oliver Wygan, chaplain, deceased, to Henry Makepeace of Chepyng Dassett of his whole right and title in the lands . . . etc. of Fenycompton and Marton, lately belonging to Oliver Wygan, clerk, deceased."[129] The last deed is seventy-five years before George Willis is born.

13. George Weymouth[130] was a Bristol merchant. He arrived on the Maine coast in 1605 and captured native Indians (Tahanedo, Amoret, Skidwaros, Mannedo, and Assacomoit) from the Pemaquid River and took them back to England. Tahanedo was to be sent back to the shores of Maine in 1606 by another adventurer, Martin Pring.[131]

14. Robert Aldbridge and Gyles Elbridge were merchants of Bristol who were allotted the eastern border of the English Proprietary Divisions of land on 29 February 1631–32, between the Damariscotta and Muscongus Rivers in what is now Maine. Both of these men lived in Bristol within five miles of the estate of Sir Ferdinando Gorges. Both men appear to be acting on their own and not as agents of the Bristol Merchant Ventures. Their lives in Bristol are easily traced, and I found no connection to Thomas Wiggin.

15. Alexander Shapleigh of Kittery in the province of Maine. Alexander Shapleigh from Kittery Point, Kingsweare,[132] Devonshire, England, built the first house at Kittery, Maine, in 1635. "Godmorrock," a castle of Kingsweare, Devon, is the ancient seat of the Shapleighs. I found no connection there between this family and Thomas Wiggin. I doubt he knew Alexander previous to 1630.

---

[128] Ref: L1/97; dated 12 Jan 1 Henry Vii (1486).

[129] Ref: L1/112; dated 1 July 17 Henry VIII (1525).

[130] In 1602, he led an unsuccessful search for the Northwest Passage; writing *The Jewell of Artes*, a manuscript on navigation, shipbuilding, and fortifications after returning to England. James Rosier, biographer, wrote *A True Relation of the Most Prosperous Voyage Made this Present Year 1605*. Rosier had been hired to chronicle the voyage of Waymouth in 1605 that ended up at the Pemobscot.

[131] Pioneers of Maine Rivers, Wilbur D. Spencer, 1930, Lakeside Printing Co., Portland, ME.

[132] Of interest here is a Richard Cater who was b. 1611 at Kingsware, Devon, and moved to Dover, Bloody Point, New Hampshire, in 1643.

16. Thomas Lake is so often styled "an associate of Wiggin." b. 1615 and baptized 11 August 1615 in Tetney, Lincolnshire, England; d. 16 September 1676; killed by Indians and left a large estate; m. Mary Goodyear, daughter of Stephen Goodyear,[133] a prominent merchant and goldsmith of London. They had eleven issue. His daughter Anne Lake m. John Cotton Jr., son of Rev. John Cotton of Boston.

The two were involved in some early patents in Maine to which Thomas Wiggin was a witness. I found no connection between Wiggin and Lake in England.

17. The Cater Surname

The Cater family of Bedfordshire and London was affiliated with the Wiggin clan with the marriage of Hannibal Wiggin, son of Vicar William Wiggin of Bishop's Itchington and Offchurch, Warwickshire, (brother of Captain Thomas Wiggin) who married Anne, the daughter of Bernard Cater (merchant of London), and sister to Andrew.

Richard Cater[134] was born in 1601, the same year as Thomas Wiggin, and came to Dover, New Hampshire, in the 1635. So far, I have not found a document tying the two men together, but it's not a far stretch of the imagination to connect them!

- Richard Cater, b. 1611 at Kingsware, Devonshire, England, immigrated to Bloody Point, Dover, New Hampshire, in 1635.
- Richard Carter[135] died before 1684, and it is from him the Carter's Rocks, which he owned at one time, was named.[136]

18. Thomas Lewis (1590–1640) of Shrewsbury, Shropshire, came to New England in 1628. He resided at Saco, Maine, and was a tavern keeper.

---

[133] Immigrant to Connecuitt, where he was deputy governor.

[134] Richard Cater/ Carter; Richard Carter was living near Pine Point before 1648. Among his descendants were John and Richard Carter, who owned land in the vicinity of Broad Cove in 1719.

[135] As previously noted, the surname went through a spelling change. It's not uncommon to find it as Cator, Cater, Carter all in the same record.

[136] When the town was fighting with the federal government in the 1950s about the construction of Pease Air Force Base, there was a petition presented. The name occurring on the petition is a *William Cater.* He apparently took the original spelling of the name back and used it when signing the petition against the construction of the base . . . . that ultimately cut the town in half and took hundreds and hundreds of acres of land from these founding families! (research of Peter Wiggin of Stratham, 2009)

19. Rev. James Parker (1559–1631), Archdean of Cornwall, resided in Maine, Dorchester, Weymouth, and later immigrated to the Island of Barbados.

20. George Vahan was in Portsmouth in 1631; sent by Mason the patentee. He left by 1634, never to return.

21. Henry Watts, baptized 1602. He came to New England with Edward Hilton and was a fishmonger; he died abt. 1697.

22. Richard Vines, born 1585 in Biddeford, Devon, England, and died in Barbados in 1651; was sent to Maine by Sir Ferdinando Gorges to start a settlement. He removed to Barbados abt. 1645.

23. John Winthrop: 1587–1649

I am not going to dwell on John Winthrop as you likely know all you need to about him. His tone in his early letters seems to indicate he had no idea who Thomas Wiggin was, but he later came to say that Thomas was "divers times amongst us," and the two became solid allies when Thomas Wiggin uncovered the plot to discredit John Winthrop and went to bat for him in 1632, even writing a letter on his behalf (or at least given credit for having written that letter). Perhaps a word about his sister is appropriate here as her son was to give them an inside track on British politics in years to come.

John's sister, Lucy Winthrop (1600–1679), married Emmanuel Downing (1585–1660). Emmanuel was the father of Sir George Downing (1623–1684), who was a graduate of the first class at Harvard College (1643). He was well known for his diplomatic services under both Cromwell and Charles II. Downing Street in London, where the prime minister's residence is located, was named for him.

The Lords

William Fiennes[137] (pronounced "Fines"), born 28 May 1582 at Broughton Castle, died 14 April 1662 at Broughton Castle, near Banbury, Oxfordshire, England. He was the 8th Lord Saye and Sele, 1st Viscount Saye and Sele (b. 1582 and d. 1662), and was a prominent opponent of King Charles. He was the only son of Richard Fiennes, the 7th Lord Saye and Sele, educated at New College, Oxfordshire, and succeeded to his father's lordship (barony) in 1613.

Member of the House of Lords and a close friend of Oliver St. John, Francis Russell (4th Earl of Bedford),[138] Robert Greville,[139] 2nd Baron Broke (AKA Brooke), John Pym,[140] and others. These are the men who worked together in two companies founded for the colonization of America. The Providence Island[141] Company was to further the settlement of the Caribbean island of Providence,[142] and the Saybrook Company was formed to settle Connecticut.[143,144] The Saybrook Company had an interest in the Dover Patent[145] in New Hampshire from 1633 to 1641.

William Fiennes did not favor the dissolution of the monarchy, and when King Charles was beheaded, he retired to an island he owned in the Bristol Channel (Isle of Lundy) and did not return until after the Cromwellian era.

Banbury Castle, Banbury, Middlesex, was the ancestral seat for the lord, and it is located less than ten miles south of Bishop's Itchington and formed the southern end of what I call the "Puritan triangle"[146] of the midlands.

---

137 Affectionately called "Old Subtlety"

138 (1593 to May 9, 1641): His daughter, Catherine Russell (died 1 Dec 1676), became the wife of Robert Greville, 2nd Baron Brooke. His other three daughters all married earls too. Greatly trusted by Pym and Oliver St John and supported by Clarendon. Styled one of the "great contrivers and designers" in Parliament.

139 See next section

140 Treasurer of the Providence Island Company; helped impeach George Villiers, 1st Duke of Buckingham; a leader in Parliament of many causes; b. 1583- d. 1643

141 Now *Providencia,* part of Colombia

142 Now *Providencia,* part of Colombia in the Caribbean

143 Settled in 1635 by deed obtained from the 2nd Earl of Warwick

144 John Winthrop the younger (1606–1676) was their governor at Saybrook.

145 1633 bought a plantation at "Cocheco"— now Dover, New Hampshire

146 More on the Puritan Triangle later

While the lords were an important force behind settling New Hampshire (and Connecticut), they lost interest after a few years because of the failure of their plan to establish a hereditary aristocracy in New England. Due to this reason, they turned their attentions to the Caribbean.

In 1641,[147] they sold the Dover patent to Massachusetts; and in 1644, they sold Saybrook to Connecticut.

In 1649, following the beheading of King Charles, William Fiennes withdrew from public life and self-exiled to the *Isle of Lundy* in the Bristol Channel. He did not return until the end of the Cromwellian era.

BROUGHTON CASTLE

The family seat for Lord Saye and Sele was a castle located west of Banbury, Oxford, that I had visited in the 1970s. I had a return visit scheduled in 2007 after much correspondence with the present Lord and Lady Fiennes and their son. Both of the present family monarchs were so helpful to me in my research, and my son and I were so looking forward to meeting with them in 2007, but I fell and shattered an arm the day before our meeting.

I was initially so hopeful of being able to search the lord's library for any correspondence between Captain Thomas Wiggin and his employer. However, that library is apparently long gone. There was a break in ownership of Broughton Castle a few generations ago, and a lot of the family archives disappeared. The lord's son, Michael Fiennes, tried his best to find anything for me to see and even put me in touch with his parents in that quest. We were not successful in finding any surviving documents.

The Fiennes family has a rich heritage going back to Sir John de Fiennes, commander and defender of Dover Castle (Hampshire County) under William the Conqueror. Sir John was also in charge of the Cinque Ports.[148]

Broughton Castle helped to create English history—if not world history. The Royalist headquarters was less than twenty miles away at Oxford. Most of the early conspirators against the Royalists were members of Parliament, and

---

[147] 1641 saw the loss of *Providencia* to the Spanish

[148] Cinque (pro: "sink" ports) established in 1155 by Royal Charter and consisted of five ports: Hastings, New Romney, Hythe, Dover, and Sandwich and supported by the two ancient towns of Rye and Winchelsea, a series of coastal towns in Kent and Sussex at the eastern end of the English Channel. These ports were all originally military and commercial ports, but are now all used by small craft and entirely ceremonial in nature. Since the original confederation was formed, about seven more ports have been added: Lydd, Folkeston, Faversham, Margate, Deal, Ramsgate, and Tenterden. The original ports were also to maintain ships ready for the Crown to use when they needed them, and in return, they were granted an "exemption from tax and tallage."

they met in this castle. The castle was to become a stalwart against all odds and quite the opposite of its image today of grace and serenity.

During the English Civil War, William and his four sons supported the Parliamentarians and raised four troops of Horse Guards; they fought at the Battle of Edgehill in 1642. Soon thereafter, the local Royalists, who were superior in numbers, laid siege to Broughton Castle and captured it. Banbury itself was burned several times.

FAMOUS FIENNES ANCESTORS

The Fiennes ancestors did not shrink from their ambitions and were always in the forefront of political activities. On 4 July 1451, James Fiennes (6th Baron Saye and Sele) was beheaded by Jack Cade after being dragged from the Tower of London, where he had been sequestered after being banished from office due to adhering to the party of William de la Pole, Duke of Suffolk.

James's brother, Roger, married the granddaughter of Thomas Dacre ("Lord Dacre") named Joan Dacre.

William (2nd Lord Saye and Sele), the son of the above James, was vice admiral to Warwick, Lord High Admiral of England, and died in battle in 1471.

Another William was the employer of Captain Thomas Wigan. This William was created a viscount by King Richard and was again constituted by King Charles, upon his restoration, as Lord Keeper of the Privy Seal. William Fiennes died 14 April 1662.

This is also the man who I believed would have bestowed the rank of captain on Thomas Wiggin before his return to New Hampshire in 1633, as leader of a group of settlers, even if he had never owned a ship. Both Lord Saye and Lord Brooke had the ability to convey such rank, and it would have been in their best interests for our ancestor to carry such a rank. So whether Captain Wiggin ever owned a ship is immaterial regarding his rank.

LORD BROOKE

Fulke Greville, Lord Broke/Brooke, was born 3 October 1554 at Beauchamp Court, Warwickshire, into a wealthy family. He was educated at Shrewsbury School (Shropshire) alongside the man who would become his one true love, Sir Philip Sidney. Fulke also became a fast friend of Sir Edward Dyer, Samuel Daniel, and Sir Francis Bacon. After leaving further education at Jesus College, Cambridge, he went to the court of Queen Elizabeth I. Holding numerous offices (Secretary of the Principality of Wales for forty-five years) and four terms in Parliament, he was Treasurer of the Navy (1589–1604), Chancellor of the Exchequer (1614–1622), made the 1st Baron Brooke by James I in 1621, and was endowed with both Knowle Park and Warwick Castle.

Greville's life was to be cut short by a servant who stabbed him on 30 September 1628 when he became disgruntled over a will Greville had written. Greville is buried in St. Mary's Church, Warwick.

One of the things Lord Brooke is so well known for are his writings. They were all published posthumously, except for a few verses in anthologies (1609) published as part of *Mustapha*. His most famous work is his dedicated writing to his friend, Phillip Sidney, titled *The Life of the Renowned Sir Philip Sidney*. It was written between 1610 and 1614 but not published until 1652, well after his murder in 1628.

Robert Greville, 2nd Baron Brooke (1608–1643), would have been Thomas Wiggin's employer in 1633. Robert was the cousin and adopted son of Faulk Greville. Robert commanded the Parliamentary forces of Warwickshire and Staffordshire in the Civil War and was killed while besieging Lichfield Cathedral on 2 March 1643.

The Shakespeare Trust holds almost all the deeds and records pertaining to the baron's holdings in Warwickshire, and they include records for Chesterton and Kingston.[149] DR78: The Willoughby de Broke collection, Vol. 2 (covering nos. 1409–1747), is a handwritten calendar compiled by E. G. Tibbits in the late 1930s of subsequent deposits made up to that time. The material comprises further deeds, marriage settlements, estate accounts, personal papers, and inventories, mainly sixteenth to nineteenth century, primarily relating to Warwickshire but including some out-county material.

The Verneys of Compton Verney (located just south of Kingston), who also held the title of Barons Willoughby de Brooke, are also included in these holdings. The close proximity of Compton Varney, Kingston[150], Chesterton, and Bishop's Itchington placed a young Thomas Wiggin right in the middle of a huge resource of titled gentry.

Butler Wiggin, the last of the Wiggins to occupy King's Farm[151], was affiliated with these same families.

---

149 Kings Farm is the land where I found records of ownership by Butler Wiggin/ Wigan.

150 In Old English "ton" as a suffix denoted a farm or place.

151 The district/parish is known even today as Kingston; the farm within that district is called King's Farm or Kings Farm, depending on the record.. It is situated just on the west side of Bishop's Itchington extending towards Chesterton where the windmill is located. Today this farm is considered the family seat of the Wiggin Clan of Bill Wiggin, member of parliament. This clan is not attached to Captain Thomas Wiggin.

Surname and Given Name Origins

MEN NAMED *THOMAS WIGGIN*

Deciding to find all the men named *Thomas Wiggin* in the British Isles born between 1580 and 1620 with the International Genealogical Index,[152] church records, deeds and court records, and more—in each county, I identified over 150 men carrying the name *Thomas Wiggin,* with variant surname spellings. Now I had to bring that list down to a manageable size—a task that took years. Using the map[153] of counties for the Tudor Era, I progressed county by county, compiling records on men named *Thomas Wiggin.*

Thomas Wiggin did not come from Lincolnshire, Lancashire, Suffolk, Norfolk, or Oxfordshire as claimed by so many authors and historians. Knowing a document of birth in those counties had never been found did not mean I was comfortable ignoring them. I searched them all and did find men named *Thomas Wiggin* in some of them, but none who had gone missing from the local records or who fit a time line to be Thomas Wiggin of New England. I am not surprised by those results, but I feel comfortable knowing I have done my own research in an effort to validate claims for his birth within that five-county area.

NORFOLK

Norfolk county is one of the four places Thomas Wiggin is said to be from because a "Wiggin Farm" was found close (it was really over 10 miles away and down what was a very rough Roman road) to the church where Reverend Leveridge[154] was preaching prior to coming to New Hampshire. I searched every

---

152 Hugh Wallis has the IGI site: http://freepages.genealogy.rootsweb.ancestry.com/~hughwallis/

153 See county map in the beginning of this book's Section I.

154 Leveridge is one of those of unknown ancestry, and we speak more of him in another section.

record for this county, trying to make a connection, and could not make one that would hold up to scrutiny.[155]

I did come across a very interesting connection between the MASON and WIGGIN families. Boyd's Index showed a Joan Mason marrying Thomas Wiggen in Heacham, Norfolk, but I never found them in the Heacham records. I did find them in the records of Holkham, 1542–1812, V1 (496,683) to wit: *1615, Wiggen, Thomas and Mason, Joan, 14th June.* In 1630, I found Joan Wiggen marrying John Hernes on 22 July, indicating Thomas has died. There were other Masons found in the records from 1561 to 1633 and also a Margaret Wiggen (1599) who married a William Mason. This is the county that Captain John Mason also came from and whose descendants married into the Wiggin family of New Hampshire. Records of a display of bad blood between the Mason and Wiggin grandchildren in New Hampshire and the marrying of Thomas Junior's daughter to the Mason heir indicated a strong possibility of a history. This whole combination of Mason-Wiggin records was of particular interest to me when I assumed Thomas Wiggin was born in 1592. None of it fits with a Thomas born 1601. Captain John Mason only had one daughter who married a Tufton, and her sons took the name Tufton-Mason to comply with their grandfather's will and claim their New England inheritances. I did not rule out this relationship for Thomas Wiggin for a decade or more until I had to consent I never could find any more connections to substantiate this being Captain Thomas Wiggin's involvement.

LANCASHIRE

Lancashire County was another county I spent years researching as one of the places claimed to be the birthplace of Captain Thomas Wiggin. It is certainly one of the strongholds of the WIGGIN/WIGAN clan. You find the name spelled *Wigan, Wigane, Wigging, Wiggines, Wiggon, Wygan, Wygane, Wiggin,* and so forth, with the modern preference of *Wiggin.* The National Archives preference for records of the town of Wigan is "Wiggin," even if it's spelled *Wigan* in most titles. Court records are mostly held under *Wiggin* as that's the way *Wigan* is pronounced in Lancashire.

If you do not become as mesmerized by Chorley, Lancashire, as I did, there's something wrong with your research mind. I so wanted this to be where our Thomas Wiggin came from that I spent years researching every single record on Chorley I could find. I still find it very odd that there is every single Wiggin given name in multiples in Chorley, but not the given of Thomas in the

[155] Discussions with the local archivists revealed she thought it impossible someone living 10 miles away, down a very rough Roman road, would even attempt to go to church under travel conditions like that.

years of concern. I simply can't explain that one. The closest I got was a Thomas b. 1605 to James Wygan of Chorley.

There was a Thomas Wiggin who married in 1598 to a Janet Parker, but I never found any issue born to them. I believe he's the father of another Thomas b. 1605 in Bury, Lancashire, but I could not prove that one either. None of them seemed to fit, and none of them appeared to leave the county.

Chorley, Lancashire, has a huge contingency of Wiggins including an Andrew,[156] who was baptized on 20 May 1558, the son of Roger Wiggan. Roger is also the father of a Cecily (July 1580), and Roger was buried 12 April 1583. I never found any more records on this Andrew, and the name *Roger* does not carry down through Captain Wiggin's line in America. Other given names in this line are *Hugh, Oliver,* and *Robert.* Heapie, Lancashire, was another place name with the clan showing up in large numbers.

STAFFORDSHIRE

Staffordshire County holds so many *Wiggin* (consistently spelled that way) names that it took me several years to figure them all out. Two Mary Wigginses were buried at St. Mary, Aldridge: one on 15 July 1662 (a widow) and the other on 20 June 1666 (wife of John Wiggin). There were also two burials for Thomas Wiggin at Aldridge: one on 2 July 1667 and one on 4 December 1670, both in the churchyard. What got me started on these two *Thomas* men was a marriage record between a Thomas Wiggin and Mary Comberladge in 1621. The date fit as that would have been at the end of our Thomas Wiggin's apprenticeship. However, both Sue Lowe[157] and I thought more likely she is the Mary buried in 1662 as "a widow." Thomas predeceased her. The Thomas of St. Matthew, Walsall, Staffordshire, showed no issue in the registers.

I also found the surname spelled *Wiggaine* and *Wiggayne,* which I thought were interesting variants.

Sue Lowe[158] told me the early Aldridge parish registers were missing (or destroyed), and the one remaining dates from 1660. The first entry in 1660 (July 1) was for William Wiggin, son of Thomas and Anne Wiggin. Other personal names found were *Henry, Arthur, Joseph, Elizabeth, Samuel, Catherine, John,* and *Thomas.* In correspondence with other researchers in Staffordshire and other archivists, they told me they were "not missing a Thomas and did not feel their Thomas ever left the county."[159] I'm inclined to agree with them.

---

156 Chorley PR, 844,801, item 4, 1548-1653; 942.72 B4L V 38

157 A fellow researcher who worked with me for quite some time.

158 Private researcher of the Lowe clan I worked with over a long period of time.

159 Various correspondences with fellow researchers in England, including local archivists.

Northumberland County: William Wigan, b. 1564 in St. Helens, Auckland, had two issue, Elizabeth in 1590 and son Thomas christened on 2 July 1592. That one got me excited due to the date! However, this Thomas married and was having issue at a time he would have been in New England. So he's not Captain Wiggin of New England either.

LONDON and SURROUNDING AREAS

I found a lot of Wiggin families in London, Middlesex, and Westminster with multiple Thomases. The London Thomas Wiggin, with a birth date of 1592, became a top contender for Captain Wiggin, and I carried him on my list for decades; I was just unwilling to let him go.

Middlesex and Westminster were both quickly eliminated as possible candidates with ongoing church records. Westminster[160] has a large family of Wiggins well-documented in church records. The London population is so mobile, with whole families moving in and out of the city with the seasons. They had country estates to manage as well as business activities in the city. This clan will be covered in other chapters.

THE IRISH 1630

The problem with searching Irish records is they are all owned and controlled by the Catholic Church. The church is difficult to work with. You have to submit a written request for a lookup and only get partial answers. You're never allowed to view a document in its entirety. That nagging feeling of "what was omitted" is always with you. The online sites for Irish research only have records from 1700, and even most of them are nineteenth-century records.

Knowing at least one claim of Captain Wiggin being Irish dictates I search those records thoroughly as they are found at the Salt Lake Repository. There is a William[161] Wiggin in the 1629 muster rolls for Northern Ireland.[162] I found *Andrew, Alexander* (two of them), *Thomas,* and *William Wiggin* on the Fermanagh 1630 muster rolls. A Thomas and one Alexander Wiggin are reported as having "no armes." Another Alexander and an Andrew Wiggan have "swords only." Sir William Cole, the Fermanagh patent holder, came from London and has family ties in Devonshire. Were the Wiggin men already in residence when Cole

---

160 I include Westminster and London under the same heading here as they are so often thought of as one and the same; however, London itself is only one mile square. Today the cities meld into each other.

161 Barony Magerbuy Sir William Cole knight undertaker of 1,000 Acres: http://www.ulsterancestry.com/muster-roll_1663.html; 1,000 acres to Jerome Lindsey, Esq., Leith, Edinburghshire. Sold to Sir William Cole, 16 October, 1612.

162 *The Book of Scots-Irish,* Robert Bell, 1988, p. 163.

arrived, or did he bring them with him and are they related? We likely will never know as the records are so scant.

I found *Thomas Wiggin* in Churchill, Fermanagh, records on Lough Erne, and he was a farmer. I also found a *William Whitinge*[163] in the same 1630 muster roll. The surname *Whiting* is also strong in the same midland counties with *Wiggin.*

Of special interest in the same Irish muster roll of 1630 are Thomas and William Barefoote (musket only). Captain Wiggin's son and namesake, Thomas Wiggin Jr.,[164] married Sara Barefoote in New Hampshire. However, she and her brother, Governor Walter Barefoote, both came from London and were the children of a Benedict Barefoote.[165]

There are other Irish Wiggin clans that use the name *MacWiggin* and *MacGuigans,*[166] found at Gallinderry on the Derry-Tyrone border, who become Anglicized to *Wigan.*[167] I could not find a *Thomas* among them.

The eliminating factor for them all was the date *1630.* If these men had been born in England or Scotland and migrated to Ireland during the 1610 colonization, I would have found their birth records.

None of them showed any propensity for sailing and were strictly farmers showing up in muster rolls when Captain Thomas Wiggin was in New England, so that eliminates them.

SCOTLAND

Scotland, which was very active in the colonization of 1610 Ireland, has *MacEochagain, MacQuiggin,* and *MacQuiggan* in their records, mostly in Argyllshire and Kintyre.[168] No *Thomas Wiggin* was found.

ISLE OF MAN

Isle of Man, a protectorate of England located between England and Ireland, has both *Mc* and *Mac* with *Quiggin* before 1570. Most surnames changed on the Isle of Man between 1570 and 1620 to comply with new laws to Anglicize

---

163 William Whiting of London was the brother of Katherine Whiting, Captain Thomas Wiggin's wife of 1633.

164 1640–1700

165 See chapter titled "Pedigrees."

166 Sep of Cenel Eoghain

167 The Surnames of Ireland, 941.5 D4mc, 1969; Anti-Irish Surname Law, 1429 Tynwald Court and the Irish 3rd Art. Statute of Kilkenny of 1367; every Englishman must use an English name, dress, mode of riding, according to his estate; use of Irish Language even amongst themselves meant loss of lands and tenements.

168 Ibid.

surnames.[169,170] The *Mc* and *Mac* were dropped, and the name became *Wiggin*. I did not find a *Thomas Wiggin* in the Isle of Man records. The one connection relates to his taking a notary report in the 1620s for the Countess of Derby while she could have been residing in London.[171] The countess has an interesting history and connection to the Isle, and that too is covered in the London chapter.

GIVEN NAMES

Given names in the era of Captain Thomas Wiggin followed a pretty set pattern. Grandfather, father, grandson . . . *John, William, John, William* . . . for first sons. Following the first son's name, other sons were named for the wife's father and then for the father's brothers (especially if they didn't have sons), the godfather, close friends, and the like.

Vicar William Wiggin names his first son John. Therefore it's likely that his father's name was John. Son John names his first son William, and thus it goes down through the generations as *John, William, John, William,* and so forth.

The London Thomas Wiggin's father was a William, and the pattern remained *William, Thomas, William, Thomas,* and so forth.

Given male names also followed a pattern (normally) of either royal names or biblical names: the royal names *Richard, William, John, Thomas, George, Henry,* and the like, or *Moses, David, Isaac,* and other biblical names.

This presented a problem when searching Captain Thomas Wiggin's genealogy as he names his first son with Katherine, Andrew. When I finally traced Captain Wiggin to London during his apprenticeship years, I found him associated with the merchant family named Cator. Bernard Cator had a son Thomas's age named Andrew Cator.[172] Thomas's brother Hannibal Wiggin married Andrew Cator's sister and resided in London for a period of years.[173]

Andrew Cator of London (Kent and Bedfordshire) is the same approximate age as Thomas Wiggin, and he lives on Coleman Street, London, along with the Whiting family and others of the Puritan persuasion. Coleman Street was long recognized as a Puritan hotbed of activity in London. The Whiting family was also searched to see if there was an Andrew in evidence, and there wasn't.

---

169 Anti-Irish Surname Law, 1429 Tynwald Court and Irish 3rd Art. Statute of Kilkenny of 1367; every Englishman must use an English name, dress, mode of riding, according to his estate; use of Irish Language even amongst themselves meant loss of lands and tenements.

170 Surnames of the Manx, L. Quilliam, erosion of Mac had taken place by the beginning of the 17th c., when BMD's began to be recorded.

171 See chapter titled "London."

172 Hannibal Wiggin, brother to Thomas Wiggin, marries Andrew Cator's sister.

173 More on this connection in the chapter titled "London."

Since Katherine's mother was a Patterson/Paterson (Scottish surname), I was especially interested in that line, but it was not fruitful. The Whitings are from Marcham, Kent, and a student of the line will find a document called "the Sentence of William Whiting in London, 1633"[174] of interest. It deals with the distribution of the estate of William Whiting Sr. in regards to his children and wife.

The only other Andrew I could find that might have had influence on a young Thomas Wiggin was Andrew Knightley of Offchurch, Warwickshire. He was born in 1588 so was old enough to have patronized a young Thomas. Following the death of Thomas's mother, about 1603, his father took up the vicarage at Offchurch, and he is buried in that church chancery. It's conceivable to think Thomas may have gone to work with his father on occasion prior to his apprenticeship at age fourteen. However, they don't appear to have lived as a family in Offchurch, so I think this is a stretch of the imagination. While we are imagining scenarios, consider this Andrew Knightley may have been a mentor/educator in young Thomas Wiggin's life.

Andrew Knightly never married nor had issue, but his name was carried down through cousins and brothers. The Knightleys of Offchurch were Catholic, while Vicar William Wiggin was Church of England. However, in later life, Thomas Wiggin never had an issue with his own children marrying into royalist families, nor did he have a problem dealing economically with royalists of Maine. He eventually aligned himself with the Puritans of Massachusetts based mainly on the charter they brought with them in 1630 giving them jurisdiction over that portion of New Hampshire Wiggin dwelt in.

Our ancestor clearly valued economics over religious concerns.

SURNAME ORIGINS

Variant common spellings include—but are not limited to—*Wigin, Wigan, Wigen, Wiggen, Wiggan, Wiggon, Wygan,* and *Wiggin,* all with or without the final "s". It depended upon where the scribe/clerk had been educated as to how the name was spelled, or on local dialects and customs. Or if the person bearing the name was educated, then it was likely spelled how he/she deemed it correct. You will find one man's name spelled a dozen different ways in the same parish and church records. Limiting yourself to one spelling, or even two, is to deny yourself a total history for any surname in any given parish.

The Salt Lake Repository has a section of the British Isles floor dedicated to the study of surname origins. Depending on the author or source you gravitated

[174] Archives to Archives (a2), PRO England, Kew, Surrey, England.

to, you found the meaning of *Wiggin* to be a "wig (e.g., bug as an ear wig)." One source called it a "warrior."

Name changes occurred through the ages in a variety of ways. Fifteenth-century laws made the use of *Mc* and *Mac* prefixes illegal on the Isle of Man,[175] so the C-K-Q surnames changed, and *MacWiggin* became just *Wiggin*. The Tudor attempt at anglicizing Ireland, especially from 1570 to 1620, was successful, so the Isle of Man fell into the same naming pattern.[176]

Scotland gives us *MacQuiggin, MacQuiggan,* and the other variants, which found their way into Ireland. Gaelic[177] origins for the name are well–documented, and *MacQuiggin* became *MacWiggin.* And still, by the late sixteenth century, the *Mac* was dropped. *Wiggin* (without the final "s") is found on the muster rolls of 1629 Northern Ireland. By the late eighteenth century, the final "s" seems firmly attached to the surname, and most of the immigrants to Colonial America sporting that final "s" can trace their ancestry back to Irish roots.

MacGuigan is found almost exclusively in Ulster and most common in County Tyrone. The MacQuigans were a Sep[178] of Cenel Eoghain, found at Gallinderry on the Derry-Tyrone border. In Scotland, the name is found in Argyllshire and Kintyre and is a corruption of *MacEochagain* and is thought to be of Irish origin.

It is accepted by all historians that when William the Conqueror[179] ordered the first census of England, now called the *Domesday Book,*[180] the citizens of his new kingdom had to be identified by something besides a call name, so they took surnames generally based on where they lived, occupations, or their father's call name. They also used landmarks, rivers, and personal traits for surnames. So Edward, son of John, became Edward Johnson. William had a son named George, and he became George Williamson. Father and son could have entirely different last names too, like John of the Cross[181] (John de Cross) of Wigan, Lancashire, might have a son who was called John of Wigan (John

---

[175] The Surnames of Ireland, 941.5 D4mc. 1969, p. 184.

[176] Anti-Irish Surname Law, 1429 Tynwald Court and the Irish 3rd Art. Statute of Kilkenny of 1367; *every Englishman must use an English name, dress, mode of riding, according to his estate; use of Irish Language even amongst themselves meant loss of lands and tenements.*

[177] Dictionary of English and Welsh Surnames, With Special American Instances; CharlesWareingBadsley, M.A., Genealogical Pub. Col., Inc. 1980

[178] "Sep" in Celtic genealogy means a division of; a part of; affiliated with.

[179] William the Conqueror (French: *Guillaume le Conquérant*) (circa 1028 – 9 September 1087)

[180] The Domesday Book was commissioned in December 1085 by William the Conqueror, who invaded England in 1066. http://www.domesdaybook.co.uk/

[181] There was a cross in Wigan, Lancashire and everyone living near it was called "of the cross."

Wigan) or John, son of John of the Cross. It makes genealogy research a bit complicated.

The town of Wigan,[182] Lancashire, England, sports a tree on its coat of arms that is said to be the "wigan tree," a type of ash. It's also visible on the signage outside the local Wigan Tree Pub.

County Norfolk,[183] England, the antiquity of the name is found in other forms. *Wigginhall*—variant of *Wiggenhall* and *Wiggenhul/ Wigginhul* and so forth—testifies to the validity of ancient places named for a surname. The parish name is said to date back to the thirteenth century, when John de Wiggenhale, a descendant of a follower of William the Conqueror, was owner of the manor. Both John and Thomas de Wigginhall/Wiggenhall are found in the old deed records. Thomas de Wigginhall's name is also found stamped in a teaser, which was found at Bawsey Saint James, and his term of office as prior of Castle Acre came to an end in 1376, so that dates the teaser for us. Parishes in Norfolk include Wiggenhall St. Germans, Wiggenhall St. Mary Magdalen, and Wiggenhall St. Peter. Wiggenhall is an Anglo-Saxon place name meaning "haugh" (enclosure) of Wigg (an Anglo-Saxon personal name meaning "beetle").

The name *Wigan*, *Wiggin*, and its variants were of Breton origin and did not appear in Norfolk County until after the Norman Conquest.[184] *Wiggenhall* is said to have evolved into *Wignall*, *Wignull*, and other variants. The Wignalls[185] descended of Ralph Baynard, who held the lands of Wiggenhall at about 1066.

Whether you spell the surname with the final "s" or not, it's a fascinating subject as to how that "s" finds its way onto many surnames. One explanation is to be found in a dictionary giving "Wigan as the Baptised son of Wigan v. Wiggin." It's debatable whether the name *Wigan* comes before the town, or if the town is named for a man.

In its Germanic form, the spelling of *Wigant* comes from *Wigan*, meaning "to fight."

PLACE NAMES: Place names like *Wigginhall*, *Wigginton*, *Wigginhill*, and so forth, are found all over England from ancient times. You will be hard-pressed today to find anyone surnamed *Wiggin* living there, if one ever did.

---

[182] Pronounced Wiggin; hard "g"

[183] Norfolk Hundred Ross of 1275 list William Wygeyn, and the Domesday Book of 1086 gives us *Wighen* and, in 1163, *Wigein*.

[184] Correspondence with Susan Maddock, Principal Archivists, Norfolk Record Office, Norwich, England, dated 1 Feb. 2005.

[185] The Wignall line coming into Colonial America with Judith Wignol, b. 1597, who married Renold Forester Sr., b. 1594, and their daughter, Sarah Forester, who m. William Story of Ipswich, Massachusetts.

Warwickshire has Wiggin's Hill located near Sutton Coldfield, with the ancient spelling of *Vygenhul.*

ANCIENT RECORDS

Bedfordshire, 1310, Walter Rufus held a messuage and 46 acres of land of Walter Wigan, which is the origins of Wiggon's Manor, later found in Cople. In 1613–14, a Walter Wiggin still held considerable property in the parish. Chicksands Priory, owned by Cople Manor, originated with a grant by *Adeliza*, wife of *Wigan*, which is mentioned in the foundation charter of Payn de Beauchamp.[186]

Norfolk Hundred Rolls of 1275 list William Wygeyn, and the *Domesday Book* in 1086 lists *Wighen*[187] and in 1163 *Wigein.* Norfolk seems to be a popular place for the surname *Wiggin.* That's the east coast of England while Wigan, Lancashire, is the west coast.

The following document is a significant find as it ties the Wiggin clan of London to the town of Wigan in Lancashire. Since Thomas Wiggin of London is one of my candidates, I am doubly interested in this record:

> 1347:[188] March 8 Westminster: P. 51: Enrolment of grant by Walter son of William son of Walter de Wygan to John de Wygan, citizen of London, of all the messuage and lands which he now has in the town or territory of Wygan, also of the reversion of a messuage there which Mabel late the wife of William son of Walter, his mother, holds for life of his inheritance, with reversion to him, for rendering a rose yearly at Midsummer for all services and demands. Witnesses: Richard Lacer, mayor of London, John de Gloucestr(ia) and Edmund de Fermenhale, sheriffs of London, Kreginald de Throrp, Robert de Asshe, Thomas Gyles, William de Waltham. Dated at London in the church of St. Bride, Fletestrete, in the suburb of London on 1 March, 20 Edward III.[189]

---

186 A History of the County of Bedford; Vol 3 (1912), pp. 238–42; Bedford, 7 Edw. II. No. 11; British History Online.

187 1086, Wighen was ancestor of the de la Mare family: From Woodditton: Manors and Other Estates; A History of the County of Cambridge and the Isle of Ely: Volume 10: Cheveley, Flendish, Staine, and Staploe Hundreds (north-eastern Cambridgeshire) (2002), pp. 86–90.

188 Source: Calendar of Close Rolls, PRO, Edward III, Vol. VIII, AD 1346–1347; pub. 1905, London, His Maj'ty Stationery Office, Fleet Street, London.

189 Coronation 1 Feb 1327, making this record AD 1347.

Here is a memorandum that Walter came into chancery on 4 March and acknowledged the preceding deed:

> Enrolment of indenture made between John de Wygan, citizen of London, and Walter son of William son of Walter de Wygan testifying that whereas Walter granted to John by the preceding chapter all his lands in the town or territory of Wygan and the reversion of a messuage which Mabel his mother holds for life in that town, John grants that if Walter pay to him or to Joan his wife 6 marks within three years from the date of these presents, then the said charter, the seisin of the messuage delivered to John by virtue thereof, the attornment of Mabel for the said messuage and the enrolment of that charter shall be of none effect, and Walter grants that if he does not pay that sum then the said charter etc. shall remain in force. Dated at London in the church of St. Bride, Fletestrete, in the suburb of London, on 2 March, 20 Edward III.[190]

And, lest you think this Wiggin of London is an insignificant man, read on:[191]

> P. 414 (ibid): Dec 8: William Trussel of Cubbesdon and Warin Trussel his brother, John Brocas, knight, John de Bedeforde, skinner, Thomas de Walden, spicer and Richard de Mallynge, vintner, citizens of London, acknowledge that they owe to *John de Wygan, citizen of London,* 3,000 (lbs); to be levied, in default of payment, of their lands and chattels in co. Berks. (Cancelled on payment)

Three thousand pounds in the fourteenth century is equal to about 48,000 British pounds sterling today. This same *John de Wigan* can be found in more Close Rolls[192] with people who owe him money. John de Wigan is a "money man" (i.e., banker).

> P. 415: (ibid) 1347: (Membrane 8d -- cont.) Enrolment of indenture testifying that whereas William Trussel of Cuddesdon, Warin Trussel his brother, John Brokas, Knights, John de Bedeford, skinner, Thomas de Walden, spicer, and

190 Ibid.

191 No two sources agree on the multiplier to compare money in the 14th c. to today's. It's probably a multiplier of 15.

192 Close Rolls were begun in 1204 to keep track of charters issued by government; written on sheets of paper, stitched together into long rolls to form a yearly record.

> Richard de Mallyngge, vintner, citizens of London, are bound to John de Wygan, citizen of London in 3,000 (lbs) by the preceding recognizance, to be paid at the octaves of Hilary next, John de Wygan grants that if they deliver the body of William Trussel son of John Trussel who is committed to the custody of the said John de Wygan, WARDEN OF THE PRISON OF MARSHALSEA[193] of King's Bench, at the octaves of Hilary next, to the warden of that prison, then the recognizance shall be null and void, but if they do not, it shall remain in force. Witnesses . . . etc. . . . Memorandum that William, Warin, John, John, Thomas, and Richard and the said John de Wygan came into chancery at Westminster of 9 Dec and acknowledged the preceding indenture.

John de Wygan was a warden of an important prison, and I can envision him as a strong-minded, imposing figure no one would want to challenge. John is of the parish of St. Bridges, London; however, the "de Wygan" shows he was originally from Wigan, Lancashire. He is likely the first of the clan in London.

WIGGIN CLAN OF WARWICKSHIRE

> Apparently, the manor of Shrewley[194] afterward came by some means into the hands of the king, and it appears to have been part of the fee of which Henry I[195] enfeoffed Wigan, his marshal. Wigan seems to have forfeited it, but it was restored to his *son Ralph*, who held it by the *service of Marshalsey*. Ralph paid relief for his estates during the years 1163–1165.[196]

This is likely the tie to Lancashire as Wigan, the marshal, ended up in London but was from Lancashire. His owning land in Warwickshire could be one of the missing links to Lancashire and the London clan.

This record places the Wiggin clan in Warwickshire about the time of William the Conqueror and also ties in with the Lancashire Wigan records.

---

193 Note: the Prison of Marshallese was near the present-day Mermaid Court in Southwark on Borough High Street. Not much of it remains today excepting the gate. It was built some decades prior to the Peasants' Revolt in 1381. At first, it imprisoned men found guilty of offences against the Court, pirates, smugglers, and other crimes committed at sea. It was a favorite prop for Charles Dickens stories.

194 http://www.british-history.ac.uk/report.aspx?compid=57144&strquery=Ralph de Wigan.

195 Coronation 5 Aug. 1100; reigned to 1135.

196 British History online: http://www.british-history.ac.uk/.

One of the oldest records I found that sets the surname preWilliam the Conqueror was in August of AD 800:

> Wirhn de Wyggyntun ppet vicar Ecclie de Edlingeham[197]
> Translation: William de (of) Wiggin-ton (the town of Wigan), perpetual vicar of Edlingeham, Northrumbia. [198]

This William de Wiggin "ton" is significant as it shows a place name of *Wyggyn* (ton/tun=town or farm) almost three decades before William the Conqueror ordered the Domesday survey, and that the town's name was being used by citizens as a surname. So is the surname Anglo-Saxon or Danish in origin?

SALADIN MANUSCRIPT ON SURNAME *WIGGIN*

Having researched all the above materials, and more, over a period of several years and several sites, I was ignorantly happy with it until July of 2007 when a man e-mailed his way right into my life. Carlos Wiggen,[199] then of Switzerland and Uruguay, had also been collecting materials on his surname. His findings bear so much relevance to the English origins of the name that we have to address his materials here. Carlos has given his kind permission for me to present his findings to you via his manuscript.[200] I will not attempt to quote his entire article on the origins of the surname.

Carlos says the reason why there appears to be so many different ways of writing the surname, and different interpretations, is two Old Saxon words have been mixed up. The difference comes between interpreting the short, open "i" and the long, closed "i".

WIG (Indo-German "uegh") means "way." In the oldest Saxon text, the *Heliand*, it is written "uuiggeo"; and as a verb, it means "move, drag, and journey."

WIG (long "i") means "fight," and "wigand" is adverbial: a fighting person (i.e., a fighter). In Old Saxon, "uuigand."

---

197 A history of Northumberland, in three parts, part 3 of Volume 2; pg. 124; by James Raine; pub. MDCCCXXVIII.

198 The Kingdom of Northumbria was a medieval Anglian kingdom in what now constitutes northern England and a portion of south-east Scotland. Common to the Anglo-Saxon era.

199 Carlos Wiggen, b. Norway 1950, pub. novels, plays, scripts for movie and TV; speaks four or more languages, holds two PhDs, attended University of Bergen and the University of Oslo.

200 Allorix.ch; Die Namen Wey, Wiggen and Verwandtes; Von Dr. G. Saladin, Zeitglocken Nr.5 vom 7, Marz 1930, a manuscript on the origins of the surname Wiggen, written in German.

Old English is an amalgamation of at least five ancient languages and a morass of inexactitudes and caprice. There are two more Old Saxon words to consider:

1. *Wih* (long *i*) meaning "sanctuary." In the *Heliand*, it is written *uuih*. In the olden days, it often meant a "sacred grove," thus an enclosure containing something "holy." In modern German, *wiege* means "cradle." The same concept seems to be behind the wedding ceremony, symbolically enclosing the couple in the holy union.
2. *Wik* (short *i*) meaning "dwelling place," from the Latin *vicus*, from the very *wikan*, meaning "to retreat, recede."

Kan, as found in *Wickan* and *Wikan*, is just a hardening of *Wigan/Wigen*. *Kan* has no meaning, as it's a present one- or three-person verb based on *kunnan*, meaning "know-how." It makes no sense to attach it to *Wi*.

Wigand, on the other side, is a fighter; it has nothing to do with *Wiggen/Wiggin*.

Gan (Wigan) has to do with Old Norse, bordering on Lapp language. Dr. Saladin mentions *awiggongangan*, meaning "going on erratic ways," such as "going astray." *Wiggon* is here dative plural of *Wig/Wyg*, "the ways I am currently on."

It follows that *Wiggen/Wiggin* is an adverb with a meaning in the direction of "from Wig" or "of Wig." From there, it became a proper name—for example, like calling someone from Texas "Tex."

Dr. Saladin demonstrates *Wig* came to mean "a place where roads meet," then "a clearing/place in conjunction with roads." He's right; forget the *warrior* rhetoric. If we want to stretch the interpretation toward the martial, then go for "watcher/defender," says Carlos.

So the oldest form of the surname is probably *Weigan*: *Wei*, meaning "way," and *gan*, "a forking in two" (i.e., a road junction). Dr. Saladin tries to lead the word back to the Roman *via*, still Latin for "road." It is a fact that the first place name *Wiggen* he has found is at a junction of two roads that existed in Roman times.

Spreading High German over the British Isles is obviously a historical event stemming from the Saxon invasions with Hengist and Horsa, when Roman rule was breaking down in the fourth century. The linguistic germs producing "the Wiggen complex" were certainly there already in the early Middle Ages, way before the Vikings. They began raiding monasteries in the tenth century.

Here's a short history lesson. The Vikings, especially the Norwegian strain, peaked about 1150, with influence in the archipelagoes in the North Sea, which included Orkney, Hebrides, Ireland, Isle of Man, and parts of Wales.

East Anglia was in the hands of the Danish Vikings, and the Swedish Viking did not exist yet.

Carlos says, "An important point here is that the name *Wiggen* does not occur even once in the relevant texts of that day and age, neither in the annals of the kings of Norway, written in Snorri, nor in the Icelandic Sagas. Although men carrying the name of *Wiggen* and variants may have entered with William the Conqueror, my guess is that it was spread by the Saxons. The Saxon tribes spoke a language found in elements of old dialects from central Switzerland, as Dr. Saladin has pointed out."

Wigan, on the River Douglas, Lancashire, has long been claimed by many as the birthplace of Captain Thomas Wiggin. The borough of Wigan is an ancient town going back to Roman occupation and was situated on the main Roman road from Chester to Lancaster. Roman artifacts and coins have been discovered at the banks of the river, dating from the mid-tenth century. The Danes held sway over Wigan, as did the Anglo-Saxons. The old streets in Wigan are still called "gates" (as in Standgate, Wallgate, and so forth), which is from the Old Norse word *gata*, meaning "street."[201]

The history of the town still does not define the origins of the name *Wigan* (pronounced "Wiggin" in the local dialect) and assumes it came from a personal name. With the input of Carlos Wiggen's work on Dr. Saladin's manuscript, we are now better aware of the name's origins; and the town of Wigan, Lancashire, seems to fit the picture nicely. It is located on a Roman road on the bend in the River Douglas and would fit the description of *Wiggen* as presented by Dr. Saladin.

I am content with the meaning of *Wiggin* as coming from the ancient Roman usage, meaning "a junction or splitting of a road; a haugh or tower appearing at a junction that was used for guarding that road." Taking into consideration where all the place names of *Wiggin*[202] appear in England, it makes more sense to believe Dr. Saladin has the correct definition. It also explains why there are so many clans of Wiggin all over the British Isles that are totally unrelated.

---

201 The history of the Borough of Wigan is readily available in numerous websites on the Internet. All quote the same data and origins of the name. British History Online has an excellent explanation of the borough. One can also purchase the set of history books on the Borough of Wigan.

202 *Wiggin*, in one spelling or another, is found in every county of England.

Early Given Name Conventions

1st son = father's father
2nd son = mother's father
3rd son = father
4th son = father's oldest brother
5th son = father's second oldest brother or mother's oldest brother

1st daughter = mother's mother
2nd daughter = father's mother
3rd daughter = mother
4th daughter = mother's oldest sister
5th daughter = mother's second oldest sister of father's oldest sister

Given names frequently were derived from a close friend who had no children (or no sons), godparents, or historical figures.

Kings' names were great favorites, and families would use them over and over again. Thomas, William, George, Henry, and so forth, came down every branch of the tree.

Another pattern was the use of biblical names like Moses, David, John, Mark, Matthew, and the like.

There were no fast rules, but traditions/conventions were strongly adhered to.

FAMILY TREES[203]

See that little leaf up there, the one on the top that branch; see how tall, strong, and straight the trunk circled with limbs so strong; on a windy day the leaves shimmer as if excited and want to talk to each other; come fall they glide on the wind, becoming history.

—Joyce Elaine Wiggin-Robbins (2015)

203 Photo by Arthur R. Mullis

PEDIGREES AND FAMILY TREES

In order for the following chapters to make sense, I present here a short pedigree on Captain Thomas Wiggin. I go into the pedigree in depth in following chapters.

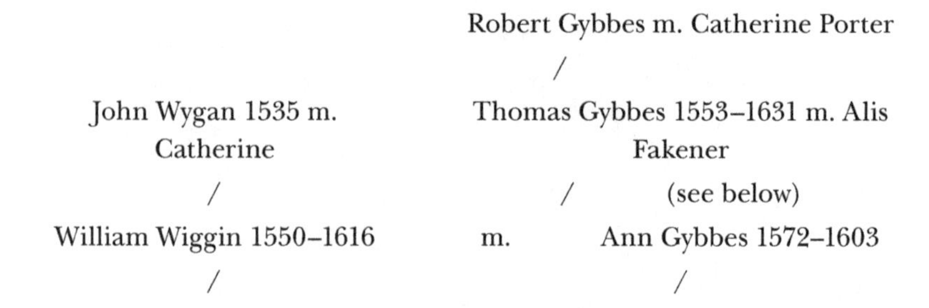

Captain Thomas Wiggin 1601–1666

m. (2) Catherine Whiting
11 July 1633, Saint Margaret's, Fish Street, London, England

Issue:

1. Andrew Wiggin 1635–1708
2. Mary Wiggin 1637–1700
3. Thomas Wiggin 1640–1700

ALIS FAKENER (Faulkner), born 14 May 1545 in Alveston, Warwickshire, England, was the daughter of Jefferie Fakenor (1510–1578) and an unknown mother. She had two daughters by him, Ann and Margaret Gybbes, b. Nov. 1575. Nothing more is known of Margaret.

The Fakener/Fawkener/Faulkner Surname

The Faulkner family appears in Alveston, Warwickshire, about 1540 and disappears by 1635—the year William Fakener's will was probated (prob/11/167; image 116; PRO, the National Archives, Kew, England). William, born 1551, Alis's brother, married Marjory Tyler and had three issue: William Junior, Frances, and Marie. Alis Fakener[204] (Faulkner) was the first wife of Thomas Gybbes, and Anne, their daughter, is recorded in the Honington[205] church registers as the child of Thomas Gybbes.[206] On 28 Nov 1575, a second daughter, Margaret, is born to Thomas and Alis and baptized in St. James, Alveston, Co Warwickshire.

ANN GYBES was born 18 April 1572 in Honington, Warwickshire.

WILLIAM WIGAN/WIGGIN and ANN GYBBES/GIBBES had the following issue:

1. Katherine, 18 July 1591
2. John, 14 Feb 1592–14 Jan 1634
3. Edward, 1 Feb 1594
4. Haniball,[207] 7 Jan 1596–abt 1639
5. William Junior, 18 Feb 1598
6. Thomas, 20 Sep 1601
7. Rychard,[208] 1 Mar 1603

Vicar William Wiggin and Ann Gybbes's marriage is recorded in two places:[209] The Lillington, Warwickshire, and the Bishop's Itchington,

[204] Alis Fakener born: 14 May1545 Alveston, Warwick, England
Marriage: Thomas Gibbes 19 Nov 1571 Alveston, Warwick, England.
IGI Batch Number: C039672 (Note the date of the marriage is less than nine months before Ann was born.)

[205] 1572, Sept 18: Ane (sic), d of Tho Gybbes; The Register Book of Honnington in the Co of Worcestere; 1571-1812, transcribed by J. Harvey Bloom M.A. In the same register book there is a Wyllyam s of Tho Gibbes, 1580, April 10.

[206] The Register Book of Honnington in the Co of Worcester; 1571–1812; Vol 7, dated 18 April 1572 "Ane/Anna, d of Tho Gybbes"; transcribed by J. Harvey Bloom, MA.

[207] You will find his name spelled *Haniball* and *Hannibal.*

[208] You will find his name spelled *Rychard* and *Richard.*

[209] Dr. Penny Upton found it recorded in Lillington but the Archivists at the church didn't have a record of it there.

Warwickshire, registers with the same date of 21 August 1590. There is a reason for the double entry as William Wiggin lived in Itchington but worked in Lillington. Anne Gybbes was residing with her father in Lillington at the time of her marriage.

Vicar William Wiggin earned ten British pounds sterling for his annual work as a clerk in Lillington, Warwickshire.[210] He probably didn't get much more than that as a Vicar.

Ann Gybbes disappears from the records after the birth of her son Rychard in 1603, who was christened in Bishop's Itchington. Dying in childbirth was not uncommon. All her children's christening records are found in the Bishop's Itchington parish records but there is no death record for her.

Katherine, first born and probably named for her grandmother Katherine[211] Porter, marries a Smith.[212] She and her children are remembered in her father's will, though her children are not named. Hannibal was easier to trace due to his unusual name. He will be dealt with later. John and William both remain in Warwickshire and are covered later. A Rychard Wiggin appears in both Gloucester and London records, and it's difficult to know if it's the same man or two different men without spending a great deal of time on the search, which I did not do. I don't know what happened to Edward either, but I did find one in Gloucester. All these names are common in every generation, in every branch, of the Wiggin/Wygan surname and its variants found all over England.

The Gybbes/Gibbs are said to be Bretons who arrived with William the Conqueror[213] and are recorded at the Battle Abby, the site of the Battle of Hastings.[214] There are those who claim the surname can be traced back to North Africa—to the Carthage reign and thus back to the Phoenicians, who descend of the Canaanites. Others claim it's an old Scottish-Pict name first found in Inverness-shire.

Following the death of Ann Gybbes's mother, Alis Fakener, her father, Thomas Gybbes,[215] marries second wife Margaret Wilkes, the widow of Sir

---

210 Thesis work of Dr. Penelope Jayne George Upton: Change and Decay: The Warwickshire Manors of the Bishop of Coventry and Lichfield from the Late Thirteenth to the Late Sixteenth Centuries; Submitted for the degree of Doctor of Philosophy at the University of Leicester, September 2002; pp. 161, 162, and 195.

211 The *C* and the *K* of this name are interchangeable.

212 Check out the Raleigh pedigree. There were Smiths in Bishop's Itchington, but I've been unable to find out what Katherine's husband's given name was. Their children are acknowledged in the vicar's will, but he does not give their names.

213 1028–1087

214 14 October 1066 between the Norman-French army of Duke William II of Normandy and an English army under the Anglo-Saxon king Harold II

215 Will of Thomas: Prob 11/160; image 362; PRO, Kew, England; Wife Margaret outlives Thomas Gibbs and is executrix.

Francis Dymock (and they had a daughter named Ann Dymock, who married Sir Walter Earle[216]).

Margaret Wilkes has two sisters and is coheir to her brother, who died without issue.

> Hodnell DR 18/1/487*19 August 1614*[217]
> These documents are held at *Shakespeare Centre Library and Archive*
>
> Contents:
> Exemplification of an Order in Chancery, dated 22 plaintiffs, and Sir William Kingesmill and Lady Anne his wife, Erasmus Dreyden and Frances his wife (which said *Anne and Frances were the other sisters of Robert Wilkes*), Sir Henry Kingesmill and John Dreyden, defendants, concerning the manor of Hodnell and lands in Hodnell, Ascott, Hooks End, Whittington and Radbourne.
>
> Note: Hodnell is on the East boundary of Bishop's Itchington. June 1612, in a suit between Thomas Gibbes, Esq., of Hodnell and Margaret, his wife (sister and coheir of Robert Wilkes, Esq.)

Thomas Gybbes and second wife, Margaret, have two sons: Edward and Thomas (1561–1578). Edward died a young man, leaving a daughter, Frances, who was married to Sir John Rayney, Baronet. They had a son, Edward, who died in 1703, leaving his namesake son, Edward Junior, who died with no male issue.

> John Rayney, Esq., of Wrotham and West Mailing in Kent received the honour of knighthood at the coronation of Charles I and was created a Baronet 22nd January 1641. He married Catherine daughter of Thomas Style, Esq., of London and had four sons and three daughters John, Thomas, Richard, William, Susannah, m. to William Selby, Esq., of Ightham; Elizabeth m. to Sir John Chichester baronet and Martha m. to Nathaniel Bonnel of London merchant. He m. secondly *Frances daughter of Edward Gibbes, Esq., of Warwickshire and had by her a son Edward who had issue: Sir John Rayney who*

216 There are numerous House of Commons records on him.
217 All records shown here indented are from this source.

served as sheriff of Kent in 1615, died 3rd March 1660 and was survived by his son II Sir John Rayney of Wrotham and West Mailing who married Mary daughter of Jeremy Blackman, Esq., of Southwark and dying about 1680.

Thomas Gybbes/Gibbs does not mention William Wiggin and Ann's issue in his will of 1631, but they are all of age. He has children with second wife Margaret who had inherited the Hodnell estates. Thomas does bequeath the remaining interest in his estates to his two surviving brothers, Tristram and Edward.

In his will,[218] Thomas calls Margaret "my now wife," which is the common language to signify there was a previous marriage(s). Since daughter Ann is deceased, he does not mention her. There is also no mention made of Margaret's daughter from her first marriage. He also refers to an "indenture" made between himself and Margaret dated "first day of December in the fortieth year of the reign of our Queen Elizabeth I" wherein, apparently, they agreed his brothers Tristrim and Edward Gibbs are to oversee the lands of Hodnell, Old Hodnell, and Watergall for his wife and children named Frances, Thomas, and Edward. Thomas maintained a home in London, and in the record of his death (Bishopsgate), he is called "merchant." He died in London in 1631.[219]

Thomas Gybbes/Gibbs was buried in Lillington, Warwickshire, 1631.

Sir Ralph Gybbes (1555–1613) m. Gertrude Wroughton (1552–1611)

/

Mary/Maria Gybbes/Gibbs m. Walter Raleigh (1586–10 Oct 1646)

Issue of Walter Raleigh and Mary Gybbes:

- Carew, baptized in 1638 and buried in January 1639
- Elizabeth, b. 1635
- John, abt. 1631
- Maria
- Walter, b. May 1630
- Lucy
- Dorothy, b. March1623
- Henry, abt. 1626

---

[218] His will is dated 8 Sept. 1631. (PROB/11/160; image 362).

[219] Probate Acts in the Prerogative Court of Canterbury, 1631: Gibbs, Thomas, of p. St Helens in Hodnell, alias Watergall, co. Warwick, (Esq.) but deceased in p. St. Boltoph Bishopsgate, London. Will (103 St. John) pr. Sept. 8 by relict Margaret.

- George, abt. 1625

Sir Ralph Gybbes (1555–1613), son of Robert Gybbes (1528–?) had a daughter named Mary/Maria (1600–?) who wed Reverend Dr. Walter Raleigh, priest, between 1620 and 1623. He was the second son of Sir Carew Raleigh, second son of Sir Walter Raleigh, the explorer. Dr. Raleigh has a colorful history and was a great favorite of Charles I. However, he was taken into custody in July 1645 and harshly dealt with. Eventually, Raleigh ended up in the custody of a man named David Bennett, a shoemaker, who murdered him as he was penning a letter to his wife. Dr. Raleigh's papers were preserved, and they are titled *Reliquiæ Raleighanæ*, being discourses and sermons on several subjects.

Dr. Raleigh's son fought for justice, but little was forthcoming. Marie was executrix of her husband's will, and little else is known of her after that.

Cautionary Note: You will find public postings of Marie/Mary Gibbs/Gybbes being married to Sir Walter Raleigh, which gives the wrong impression. He was Reverend Dr. Raleigh, the priest, son of Sir Carew Raleigh, son of the navigator.

The second Sir Walter Raleigh, second-born son of the navigator, was killed in action fighting alongside his father in Spain. Sir Carew Raleigh, third-born living son and brother of Sir Walter Raleigh II, was surviving heir to his father, Sir Walter Raleigh I. (Sir Walter Raleigh I had a first son who dropped out of the records, so we assume he died young.)

BAREFOOT[220]

Thomas Barfoot m. Katherine
/
Edward Barfoot (1550–1598) m. Winifred Hildersham (1555–1613)
/
Thomas Barfoot (1586–1631) m. Sarah Culverwell (1600–1638)
/
John Barfoot (1616–1671) m. unknown

Issue of John Barfoot and Unknown:

- Sarah, 1642–1711
- Walter, 1636–1688
- Mary, 1632–1694

[220] You will find the surname spelled *Barefoot*, *Barefoote*, *Barfoot*, and *Barfoote*

Winifred Hildersham (1555–1613) was sister to Arthur Hildersam.[221] Arthur married Ann Barefoot, who must fit into the same family line shown in this pedigree. Winifred married twice, and Thomas Barefoot married his half-sister, Sarah Culverwell. Sara Barefoot (b. 1642) married Thomas Wiggin Jr. of Dover, New Hampshire.

Due to the interest in royal connections, I present the ancestry of Ann Pole/Poole here.

Geoffery Pole m. Edith SaintJohn

/

Sir Richard Pole/Poole (1462–1505) m. Margaret Plantagenet (1473–1541)

/

Geoffrey Poole (1494–1558) married Constance Packenham (1498–1570)

/

Anne Poole (1530) married Thomas Hildersham (1530)

Issue of Thomas Hildersham and Anne Poole:

- Arthur Hildersham, 1563–1631
- Winifred Hildersham, 1555–1613

NOTE: Blessed Margaret Pole, Countess of Salisbury. Daughter of George, Duke of Clarence, who was a brother to King Edward IV and King Richard III. Executed in 1541 at the command of King Henry VIII, her cousin once removed.

Issue: Henry Pole, 1st Baron Montagu; Cardinal Reginald Pole; Sir Geoffrey Pole; Sir Arthur Pole; and Ursula Pole.

221 Hildersam or Hildersham, Arthur (1563–1632), Puritan divine, son of Thomas Hildersam by his second wife, Anne Pole, was born at Stetchworth, Cambridgeshire, on 6 Oct. 1563. He was of royal descent through his mother, a daughter of Sir Geoffrey Pole, brother to Cardinal Pole.

Wedding Rings

There was no stronger tie in seventeenth-century England than a wedding ring. When in trouble or need, a man would go to a relative by blood or marriage for assistance. Marrying back into one's own bloodline insured not only social standing, but landholdings. Titled gentry needed permission from the Crown to marry because if they died leaving underage issue, the Crown was responsible for those children until they were of marriageable age. In the case of daughters under the Crown's care, their marriage right was often "sold" in order to increase the royal coffers.

Marriage required readings in the parish church and a marriage intention license, but did not require a church wedding. Once the "intention" was filed, they could just live together and were considered married. The "intention" was filed by a bondsman who put up a pledge of money stating the marriage would be legal. If it wasn't, he lost his money. That seldom happened. The information on an "intention" form isn't very accurate. If an immediate wedding was required, and bans could not be read in the parish church, a "special license" could be applied for with the bishop.

Arranged marriages, of sorts, were popular. A man often contracted to marry an underage girl and then waited for her to become of age. It was not uncommon for a twenty-year difference in ages. Thomas Gybbes's second wife was a ward of the Crown, and her marriage was sold initially to a man who died leaving her with a child. She then married Dymock (no issue), who died, and third she married Thomas Gybbes and had three more children.

Men had to finish their apprenticeships before marriage; in England, they could not work a trade without an apprenticeship, and the terms were strict. Bound to a "master" until age 21 (seven years), sometimes securing a job at the end of the term; sometimes apprentices received a suit of appropriate clothing and entry into a trade guild. They often married right after finishing their apprenticeship.

Captain Wiggin's generation was finding it harder and harder to build on the affiliations of their fathers and grandfathers. The political scene was escalating toward anarchy, and the religious scene was feeling the unrest. Making a marriage based on alliances alone was not going to maintain the inherited safety net it always had. However, for men like Captain Wiggin who were not intimidated by starting over in a "howling wilderness," the world was indeed his oyster. Wiggin had a lot of places to choose from to start over, but as I build his life in England, you will come to see the traditions he carried with him and why he didn't abandon these traditions.

Two of the vicar's sons remained in Bishop's Itchington parish, and for another hundred years, his descendants remain in the area. Butler Wiggin[222] had ties to some very important men of his time and had a home in London as well as owning Kingston Farm[223] in Bishop's Itchington. Kingston could have been the family land all along. It was in Chesterton, which is the parish to the west of Bishop's Itchington and where the famous windmill is found still standing today. Butler married the sister of Sir Richard Ladbroke, mayor of London. (Richard Ladbroke's father had also been mayor of London). Butler is often found in the English records.

In between Butler and Vicar William, the children were making good marriages; Mary (b. 1643), great-granddaughter of the vicar, married into the Poole line. The Pooles are nearly all "Sir Knight" and stem from royal bloodlines. Mary Wiggin's husband (Richard Poole, b. 1633) goes back into the POPHAM[224] line as well.

Marriages were hugely important, and those wedding rings were not to be trifled with. Relationships through marriage were strong and reliable.

While the first marriage of Captain Thomas Wiggin remains unproven, you can be sure it was a well-connected marriage. Everything I found indicated a London marriage, and she likely died in the plagues of that city. There was a marriage in Westminster we will discuss in more detail in section II.

Wedding rings that carry into the pedigrees and have marriage ties into the Gybbes-Wiggin line:

---

[222] 1709–1766; Will of Butler Wigan of Chesterton, Warwickshire Date 04 August 1766 Catalogue reference PROB 11/921; Kingston Manor, a half mile southeast of the church, is an L-shaped house of stone, of which the southwest wing was built in the 16th century. It has low six light mullioned windows, and a massive projecting chimney-stack with four diagonal shafts (From: "Parishes: Chesterton," A History of the County of Warwick: Volume 5: Kington hundred (1949), pp. 42-46.); Memorandum of Agreement between [John PeytoVerney] Lord Willoughby de Broke and William Webb, Tharp, Warwicks. for the tenancy of Kingston Farm, late in the occupation of Butler Wigan, at £250 p.a; WCRO, DR7/2: Feoffment dated 3 June 1751. Mr Butler Wiggin to Richard Wiggan (his brother);
Wigan, Butler, brother-in-law of Sir R. Ladbroke. 29 Jun 1766. (L.M. 379.); 1766: June 29: death of Butler Wigan, brother-in-law of Sir Robert Ladbroke reported in *The London Magazine*, or, *Gentleman's Monthly Intelligencer*, By Isaac Kimber, Edward.

[223] This farm is now the family seat of the Wiggin family.

[224] 1607, Popham Colony was founded at the mouth of the Kennebec River but was short-lived.

DRAKES-PREDEAUX-VILLIARS-BOTELER

1627: Captain Thomas Wigan/Wiggin paid a visit to Sir John Drake of Devonshire to get help with securing a letter of marque and reprisal against the French.[225] There was a good reason Wiggin paid a call on Drake, aside from Drake's connection to the Admiralty:

Humphrey Prideaux (two daughters, Elizabeth and Margery)
(1487–1550) / /
/ / 1st
Elizabeth Prideaux m. Robert Drake Margery Prideaux m. Robert Gybbes
(1523–1572) / (1528–1600) (1512–1554) / / (1528–1586)
Sir John Drake (d. before 1666) Margaret /
m. Hon. Eleanor Boteler* Elizabeth /
Issue: Elizabeth** m. Jane /
Sir Winston Churchill Sr. Robert m. 2nd Catherine Porter
(four sons including)
/
Alis Faulkner 1st m. Thomas Gybbes (1553–1631)
/
Ane[226] Gybbes (and Sister Margaret)
b. 1572 d. abt 1603
m. 1590 Vicar William Wiggin
/
Captain Thomas Wiggin (b. 1601–d. 1666)

*Their daughter, Honorable Eleanor Boteler (d. 1666) married Sir John Drake (d. 1666).
**Their daughter, Elizabeth Drake, married Sir Winston Churchill (b. 1620–d. 1688). Sir Winston Churchill (b. 1620–d. 1688), progenitor of the Churchill family made famous by Sir Winston Churchill of WWII England.

It's interesting to note that Vicar William Wiggin's second great-grandson marries a Butler, names his son Butler Wigan/Wiggin, who occupied King's Farm, Chesterton, Warwickshire, and had business dealings with the Rich family of Warwick Castle. Butler Wiggin married Mary Ladbroke, whose brother was mayor of London, and whose father had also been mayor of London. The family seat was Ladbroke, Warwickshire, close to Bishop's Itchington.

---

225 More on this subject in the chapter titled "1627" in the Thomas Wiggin section.
226 You will find her name spelled *Ane* and *Ann*.

Sir George Villiers, Duke of Buckingham_(1592–1628)

Sir George (1550–1604) married 1st Audrey Saunders (d. 1588) and had a daughter Elizabeth Villiers.[227] Elizabeth married Sir John Boteler, 1st Baron Boteler of Brantfield (b. 1566–d. 1637). Sir George is also the common ancestor of fifteen British prime ministers. Boteler married, before 1609, Elizabeth Villiers, daughter of Sir George Villiers, of Brokesby, co. Leicester, half-sister to George Villiers, 1st Duke of Buckingham. They had two sons and six daughters. The surname *Boteler* became *Butler* and figures into the pedigree of Butler Wiggin, who was named for his mother's surname line.

Ane/Ann Gybbes

Born 18 April 1572 in Honington,[228] Warwickshire, England; daughter of Thomas Gybbes and Alis Fakener/Faulkner.

Died about 1603 with the birth of her last child/son, Richard, Bishop's Itchington, Warwickshire, England; may be buried in Lillington.

Parents: Thomas Gybbes/Gibbes and Alis Fakener/Faulkner.

Alis Fakener/Faulkner: Born 14 May 1545 in (St. James Church) Alveston, Warwickshire, England,[229] and daughter of Jefferie Fakener. This surname is quite confusing in the variations of the spelling. It evolves into Faulkner. Alis was 28 when Ane was born. There is also a son, Wyllyam, born to Thomas, and then they all disappear from the Honington church registers.

Married Vicar William Wiggin on 21 August 1590 in Lillington, Warwickshire; the marriage is also recorded in Bishop's Itchington Saint Michael's church, as the vicar was a resident there.

Genealogy: Ane Gybbes (1572)> Thomas (1530)> Robert (1489)> Thomas IV (1457)> Thomas III (1405)> Thomas II (1377) > Thomas I of Honington, Warwickshire b. abt. 1350.

Surname variations: Gybbes, Gybbis, Gybbs, Gybbe, Gibbys, Gybbes, Gibbe, Gibbes, Gibb, Gibe, Gib, Gibs, Gibbs, Guibe (probably original French spelling).

---

227 Her sister Anne Villiers (b. 1588) married Sir William Washington (1590–1648), brother of Rev. Lawrence Washington, ancestor of President George Washington.

228 The Register Book of Honnington in the Co. of Worcester, 1571–1812, Vol. 7; transcribed by J. Harvey Bloom., MA.

229 IGI C039672

The Gibbs family is easily traced through a manuscript titled *Memoir of the Gibbs Family of Warwickshire, England, and United States of America.*[230] This original account of the Gibbs family was penned by William Gibbs of Massachusetts and Professor Josiah W. Gibbs of Yale College in 1845, when they titled it *Family Notices.* In September of 1879, J. Willard Gibbs released the *Memoir* version.

The second tome of importance in the study of the Gibbs clan is titled *The Gibbs Family History and Their Relatives of the Olden Times* by Montgomery Gibbs, Chicago by Colvin, 1893; compiled and edited by Vernon Lee Gibbs.

During the reign of Richard II,[231] King of England, brothers John and Thomas Gybbes settled in Devonshire[232] and Warwickshire respectively. Their father was Thomas of Honington,[233] Warwickshire. The book above is devoted to Thomas of Warwickshire and his descendant. It is from this book we find the antiquity of Ann Gybbes's genealogy.

Ann was only about thirty-two when she died from childbirth in 1603. Her death left her husband, William Wiggin, with one daughter and five sons, all under the age of ten.

It isn't likely William would have kept all the children with him after his wife's death. At least the last three—Hanibal, Thomas, and Rychard—would need a lot of care. So where did they go? After an exhaustive study of William Wiggin's genealogy, I came to the conclusion he had no Wiggin relatives close by. Therefore, it is likely Ann's children went to her relatives, if only for a short period of time. The Gybbes clan surrounds Bishop's Itchington.

Ann was the daughter of Thomas Gibbs who, by his second marriage, held the adjoining lands of Old Hodnell, Hodnell, Wills Pasture, and Watergall in Warwickshire. These properties adjoined that of Bishop's Itchington, where Ann's husband, Vicar William Wiggin, was employed in the church of Saint Michael's. He was also employed as a clerk in the Lillington church.

Ann was a wife who loved her children. Even though she was pregnant every two years following her marriage, she undoubtedly kept up with the demands of her growing family. Ann's death was not recorded in the Bishop's Itchington church records, and based on her husband's records, we can conclude she died following the birth of her last child. Even though the plague was still dominating the summer months, no one else in the family died of it, so it's not reasonable to conclude Ann did either.

---

[230] Published by Press of Lewis & Greene of Philadelphia in 1879.

[231] Richard II (6 January 1367 to ca. 14 February 1400) was king of England from 1377 until he was deposed in 1399.

[232] The Gibbs clan of South Carolina descends of Robert of Devonshire.

[233] The Manor of Honington: The appurtenances of the manor included 4 water cornmills, 4 fulling-mills, and 3 dove-houses.

Her father, Thomas Gibbs of Hodnell, and his second wife, Margaret Wilkes, the widow Dymock, had three children of their own: Edward, Thomas, and Frances.

Vicar William Wiggin, being an employee of the Clergy of the Church of England, would have been encouraged by his diocese to remarry very quickly following Anne's death. I would not be surprised if the diocese was responsible for the introduction of the widow Ellen Sambrooke of Coventry, Warwickshire, to the vicar. Ellen and her unmarried daughter, named Margaret, would have filled the void left by Ann's death very nicely. Since Ellen was closer to the vicar's age, no doubt, she left a lot of the physical raising of the children in the hands of her daughter, Margaret, and the house servants.

Thomas Gybbes

Thomas Gybbes/Gibbs held houses in London, and I found several of them. "Thomas Gybbes, citizen and mercer of London . . . parishes of St. Mary Magdalene, Milkstreet, and St. Olive's Without Bishopsgate"[234] are all mentioned in ancient deeds. Just which one he resided in is something I didn't pin down. If he wanted to be close to activity, he was on Milkstreet; but if he wanted to be outside London proper, then he was at Bishopsgate. There may well have been more.

The Will of Thomas Gibbes: Dated 2 September 1631.[235] Died in London; interred in Lillington, Warwickshire.

---

[234] Deeds: C.401-C5.00, A Descriptive Catalogue of Ancient Deeds, Vol. I (1890) pp. 424–435.

[235] June 27, 1631: 155. The King's Commission to Edward, Earl of Dorset, Lord Chamberlain to the Queen, Henry Earl of Danby, Dudley Earl of Dorchester, and Sir John Coke, Secretaries of State, Sir John Danvers, Sir Robert Killigrewe, Vice-chamberlain to the Queen, Sir Thos. Roe, Sir Robert Heath, Attorney General, Sir Heneage Finch, Recorder of London, Sir Dudley Digges, Sir John Wolstenholme, Sir Francis Wyatt, Sir John Brooke, Sir Kenelme Digbye, Sir John Zouch, John Bankes, *Thomas Gibbs*, Samuel Rott, [Wrote], George Sand, John Wolstenholme, Nicholas Farrer, Gabriel Barbor, and John Farrar, appointing them Commissioners to consider how the estate of the Colony of Virginia has been, what commodities have been raised there, how the estate thereof standeth at present, what commodities may be raised there which may be more profitable to said Colony, and by what means said Colony may be better advanced and settled in future times; and to present to his Majesty their proceedings from time to time, with propositions for settling said Plantation, and encouraging Planters and Adventurers. This Commission to continue in force notwithstanding the same be not from time to time continued by adjournment. 1 *Memb.* [*Patent Roll,* 7 *Car. I., pt.* 20, *No.* 50.] *Printed in Rymer, see Syllabus, p.* 882.

1. Declares himself a resident of Old Hodnell, Hodnell and Watergall, and Wills Pasture, Warwickshire.
2. "Margaret my now wife . . . by our indenture dated the 5th Sept. the 40th year of reign of our sovereign queen Elizabeth" (1598) . . . indicates they had a prenuptial, leading me to believe Margaret was shutting out any previous issue of Thomas's from inheriting land she was entitled to through an inheritance from her brother Roger Wilkes, son of William, their father. "Tristrim[236] and Edward Gibbs, my brethren the land known as Hodnell/Watergall in the county of Warwick." His eldest son is Edward; the only brother living is Tristrim. These two are to get all the land not held by Margaret through her inheritance. Thomas Gibbs was involved in many land dealings[237] with other men. He acquired land after he married Margaret.
3. All the land his "now loving wife" inherited from her brother, Roger Wilkes, remains hers.
4. He only mentions his two sons, Edward and Thomas, and one daughter, Frances.
5. His wife is the executrix; she's to bury Thomas's body where she decides.
6. Lillington, Warwickshire, records show Thomas Gibbs Sr. was buried there in 1631.[238] The church at Old Hodnell was in disrepair, and all indications are they were not living on this property and I don't believe they ever did.
7. Even though he acknowledges a prior marriage by calling his wife, Margaret, "my now wife," he makes no mention of the two children

---

236 The same deed of 1612 mentions (1) a house in the tenure of Tristram Gibbs, with a stable toward the street on the north side, and a large garden on the south, "walled on the east side and toward a lane of the south side," abuttingwest on the garden of Frances Varney's house; and (2) a house "now or lately in the tenure of Alice, the Lady Dudley," with a paved court on the north side before the door, a stable on the north side towards the street, another paved court backwards towards the south, walled with brick, and a large walled garden on the south side.

The position of Tristram Gibbs's house can be roughly identified by the fact that a parcel of ground abutting north on Denmark Street and south on Lord Wharton's garden and ground is stated to have been formerly "part of the garden belonging to the messuage in tenure of Tristram Gibbs, Esq." The house was therefore to the north of Lord Wharton's house, and its site probably extended over part of Denmark Street.From: "Site of the Hospital of St. Giles," Survey of London: volume 5: St. Giles-in-the-Fields, pt II (1914), pp. 117–126. URL: http://www.british-history.ac.uk/report.aspx?compid=74292&strquery=Gibbs.

237 In 1611, Thomas Gybbes bought a manor called Hunningham, located a mile from Offchurch, from Sir Robert Rich (afterward Earl of Warwick). He sold the manor in 1614.

238 Warwickshire PRO: Dr. Penny Upton's research.

from his first marriage because daughter Ann is deceased, and her sister probably was too.

8. He does not acknowledge any grandchildren from Ann (his deceased daughter), but he also does not acknowledge any grandchildren from his issue with Margaret Wilkes. His son Edward had children. His son Thomas seems to disappear and he may have been sickly when father Thomas wrote his will as very little mention of him is made in the will.

Tristrim Gibbs, brother of Thomas, deserves special citation here because of his associations:

- *Item I give and bequeath to my Servant* Tristram Gibbs *the Sum of twenty Pounds and I do specially commend him to the good Favour of my Brother Robert Sydney and pray him to have a favourable Care over him and of my Servant Philip Jordayne* (will of the famous poet Sir Phillip Sydney, proved in 1589).
- Sir Phillip Sydney is interred in St. Paul's Cathedral, London, England. Born 30 November 1554 and named for his godfather, King Philip II of Spain, Sidney was the eldest son of Sir Henry Sidney, Lord Deputy of Ireland, and nephew of Robert Dudley, Earl of Leicester. One of the best educated and well-rounded men of his day, Sidney served Queen Elizabeth; courted Penelope Devereux, the future wife of Lord Rich; he married Frances Walsingham, the daughter of Sir Francis Walsingham, in 1583 and had one daughter, Elizabeth (1585–1612), later Countess of Rutland, the wife of Roger Manners, 5th Earl of Rutland (some claim she was poisoned by Sir Walter Raleigh).
- In 1586, the Sidney brothers took part in a skirmish against the Spanish; Philip was wounded in the leg and died within the month. "Farewell, the worthiest knight that lived" cried the funeral procession said to be the biggest production of the era.
- He married Elizabeth, the widow Baker.

The Gibbs family was well established in London, as was the Wiggin clan. They were all clustered around St. Giles, Cripplegate, London, and are found in the church registers.

Helena/Ellen Sambrooke Wiggin; second wife of Vicar William Wiggin

Died after 1626, Coventry, Warwickshire
Sons: Samuell Sambrooke and John Sambrooke
Daughters: Margaret Sambrooke (never married)

Grandchildren: Mary, Peter (eldest son of Samuell), Sara, John, and Ellen (children of John).

Ellen writes her will in 1626, Coventry, Warwick (prob.11/151)[239], in which she calls herself "Ellena Wiggens" but signs her name *Elen Wiggen*. Witnesses to her will are Maybell Love and Edward Love. She requests to be buried in St. Michael's Churchyard.

The Knightleys of Offchurch Bury, Warwickshire

Winifred Knightley (died 1569) was the daughter of William Knightley and Ann Hare (b. 1489 in Norwich, Norfolk) of Fawsley, Northamptonshire. She married Robert Coke and became the mother of Sir Edward Coke (1549–1633) and Dorothy Coke (b. 1551). Sir Edward's daughter, Frances, married John Villiers, son of Sir George Villiers.

Sir Edward Coke was, among other titles, Lord Chief Justice of the King's Bench.

The Knightleys were patrons of the Offchurch parish church, where Vicar William Wiggin was employed and buried.

[239] Probate number used at the National Archives, Kew, England

THE VICAR WILLIAM WIGGIN

"Do not forget to live"
Sir William Wiggane[240]

b. abt 1553–d. between 1617 and 1620

Ordained Priest by the Bishop of Gloucester 11 July 1583
Patron: Sir Christopher Wray, Knight, Chief Justice of England

There is a motto over a sundial-shaped clock on the musket ball–pockmarked, south-facing tower of St. Gregory's church in Offchurch, Warwick, England, that says "Do not forget to live." King Offa[241] of Mercia was not the only person to leave his mark on this church as Cromwell's troops, during the English Civil War in the mid-seventeenth century, also left their calling cards following the Battle of Edgehill.[242] Did they execute someone up against the

240 "Our Biographical Archive adds a little more information particularly about his position as Vicar of Messingham in Lincolnshire. I attach a copy of his page in our records" (Naomi Herbert, St. John's College Library, Cambridge, UK): "Wm. Wiggane, presented by Christopher Wray, knt., chief justice of England, by an assignment, dated 3 Aug 1578, to him of a grant, dated 10 Oct 1569, by Nicholas bishop of Linc. To Christopher Thorneton of Laughton, co., Lincs.Gent. And Wm. Paunt of the same, yeoman, to the vicarage of Messingham, vacant by death. Admitted 8 April 1585, (LRS 2, p 78). This seems to be an abbreviation of the Presentation Deed referring to the incoming Wm. Wiggane, (Ref DIOC/PD/1583/67) This also confirms the Vicar went from Cambridge University to Messingham, Lincs.

241 Offa was King of Mercia, a kingdom of Anglo-Saxon England, from 757 until his death in July 796.

242 Edge Hill and Kineton in southern Warwickshire on Sunday, 23 October 1642.

church wall? The motto and the musket ball's message seem to be some sort of offsetting vision. This church is the final resting place for Vicar William Wiggin, and the motto is a fitting one.

William Wigan/Wiggin m. 21 Aug 1590 Ane/Ann Gybbes
b. abt. 1553, d. bet. 1617–1620 b. 18 April 1575–d. aft. 1603

Issue: Katherine Wigan, b. 19 July 1591
John Wigan, b. 14 Feb 1592
Edward Wigan, b. 1 Feb 1594
Hannibal Wiggin, b. 15 Jan 1596
William Wigan Jr., b. 18 Feb 1598
Thomas Wiggin, b. 20 Sep 1601
Rychard Wiggin, b. 1 Mar 1603

The births and baptisms of the Wiggin children are all found in the registers of St. Michael's Church, Bishop's Itchington, Warwickshire, United Kingdom.

It is through the well-documented life of the vicar we will find the building blocks of character for Captain Thomas Wiggin. The vicar would have strong influence over his sons. Even if the vicar sent his youngest children to live with relatives following the death of their mother about 1603, he would maintain control of them and likely bring them home following his second marriage to the Widow Ellen Sambrooke about 1605. The vicar lived long enough to see his youngest son, Rychard, in apprenticeship. No record for the vicar's birth has been found, but it's reasonable conjecture to say he was probably the son of a John Wigan based on naming patterns of the era and could well have descended from a long line of clergy surnamed *Wigan/Wiggin* found in Warwickshire.

The vicar spells his name *Wiggin* in his 1617 will, although most of his records are found with the *Wigan* spelling. In the local dialect, *Wigan* is pronounced *Wig-gin* (hard *g*).

A void was created by the death of Anne Gybbes[243] Wiggin, the vicar's first wife and mother of his children, which makes it even more important that we understand who Thomas Wiggin's father was. Since we don't have a written record of what influences came to play on Thomas Wiggin while growing up between the ages of two and fourteen (the age to enter apprenticeship), we have to rely on what was happening in the father's life. It is from his father, Thomas, he will learn his values, morals, and receive the basis of his religious beliefs and early education.

[243] M. 21 August 1590

The next couple of years following wife Anne's death (abt. 1603)[244] are filled with daily routines of caring for his older children with the help of servants,[245] working his farmland, and performing his church and clerical duties. An opportunity comes in 1605 for Vicar William to take an assignment in Offchurch, which is only five miles from Bishop's Itchington and in the same diocese. He won't have to relocate the family, and that's a bonus. The parish is smaller and will be less demanding, which is exactly what he needs just now. His only daughter and firstborn child, Katherine, has been promised in marriage, and he knows he will lose her soon. It's almost like going through death all over again, losing Katherine. Perhaps a professional change is what he needs.

About the same time the vicar takes the assignment in Offchurch, he marries again. Church guidelines for a vicar practically demands he be married to a woman acceptable to the church hierarchy. Having an "unapproved" wife, or being unmarried, could cause him to lose his standing in the church. Helen/Ellen the widow Sambrooke[246] is about his age. She has grown children and grandchildren[247] whom she names in her will,[248] which is recorded as *Ellen Wiggins of Coventry* (although she signs it *Elen Wiggen*). Coventry is the seat of the diocese, and this marriage could well have been a church-arranged union. Ellen brings into the marriage an unmarried, grown daughter named Margaret, whom the vicar will remember in his will. No doubt, Margaret is a great help to the vicar in the care of his orphaned children. However, I do wonder if she may also be the reason Katherine Wiggin marries so young. Perhaps the home was not harmonious with this second marriage.

Offchurch—a place so filled with history it intrigues Vicar William Wiggin—is the perfect place for a man with an insatiable appetite for history. Inside the church, called St. Gregory's,[249] is an old stone coffin said to have held the remains of King Offa,[250] or his son Fremund. King Offa was king of Mercia in the ninth century, and his beloved firstborn son, Fremund, who forsook his

244 There is no death record

245 His long time servants are remembered in his will of 1617, John Bartlett, William Handes, Samuel Clarksett, Anne Miller.

246 Also spelled Sambroke

247 Children: Samuell Sambrooke, John Sambrooke and Margaret Sambrooke. Grandchildren: Mary, Peter (eldest son of Samuell), Sara, John (eldest son of John) and Ellen.

248 Prob/11/151; Ref 1044; PRO, Coventry, Warwick, 1626; National Archives, England: sons Samuell, John; daughter Margaret; grandchildren Mary, Samuel, Ellen, Peter and Sarah all surnamed Sambrooke.

249 To read a history of the church go to: http://www.british-history.ac.uk/report.aspx?compid=57126

250 Offa, King of Mercia 757-796; the Kingdom of Mercia consisted of 17 counties: Gloucester, Hereford, Worcester, Warwick, Leicester, Rutland, Northampton, Lincoln, Huntingdon, Bedford, Buckingham, Oxford, Stafford, Shropshire, Nottingham, Derby, Cheshire and part of Hertford….all called "shires".

right of accession to his father's throne to become a monk, founded a monastery on the Isle of Lundy. And it wasn't until after his father, King Offa, died that Fremund returned to the mainland to fight the invading Vikings. Fremund was the victor in a great battle known as Radford Semele.[251] However, he was then killed by one of his own men as he knelt in thanksgiving prayer; the knave lopped off his head with a sword. Legend says Fremund then stood up and carried his head in his arms for some distance, where he drove his sword in the ground and a spring bubbled up around his feet. He carefully bathed his head and then lay down and died. His body was taken to Offchurch, where his tomb[252] became a place of healing pilgrimages. I tell you this story as Vicar William Wiggin became the priest of this very important church—a church rich in history for a man who put great stock in the written word of both his Bible and his books. A more perfect vicar could not have been chosen to carry on the work of a church of this nature and history. Vicar William needed a pilgrimage of healing himself.

Fremund becomes a link to another man in the life of Captain Thomas Wiggin, known as Lord Saye and Sele[253] (William Fiennes of Broughton Castle, Oxfordshire, 1582–1662) and his occupation of the Isle of Lundy.[254] After the beheading of King Charles, Lord Saye and Sele would retire to the Isle of Lundy and not return to England until the monarchy was restored to the throne. Although probably the staunchest Puritan of them all, Lord Saye and Sele never wanted the beheading of the king. He wanted church reformation Puritan style. When he does return, he is welcomed back into royal circles and is appointed Keeper of the Seale.

The Isle of Lundy, located at the mouth of Bristol Bay, is an island steeped in mythical history that also became a haven for the Dunkirk pirates,[255] who not only terrorized shipping into and out of Bristol Bay, but the shoreline villages of Devonshire and Cornwall as well.

Situated within sight of the old church is Offchurch Bury, the manor house. It was owned by the Knightley family from Northamptonshire and occupied by a branch of the family who were Royalists with Catholic ties. Vicar William

---

251 A village about one mile south of Offchurch

252 He was moved three or more times over the ensuing centuries.

253 William Fiennes, 1st Viscount Saye and Sele (June 28, 1582 – April 14, 1662), was born at the family home of Broughton Castle near Banbury, in Oxfordshire

254 Lundy is the largest island in the Bristol Channel, lying 12 miles (19 km) off the coast of Devon, England, approximately one third of the distance across the channel between England and Wales.

255 During the Dutch Revolt (1568–1648) the Dunkirkers or Dunkirk Privateers, were commerce raiders in the service of the Spanish Monarchy... Surrendered the island on 24 February 1647 to Richard Fiennes, representing General Fairfax. In 1656, the island was acquired by Lord Saye and Sele (Wikipedia)

is more than aware of the importance of the Knightly family, patrons of his church, as Sir Richard Knightley of Fawsley Hall, Northamptonshire, is about five or six miles away and was one of the prominent Puritan movement leaders.

Vicar William will remain at St. Gregory's church from 1605 to his death between 1616/17 (date of his will) and 1620 (date of probate). He is so dedicated to St. Gregory's, he requests in his will to be buried in the chancery (20 Oct 1617: VICAR WILLIAM WIGGIN'S WILL[256]).

I eagerly contacted every archivist with a connection to Offchurch, including the diocese offices, and there are no records for the parish going back to the time of William Wiggin. Even the archivists at the Warwickshire Record Office told me a meaningless clerk burned all the records back around 1900. About then, I was feeling fate was trying to obscure my eleventh-great-grandfather's life as much as it had his son Thomas's.

Then on 10 June 2010, I received a letter from Rev. Brian Green. He included a brochure titled *Incumbents of St. Gregory's Church, Offchurch, in the County of Warwickshire*—which lists all the incumbents starting in 1328 through 2002. In the 1604 slot appears *William Wiggan.* The church is now part of the Feldon Group of churches, which also includes Bishop's Itchington. He included a picture and brochure showing William Wiggin at the church. He states they don't know who is buried beneath the flooring of the church and probably won't go seeking remains as they would probably be unidentifiable.

I had not been able to find a birth record on William Wigan/Wiggin and had to delve into the English clergy records for most of my knowledge. I found the book governing the clergy in the Church of England and discovered a man had to be twenty-three in order to be ordained a "deacon." This set William's birth date as in or before 1553.

I was so lucky to have such people as Dr. Penelope Upton and Dr. Anthony Upton[257] (Warwickshire), Naomi Herbert, St. John's College Library of Cambridge University, Rev. George Massey[258] (Messingham, Lincolnshire[259]), Lincoln Archive,[260] and the staff at the CCEd archives,[261] Archivists for the Diocese of Cheshire, and the Cheshire Cathedral[262] . . . and so many more

256 Pro 11/135; Prerogative Court of Canterbury; ref 535/455; Will of Wm Wiggin Vicar of Offchurch, Warwickshire

257 Tony Upton attended church at Offchurch at one time, and he lived near there when we corresponded. Both Tony and his wife, Penny, did their thesis work for their degrees on the English clergy. Tony also has a very impressive biography.

258 Current Vicar of the Messingham parish church

259 Jackie Walker, Clerk to Messingham Parish Council, Lincolnshire.

260 Ellen Cross, Cultural Services Advisor, Lincolnshire Archives.

261 Online site for English clergy records

262 Nicholas Fry, Cheshire and Chester Archives and Local Studies Service, Chester, Cheshire; Paul Newman of the same office.

wonderful and giving people who shared their records, time, and knowledge.[263] Their efforts made my work that much easier. I knew I could rely on them to interpret the clerical records I was finding beyond the CCEd[264] database, which is constantly growing and changing.

Definitions of Church of England:

- CURATE: Wasn't highborn (no title) and usually had a parish where the living was not good enough for a vicar or rector. A clergyman who has the charge "cure" of souls "instituted" or "licensed" by the bishop of the diocese. He is chosen by the patron, who has the right to nominate a clergyman for the parish in question. He can be removed only by resignation, exchange of cure, promotion to another benefice involving the cure of souls, or deprivation following a public conviction for some disgraceful offense. In general speech, however, the word *curate* is used to denote an assistant to beneficed clergymen—e.g., one appointed to assist the incumbent in the performance of his duties, or to take charge of a parish temporarily during a vacancy, or while the incumbent is unable to perform his duties. Assistant curates are nominated by the incumbent or the bishop, and licensed to the bishop. This license may be revoked by the bishop after due notice.
- VICAR: Same ecclesiastical status as a rector. Entitled to the small tithe and a portion of the glebe. These were allocated by an appropriator. As a parish priest, the vicar had the same spiritual status as a rector, and the forms of institution and induction are identical since, in both cases, he holds his full spiritual jurisdiction from the bishop. He also holds the freehold of church, churchyard, vicarage, and glebe.
- RECTOR: Has a historical living and can't be sacked easily; can be an honorary dean. Has the charge and cure of a parish and has the parsonage and tithes; or the person of a parish where the tithes are not impropriate: in the contrary case, the parson is a vicar.

Originally, the CCEd database had Vicar William as vicar in Bishop's Itchington by 1587, three years before he married Ann Gybbes in that church. By 2010, they had changed the assignment to Long Itchington[265] (the original

---

[263] Lichfield Diocese Di Cooper and Mithra Tonking, Archivists; Worcestershire RO, Robin Whittaker, Archivists.

[264] Clergy of the Church of EnglandDatabase

[265] *Holy Trinity Church, Long Itchington: A Historical Guide* by Archibald Payne (1970). Booklet out of print.

record just says "chington"). All his children were found to have been christened in the Bishop's Itchington records, which indicates he lived in that parish.

The Clergy Database online[266] gives us the vicar's ordination as deacon on 21 December 1576 in the Bishop's Palace chapel in Chester, Cheshire. This record tells us he did not have "letters of dismissory," meaning he was at that time a resident of the Chester diocese. This diocese covered Warwickshire and Lancashire, as well as Cheshire. So he likely was born somewhere in that area.

Chronological Events for Vicar William Wiggin:

1553: About the year of William's birth in probably Cheshire or Warwickshire.
1562: Warwick Castle is in the hands of Robert Dudley, 1st Earl of Leicester
1564: Shakespeare is born in Stratford-upon-Avon. Shakespeare dies in 1616, about the same time Vicar William dies.
1569: "I can confirm that a William Wiggane (probably the Elizabethan way of writing *Wiggan*), was the incumbent of Holy Trinity Parish from c1569. He may have, prior to his institution, served as a curate, but the actual records of this could be found in the Diocesan Archives in Lincoln. Whether this is a William Senior or the William you are looking for, I don't know, but I'm drawn to it being the same person for, in 1590, he was succeeded by Richard Rowbotham."[267] (Source: Rev. George Massey, Messingham Church[268] enquiry; 26 April 2010).
1576:[269] William Wigan, ordination, 21/12/1576; Chester, Cheshire; CRO EDA 1/3 (Ordination Register; ID 108570). Deacon.
1579: Wiggan, William. Matric. Sizar from St. John's, Easter 1579, Cambridge.
1581: Saxby, Lincolnshire, Clerical Subsidy Rolls;[270] William Wiggane; Curate, Saxby All Saints.
1583: Venn, John, and Venn, J. A., "Alumni Cantabrigienses" (Cambridge University Press, 1922–1954). The standard biographical reference

[266] http://www.theclergydatabase.org.uk/jsp/search/index.jsp.
[267] Messingham; Wm Wiggane, Curate, No graduate, does not preach; Messingham 19/6/1587.
[268] In 2010, George Massey was vicar of Messingham Holy Trinity Church.
[269] In April of 1576, in Chester, a Richard Rowbotham was ordained a priest by the bishop of Chester, and he would follow William Wiggin in Messingham Church.
[270] The "Clerical Subsidies" show the names of the churches, and sometimes of the clergy, who paid the sums assessed on them. Clerical Subsidy Rolls are found in both the PRO and Lincoln Diocesan Registry for the years in which lists of curates are printed: 1571–1603.

work for members of Cambridge University up to 1900. Vicar of Messingham in Lincolnshire.[271]

1584: A William Wiggin and Eliz. Hobson, 7 February 1585.[272] Was this perhaps a first marriage? No further records have been found. It may not be him as the name is common.

1585: Sir Wm Wiggane,[273] Messingham, Lincolnshire, vicar to Sir Christopher Wray, knt., chief justice of England. Liber Cleri: "Bred in the schools."[274]

1586: December 14, Wm Wigan, Vicar, Long Itchington,[275] Warwickshire; LRO B/A2ii/1 Institution Book.[276]

The parishioners of Itchington had been without a vicar for thirty years. No one had lived in the vicarage since prior to 1558, when Edward Keble was instituted but never lived there; and no funds had been expended on the upkeep by the holder of the advowson, Thomas Fisher. With the mansion house and church in a state of irredeemable decay, Wiggin was resident in Upper Itchington, and the chapel there was afforded full parochial rights.[277] To be

---

[271] Naomi Herbert, Librarian's Assistant, St. John's College Library, Cambridge CB2 1TP, (01223) 338711 "Bred in the schools" refers to his having been to university; also, thanks to fellow researcher John Kane.

[272] Yorkshire Marriage Reg., West Riding, Vol. III; London, Issued to the subscribers by Phillimore & Co., Ltd., 124 Chancery Lane; 1915; pp. 21.

[273] William Wiggane, cl., to the vic. Of Messingham, Stowe, vac. By death. P.- Christopher Wray, Knt., chief justice of England, by an assignment, dated 3 Aug 10 Eliz. (A.D.1578) to him of a grant, dated 10 Oct. 1569, by Nicholas bishop of Lincoln to Christopher Thorneton of Laughton, co. Lincoln, gent., and William Paunt, of the same, yeo. 8 April. A commission for induction was granted (P.D., 1583, nos. 67–69); Source: Canterbury and York Series (1909); Church of England; London; pg. 79; 1582–3.

[274] Refers to his having been to university.

[275] The villages called "Itchington" get confusing. There was a Nether, Upper, Lower, Bishop's, and Long Itchington. See map for locations.

[276] The formal act, generally recorded in a presentation deed, by which a patron indicates to the ordinary (normally the bishop) the name of the clergyman whom he wishes to be appointed to a benefice by institution; one form of an appointment to a benefice or dignity. Institution was the act by which a bishop or other ordinary committed a living to the care of a clergyman. It followed after a presentation the cleric's subscription and the receipt of letters testimonial, and was followed by induction or installation. It was the only one of these events normally recorded in the episcopal register or act book and, as such, can be regarded as furnishing the date from which an appointment commenced. (Source CCEd)

[277] Data derived from Penelope Upton, Thesis, "Change and Decay: The Warwickshire Manors of the Bishop of Coventry and Lichfield from the Late Thirteenth to the Late Sixteenth Centuries; Sept. 2002; Doctor of Philosophy at the University of Leicester; pg. 162.

strictly correct, it seems that two men served briefly before him, but very little is known about them: ex. Inf. A. A. Upton.[278]

1590: "William Wigan was married to Ann Gybbes at Lillington, Warwickshire, in August 1590 and had five children baptized at Bishop's Itchington during the 1590s, including the wonderfully named Haniball, who, according to the register, was born 7 January 1597 and baptized four days later: CRO, DR 60/1, ff. 8v, 9r, 9v, 1 Or, 33v. How the Wigan family survived on only ten pounds a year is a mystery."[279]

1601: Birth of Thomas Wiggin.

1603: Birth of Rychard Wiggin and probably the date of wife's death.

1604: Gunpowder Plot. . . associated with powerful Catholic families in Warwickshire; the Midland's uprisings are gathering pace, and a small army gathers on Dunsmore Heath. Of note here is that the Knightley family of Offchurch is Catholic. This leads to a break in family relationship with the Knightley family in the family seat in Northampton, who are Puritans. It's the Northampton branch that becomes an ally of Lord Saye and Sele.

1605:

- The birth of Sir William Dugdale (d. 1686), the famous historian who came from Coleshill, Warwickshire. He became Garter King-of-Arms. He's buried in St. Cuthbert's Church, Shustoke.
- Vicar William Wiggin assigned to Offchurch St. Gregory, where he remains to his death between 1617 and 1620.

The very long list of Warwickshire notables cannot be covered here, but of King Offa[280] we take note, as Vicar William is buried in the church founded on that legacy—literally. He's buried in the church that is said to have been built on top of King Offa's church, which he built to honor a fallen son who was said to have been killed in battle near there. The ancient religious house was probably built of inferior materials and just could not stand the test of time.

In the eleventh century, the Normans conquered England, and it was under the Normans that much of the present church was built (between 1110 and 1120). Offchurch remained in the session of the monks of Coventry until the dissolution of the monasteries in 1539, when it was granted to one of the King's

---

[278] Ibid, pg. 162.

[279] Ibid, pg. 162.

[280] King of Mercia, died 796. Ruled much of Britain south of the River Humber. Offa's Dyke is named after him and was his most ambitious project. There's a stone coffin under the porch and is said to contain the king's remains. The famous Lady Godiva, wife of Leofric, Earl of Mercia, came from Offchurch.

commissioners—Sir Edmund Knightley, whose descendants were in possession of the Bury house and its surrounding lands until 1919.[281]

Sir Edmund Knightley's descendants will become important to us as we explore associates of young Thomas Wiggin. According to one source, the church of St. Gregory is under the patronage of the Knightley Catholic branch of the family.[282] One source isn't enough to convince me.

Let's now go back a bit and look at the vicar's schooling and ordination records.[283]

Ordination records usually contain only a date, place of ordination, the ordaining bishop, and maybe some details of the individual's qualifications (like an examination of literacy), testimonials, but no genealogical information. A man being ordained was required to produce testimonials, an evidence of a title or curacy[284] to which the individual was licensed. Dates of birth and/or education may also be stated.

Naomi Herbert of St. John's College Library, Cambridge, provides the following information. "Wiggan's entry in John and J. A. Venn's 'Alumni Cantabrigienses' (1922–1954, Cambridge University Press), the standard biographical reference work for members of Cambridge University up to 1900, is short: 'Wiggan, William. Matric. Sizar from St. John's, Easter, 1579. Perhaps V. of Messingham, Lincs, 1583.' Our Biographical Archive adds a little more information, particularly about his position as vicar of Messingham in Lincolnshire. I attach a copy of his page in our records."

> Lincoln Record Society's files dated 1926, page 7: William Wiggen appears in the Clerical Subsidy Roll 1581, under Saxby[285] . . . and on page 8: Liber cleric, 1585: Messingame,[286] Sir[287] William Wigane, Vicar; ordained priest by the Bishop of

---

[281] Source: http://warkcom.net/live/welcome.asp?id=1425.

[282] Source: *A New and Complete History of the County of Warwick*; William Smith, pub. Emans of Birmingham, 1829.

[283] I would also like to acknowledge the kind assistance in tracking down education records by John Kane, resident of England.

[284] This may account for his presence in Saxby and Messingham. He had a curacy.

[285] There are two Saxby parishes in Linc. One has church records beginning in 1599, and the other, Saxby near Barton-upon-Humber, begins in 1561.

[286] This should be "Messingham" and not as spelled. There's no such place in England as Messingame. Messingham is about 80 to 90 miles from Coventry, Warwickshire. There is a ten-year gap between ordination and Bishop's Itchington church, and this assignment partially fills that gap.

[287] I have never been able to find a record of a *Sir* William Wigane. I believe the "sir" is misstated. There's no listing in the Baronetage of England. If Sir Christopher Wray, his patron, had him knighted, there should be a record.

Gloucester, 11 July 1583; bred in the schools.[288] The patron[289] was Christopher Wray,[290] knight, Chief Justice of England.

Christopher Wray,[291] knight (b. 1535 and d. 1592), had issue of one son and two daughters:

1. Wray's eldest daughter, Isabel, was married to Godfrey Flojambe of Aldwarke, Yorkshire[292] first; second to Sir William Bowes of the Scottish embassy; third to John, Lord Darcy of Aston (Lord Darcy of the North). She died in 1623.
2. Wray's youngest daughter, Frances, married first Sir George Saint Paule; was married secondly to Robert Rich in 1616, 1st Earl of Warwick.[293]
3. Wray's son, Sir William II Wray, father of, by his second wife, Sir Christopher III Wray (1601–1646), grandson and namesake of our subject.

Christopher Wray was the justice who passed sentence on Mary, Queen of Scots, in 1587. The sentence troubled him much, and he was worried Elizabeth, Mary's sister, would not think kindly of him for that sentence of death. However, it was Elizabeth who made him Chief Justice of England and knighted him.

---

288 I inquired as to the meaning of "bred in the schools," and it only refers to William having been to university.

289 Patron: The holder of the right of presentation to an English ecclesiastical benefice. Ecclesiastical benefice: An endowed church office giving income to its holder. So it appears that Christopher Wray was offering, or had offered, Vicar William Wiggin a curate or vicar position in one of his churches in Lincolnshire. We have him at two locations in Lincolnshire: Saxby and Messingham.

290 Died 1592. Had a grandson named Sir Christopher Wray. http://en.wikipedia.org/wiki/Christopher_Wray.

291 Excellent bio found at: http://www.churchmousewebsite.co.uk/Glentworth_wray.htm.

292 An ancestor of this author.

293 M. 1616, at age 56; he died 1619. No issue. Rich had five children with his first wife, Lady Penelope Devereux.

Three others—*Arthur Hildersham,*[294]/[295]*Andrew King,*[296] and *Anthony Nutter*[297]/[298]—are connected with the diocese of Lincoln. They appeared first before the ecclesiastical commission and, since they refused to answer upon the oath *ex officio,* they were committed to prison. On 13 May 1592, they appeared in the Star Chamber. At length, it was found that no illegal practices could be proved against them, and they were released on their promises of good behavior.

1) *King* was in 1595, a schoolmaster at Chesham Woburn in Buckinghamshire, and preacher there in 1605. There is no record on Andrew King in CCEd.
   Andrew King/Antonius Kinge: Ordained on 9/4/1564 at Bishopthorpe Manor (Yorkshire) Chapel as a deacon; ordained as a vicar in the same year and died of "natural causes" in 1588. This is as close as I could come to an "Andrew" King in the CCEd records.

2) *Nutter* held the rectory of Fenny Drayton in Leicestershire from 1582 to 1604–5.
   Anthony Nutter[299] was in the same diocese as Vicar William Wiggin; uncle to Hatevil Nutter of Dover, New Hampshire. In his will, dated 19 January 1633, he writes: "Clerke and the unworthy minister of Christ: and bequeaths: I give unto Hatill (sic) his (brother's) sonne for whome I was Witness at his Baptisme the somme of Three pounds over and above his parte in the aforesaid somme of six pounds thirteen

---

[294] Queen Elizabeth called him "cousin" as he descended of the Plantagenets. (http://en.wikipedia.org/wiki/Arthur_Hildersham) A Puritan and pupil of Thomas Cartwright, "father of Presbyterian" church of England.

[295] *The Presbyterian Review,* Volume 9; edited by Charles Augustus Briggs, Archibald Alexander Hodge, Francis Landrey Patton, Benjamin Breckinridge Warfield; 1888; Scribner's Sons, NY, NY.

[296] Thomas Wiggin's mother descends from the King line. It's interesting this man is named ANDREW.

[297] The NUTTER family is close to the Wiggin family in New Hampshire, and Anthony Nutter and Thomas Wiggin Jr. were the two men in Walter Barefoot's house, engaged in a fight with the Mason heir, who was also Thomas Wiggin Jr.'s son-in-law (no record on CCED for Nutter).

[298] 1584: curate: Muckstocke (Staffordshire); LRO, B/V/1/15; Overton, William/ Coventry & Lichfield, 1580-1609; CCED (same diocese Vicar William Wiggin is in).

[299] *The English Origin of Elder Hatevil Nutter of Dover, New Hampshire: With an Account of His Uncle, the Reverend Anthony Nutter, Puritan Minister of Fenny Drayton, Leicestershire, and Woodkirk, Yorkshire-* John C. Brandon- TAG- Vol. 72 (1997), pp. 263–84;Boyle, Frederick R.: Hatevil Nutter of Dover, New Hampshire, and his Descendants. Portsmouth, NH; Peter E. Randall, 1997.

shillings four pence." Anthony also gives 20 pounds British monies to John Reyner, who became the sixth minister in Dover, New Hampshire.

Hatevil Nutter arrives in Dover, New Hampshire, by 1635. Thomas Wiggin Jr. was born in 1640, so Hatevil is at least twenty years older than Junior. In 1647, Hatevil purchased a home lot from Captain Thomas Wiggin, and in 1640, it's described as "Butting on ye fore River, est; and on ye west by High street; on ye north by ye lots of Samewell Haynes; and on ye south by lots of William Story." His house stood on the east side of High Street on Nutter's Hill about 15 or 20 rods from the north corner of the meeting house lot on Hilton's Point. It is thought he lived below the falls along the river Sligo,[300] below James Stackpole.[301]

3) *Hildersham,* in 1593, became vicar of Ashby de la Zouch in the same county.

At this juncture in my investigation of Vicar William Wiggin, I decided to see just how far back I could trace the Wigan/Wiggin clan in the clergy. Occupations in any surname prior to the fifteenth century pretty much followed a pattern, so I felt strongly that Vicar William had ancestry in the church.

1200:[302] (Lancashire)
William, Clerk of Wygan
William, Vicar of Prestwich
William, Vicar of Rachedale

These records interested me enough that I purchased the two-volume set of books authored by David Sinclair titled *The History of Wigan V1 and V2,* pub. Wigan, Wall Printers; 1882. While I learned very little about our clan from the books, I did find the two volumes fascinating and very complete in their history of the parish of Wigan, Lancashire.

1432: [303] William Wygeyn, deeds and papers of Desford, Leicestershire; also named in this deed are Amicia and Walter Wygan.

---

[300] Part of Dover, NH: named for a county in Ireland; now Salmon Falls River.

[301] James Stackpole's or the Sligo Garrison (1709?) was on Sligo Road at "The Point."

[302] Cat Ref: RCHY, Lancashire Deeds, Ref RCHY 3/1; Ref RCHY 3/¼; c. 1200; Hornby Catholic Mission Papers (St. Mary's Church, Lancashire).

[303] Deeds and papers, Leicestershire, Ref DR10/1357; dated 2 Feb 1432.

1479: [304] William Wygan, chaplain, Lancashire: Demise, James Hall, rector of Northenden to William Wygan (and others), manors and properties in Lancashire and Cheshire.

1497/8: [305] William Wygan, chaplain: deed: Robert Tatloke of Liverpool to William Wygan, chaplain all properties in Mellyng, Aghton, and Lyverpull. Note: Mellyng is in the parish of Hallsall.

1498: [306] Oliver Wygan,[307] chaplain, Fennycompton,[308] Warwickshire; Quitclaim from John Shropshere and wife Alice Tubbe, sister and heir of Thomas Tubbe jun' of Fennycompton to Oliver Wygan, chaplain. Robert Tubbe, father of said Thomas and Alice.

1514: [309] William Wygan, priest; also found along with William is Thomas Wygan, layman, and Elizabeth Wygan, laywoman.

Genealogical note: Between 1504–1511, we also find John Whyhttyng (Whityny), priest; with Agnes Whytyng, laywoman; Denise Whityng, laywoman; and John in 1509 as a layman. William Whytyng is a layman in 1504.

1525: [310] Edward Wygan (Edwardus Wygan) professor of sacred theology and kinsman to Oliver Wygan, chaplain (deceased); Quitclaim by Edward Wygan, professor, etc., to Henry Makepeace of Chepyng Dassett of land in Fennycompton, Warwickshire, lately belonging to Oliver Wygan, clerk deceased.

Genealogical notes: Before we go further here, I'd like to point out the significance of the parish of Fenny Compton. It lies about 2 to 3 miles south of Bishop's Itchington, Warwickshire. It is also the ancestral home of the George Wyllys/Willis family of early New England, who owned shares in

---

304 Lanc Record Office: Rixton-with Glazebrook MSS; Cat Ref DDX 293; DDX 293/79; dated 12 Apr 1479.

305 Lanc Record Office: Molyneux. Cams of Sefton, Cat Ref DDM; Molyneux family, Earls of Sefton; Grant Ref DDM 21/11; dated 7 Mar 1497/8.

306 Ref L1/103; 18 Apr 13 hen. VII 91498; PRO records online.

307 While trying to trace the descendants of Oliver Wygan in Warwickshire, I was told by the archivists at the Public Record Office that "some well-meaning clerk burned the county records around 1900 as being old and useless." This act has more than hindered my research efforts in Warwickshire. Oliver's son Edward was of an age to be a candidate as father of Vicar William Wiggin.

308 The ancient spelling for this parish used a closed format. Fenny Compton was Fennycompton.

309 Bede Roll of the Fraternity of St. Nicholas; 1449–1521; L37.01 Archives of the Parish Clerks' Company; Section 18 of the Guildhall archives; manuscript section; London.

310 Ref L1/112; 1 July 17 Hen. VIII (1525); PRO, Kew, Richmond, England.

the Hilton purchase of 1632/33. A Makepeace (see 1525 above) daughter married into the Willis family.

The antiquity of the following record's date associated with the surname *Wiggin* is amazing. Remember the Domesday Book[311] is dated 1086 in the reign of William the Conqueror. The following Wygan certainly drew my attention as he was in the service of the Crown in the Holy Lands and represented one of the oldest records I found outside of Lancashire. Since they had a religious connotation, I decided to include them here.

> Patent Rolls of the reign of Henry III preserved in Kew, England, Public Record Office; Henry III, AD 1247–1258, London 1908:
>
> Pg. 43: 1249, June 14, Reading: "Simple protection for Wygan le Bretun, gone to the land of Jerusalem, until his return (Etsuntpatentes).
>
> Pg. 228: 1253, March 18, Westminster: "The following, who have gone on the king's service to Gascony, have letters of protection simple for so long as they are in his service there: WIGAN LE BRETUN.
>
> Pg. 347: 1254, October 16, Bordeaux: "Bond to WIGAN DE SANCTO AMANDO . . . for spices taken to the king's use by Roger the Tailor and Bonacus Lumbard; to be paid in the quinzaine of Easter next at Westminster.

ORDINATION

After university, William Wiggin required ordination, and we find that record as follows:

> 1576: [312] William Wigan, ordination, 21/12/1576; Bishop's Palace, Chester, Cheshire; CRO EDA 1/3 (Ordination Register; ID 108570). Deacon.

The diaconate was the earliest stage at which a man could exercise a useful full-time ministry as a parochial assistant. Only then would an incumbent feel disposed to pay him a modest wage. The age at which a man could be made deacon fluctuated. The first English Prayer Book of 1549 stipulated that he

[311] Held at the National Archives, Kew, England.

[312] In April of 1576, Chester, a Richard Rowbotham was ordained a priest by the bishop of Chester, and he would follow William Wiggin in Messingham church.

should be at least twenty-one years of age, raised to twenty-three years in 1662. Deacons were qualified to baptize and perform most clerical duties, but they could neither officiate at a marriage nor hear confessions. They were not authorized to celebrate Mass or Holy Communion.

When I wrote the archivists of the cathedral in Chester, Cheshire, I received a lengthy and thorough reply. Ordinations taking place in William's time were performed very quietly in a side chapel of the Cathedral as there was a lot of political unrest[313] all around them. William could have come from anywhere for ordination, as anyone with a desire and the qualifications for ordination could receive the rites at the cathedral. The cathedral's records for William's time are no longer in existence.

The archivists at Chester Cathedral[314] also said Vicar William was at the Worcester Cathedral. The Worcester Cathedral also had no records and could give me nothing in the way of a lead.

1579: Matric sizar 2 May 1579

1581: Appears in the Clerical Subsidy Roll under Saxby

1583: Instituted to the vicarage of Messingham, Lincolnshire; patron Christopher Wray, knight, Chief Justice of England, by an assignment . . .

1585: Liber Cleri, Sir William Wigane, Vicar; ordained priest by the Bishop of Gloucester 11 July 1583; bred in the schools.

1587: Willimus Wigan, 13/12/1587; Episcopi/Warwickshire (Source PRO E331, Coventry and Lich/6 [returns to First Fruits Office])

1605: William Wiggan, vicar, Offchurch, 26/7/1605 (Source LRO, B/V/1/24 [Liber Cleri])

It appears from this record that William had gone to his assignment in Offchurch following the birth of his last child (Rychard in 1603) and the death of his first wife, Ann Gybbes, at about the same time.

1616: William Wigan/Wiggin, vicar, 123/9/1616, Offchurch (Source LRO, B/V/1/32 [Liber Cleri])

This is the last clerical record for Vicar William and the same year he writes his will.

---

313 See William's timeline

314 Nick Fry, Archives and Local Studies Service of Cheshire Record Office, Cheshire

The records of Bishop's Itchington are intact up to William's leaving there, and the records of Offchurch are totally missing during his tenure as vicar there. There are no records at all in existence. What happened to those records? All the children's christening records are at Bishop's Itchington, but nothing of Ann's death. The subsequent generations at Bishop's Itchington are also found in the church records. I believe Vicar William did not keep the records at Bishop's Itchington, and they had a curate doing that. However, once at Offchurch, he took over those duties, and the records disappeared with his death. They may well have been in the library at Kingston Farm[315] and passed down the family.

Record-keeping: William had five sons, and for at least four of them, he had to find apprenticeships. His eldest son, John, remained on the family farm, so he likely did not leave home for an apprenticeship. I have not found one single apprenticeship record on any of his sons, which also leads me to believe he maintained those records and they too disappeared upon his death. I think it highly likely Hannibal apprenticed in the Cator family, as he ended up marrying a Cator daughter. This was not unusual at all for this era; more on Hannibal later.

Vicar William's will[316] is dated 20 October 1617, Offchurch,[317] Warwickshire—probated on 24 May 1620 by his eldest son, John. Interesting to note the vicar signs his surname "Wiggin" and not the spelling of the time, "Wigan." In his will, he requests burial in the chancel of St. Gregory's in Offchurch, Warwickshire, which was his last pastoral assignment. He names sons John (the eldest), William, Edward, Hannibal, Thomas, and Rychard (the youngest) and his one daughter, Katherine (married name *Smith*, his firstborn), and "her children." The mother of the vicar's children, Ann Gybbes, is deceased, and he

---

315 I traced down to Butler Wigan, who last owned this farm.Since the family had a farm, Vicar William likely had an office in his home, where he maintained all his records. One of my missions for 2007 in England was to visit the farm and try and find out what happened to the vicar's library and records. I was not able to keep that portion of my trip, so I never found out about the records.

316 Calendars of wills and administrations in the Consistory Court of the bishop . . . By Lichfield, Eng. (Diocese). Consistory Court, Consistory Court, William Phillimore Watts Phillimore, Lichfield (England)., Derby (England). District Probate Registry, Lichfield, Eng. District probate registry, Birmingham, Eng. District probate registry, Derby, Eng. District probate . . . PG 536 William Wygan, 1752, Of Bishop's Itchington . . . WILL

317 Offchurch, three miles East of Leamington, lies on the Welsh Road, a former sheep-droving road from sheep-farming areas of Wales to London.

was married to the widow Ellen Sambrooke[318] (who had her daughter, Margaret, living with her) of Coventry, and she is mentioned in the will. In his will, Vicar William delays his youngest son's inheritance for two years, which pretty much dates his death in 1620 as Rychard was born in 1603 and would not be of age until 1622/23. Since the vicar wrote his will in 1617, he was probably in poor health for about three years and certainly didn't expect to live until 1620 or he would not have worried about Rychard's age and inheritance. Thomas was right at twenty when his father dies. He and the middle sons had to be fairly settled in their lives as their father is not very worried about them. He doesn't mention any of their circumstances at the writing of the will. Each of them was to receive thirty pounds.

CCEd[319] Records

1576: CCEd Record Number 30457 21/12/1576 Ordination register: Bishop's Palace (Wigan, Willmus); this is probably where he was doing his apprenticeship as a clerk.

1576: CCEd Person ID: 30475, 1576: PRO, EDA 1/3 (Ordination Register) 21/12/1576; Bishop's Palace, Chester; deacon residence Chester diocese; Bishop's Palace (Wigan, Willmus); this is likely where he was doing his apprenticeship as a clerk.

1581: Lincoln Record Society 23 (1926) William Wiggen appears in the Clerical Subsidy Roll, under Saxby.

1582: Lincoln Record Society's files dated 1926, pg 7: William Wiggen, Clerical Subsidy Roll for Saxby All Saints.
Lincoln Record Soc. 2 (1912)
Lincolnshire patron, Christopher Wray, knight, Chief Justice of England

[318] After the vicar's death, Ellen returns to Coventry and leaves a will (1626; Prob/11/151) under the name *Ellena Wiggens* (but signs her name "Elen"), in which she names not only Margaret (still unmarried), but her sons and grandchildren as well. No mention of any of her stepchildren by Vicar William Wiggin. Sons were Samuell and John Sambrooke, and grandchildren named were Mary, Peter, Sara, John, and Ellen.

[319] Clergy of the Church of England Database

1582: CCEd Record Number 229982, 1582, Curate, Saxby, "State of the Church" Clerical Subsidy Roll. Wiggan, William; Matric. Sizar 2 May 1579.

1583: Lincoln Record Society Record: Note: Richard Rowbotham was ordained at the same time and place with Vicar William Wiggin.

1585: Liber cleri, Messingame,[320] Sir[321] William Wiggen, vicar, ordained priest by Bishop of Gloucester 11 July 1583, bred in the schools.[322]

1586: CCEd Record Number 201170, 14/9/1586, Qualification University, Vicar, Itchington; LRO book B/A/2ii/1 Institution Book.

1587: PRO, E331 Coventry and Lich/6 (Returns of First Fruits Office); 13/12/1587; Institution, ChingtonEpoiscopi/ Warwickshire (Willimus Wigan).

1590: Richard Rowbotham followed Sir William Wiggen.

1605: LRO, B/V/1/24 (Liber Cleri); 16/7/1605; Vicar; Offchurche (William Wiggan).

1616*: LRO, B/V/1/32 (Liber Cleri); 13/9/1616; Vicar; Ofchurch (William Wigan).*

Vicar William Wigan/Wiggin met the requirements for ordination as stated below:

The Ecclesiastical Law of the Church of England, Volume 1 By Sir Robert Phillimore, Sir Walter George Frank Phillimore, Charles FuhrJemmett Sweet, and Maxwell Ltd., London, 1895

[320] This should be "Messingham."

[321] I have never been able to verify this title. There is no listing in the Baronetage of England.

[322] Means he went to university . . . Oxford.

Pg. 99:
. . . No bishop shall henceforth admit any person into sacred orders which is not of his own diocese except he be either of one of the universities of this realm or except he shall bring letters Dismissory so termed from the bishop of whose diocese he is and desiring to be a *deacon is three and twenty years old* and to be a *priest four and twenty years complete* and hath taken some degree of *school in either of the two universities* or at the least except he be able to yield an account of his faith in Latin according to the *Articles of Religion approved in the synod of the bishops and clergy of this realm one thousand five hundred sixty and two (1562)* and to confirm the same by sufficient testimonies out of the Holy Scriptures and except moreover he shall then exhibit letters testimonial of his good life and conversation under the seal of some college of Cambridge or Oxford where before he remained or of three or four grave ministers together with the subscription and testimony of other credible persons who have known his life and behavior by the space of three years next before . . .

Pg. 100:
And for the regular method of examination we are referred by Lindwood to the canon upon that head inserted in the body of the canon law viz: When the bishop intends to hold an ordination all who are desirous to be admitted into the ministry are to appear on the fourth day before the ordination and then the Bishop shall appoint some of the priests attending him and others skilled in the divine law and exercised in the ecclesiastical sanctions who shall *diligently examine the life age and title of the persons to be ordained at what place they had their education whether they be well learned whether they be instructed in the law of God* And they shall be diligently examined for three days successively and so on the Saturday they who are approved shall be presented to the bishop By a constitution of Archbishop Persons of religion *shall not be ordained by any but their own bishop without letters dimissory* of the said bishop or in his absence of his vicar general.

Summary of the Vicar William Wiggin**:** Sons who went into the clergy were not—as a rule—inheriting first sons. The clergy was an avenue to success to rival military-type service to the Crown. The clergy of Vicar Wiggin's day could become wealthy through landholdings and are very prominent in deed records of England. They often banded together in their land dealings. The clergy required dedication, commitment, a lot of determination to succeed, and pristine character. Even that was not enough, as the candidate for ordination also had to have people in high positions to vouch for their moral character. They could obtain those testimonies by working as clerks in various churches, and this is apparently what Vicar Wiggin did. He is found in at least four different churches. We know from the requirements of ordination he could read, write, and speak Latin and was well-read in both religion and history.

A man of this caliber is going to make sure his sons are educated to the best of his ability, and he also would be sure they were apprenticed in occupations where they too could excel.

Descendants of Vicar William Wiggin and Ann Gybbes

Residing in Bishop's Itchington, Warwickshire

GENERATION ONE:

1. Katherine Wigan
   Baptism: 18 July 1591, Bishop's Itchington, Warwickshire, England
   Father: William Wigan
   Indexing Batch number C03990-2, England ODM; 548396

   Katherine married a Smith and is called "my daughter Katherine Smith" in her father's will. Her children are not called by their names in the will. There are several Smith men in Bishop's Itchington who could have been her husband, and their records appear in St. Michael's documents.

2. John Wigan
   Baptism: 14 February 1592, Bishop's Itchington, Warwickshire, England
   Father: William Wigan
   Indexing Batch number C03990-2, England ODM; 548396

   John is probably named for his grandfather. He married "Elizabeth" and had issue, all born in Bishop's Itchington:

   - George, b. 22 April 1621; prob. died young
   - John, b. 6 October 1622 (see next generation)
   - Thomas, b. 6 May 1625
   - Richard, b. 3 February 1627

- Edward, b. 3 June 1632
- Haniball, b. 17 August 1634; d. 23 August 1634
- William, b. 1639

3. Edward Wigan
   Born: 1 February 1594
   Baptism: 5 February 1594, Bishop's Itchington, Warwickshire, England
   Father: William Wigan
   Indexing Batch number: C03990-2; 548396

   Edward married Margeriam Wainwright Turner (daughter of Ralph Turner, born abt. 1606) of Cheshire. Nothing more is known about them.

4. Haniball Wigan
   Born: 7 January 1596
   Baptism: 11 January 1596, Bishop's Itchington, Warwickshire, England
   Father: William Wigan
   Indexing Batch number: C03990-2; England ODM; 548396

   Haniball married Ann Cater of Sandy, Bedfordshire, on 14 September 1627and had issue:

   - Anne (1633–1635) in St. Giles Parish, London.
   - John (abt. 1635–1636) in St. Giles Parish, London.
   - Mary (1638–1638) in St. Giles Parish, London.

   Ann Cater is the daughter of Bernard (1594–1625) and Joan Allen (d. 1649) of Sandy and the sister of Andrew Cater (1595–1654). There are two more sisters, Susan (1600–?) and Elizabeth (1597–?). The family has holdings in London and Bedfordshire, with a home on Coleman Street, London, along with other merchants of the day, including William Whiting. Andrew and his wife, Margery, have ten issue: two born in Bedford and eight in London. Andrew pens his will[323] on 1 June 1645, and it's probated on 20 November 1645. He states he is a "citizen and leather merchant of London." He mentions his sister "Anne Wiggen" and leaves her twenty pounds. His other sisters each get five pounds, and a niece, Margaret Whitebrook, receives five pounds. Andrew Cater owns two houses in the parish of St. Alphage, near Cripplegate, London, that he wills to his son, Andrew Junior.

[323] PRO: Prob/11/237

Because Andrew mentions his sister Anne by her married name but does not mention Hannibal, and because he recognizes a niece and does not name any children for Anne, it's safe to assume all her children and Hannibal are deceased. Because I cannot find mention of Hannibal and his family in the church records of London after the death of the third child, I believe they left London and went back to Bedfordshire. Hannibal probably died soon after and is buried in Sandy, Bedfordshire. They were likely victims of the plague.

5. William Wigan
   Born: 18 February 1598
   Baptism: 25 February 1598, Bishop's Itchington, Warwickshire, England
   Father: William Wigan
   Indexing Batch number: C03990-2; England ODM; 548396

   William m. Mary Unknown and had the following issue, all born in Bishop's Itchington:

   - Mary Wiggin, b. 10 December 1643
   - John Wiggin, b. 28 January 1645
   - Catherine Wiggin, b. 24 April 1649
   - Elizabeth Wiggin, b. 8 April 1652

6. Thomas Wiggin (AKA Captain Thomas Wiggin)
   Baptism: 20 September 1601, Bishop's Itchington, Warwickshire, England
   Father: William Wiggin
   Indexing Batch number: C03990-2; England ODM; 548396

7. Rychard Wigan
   Baptism: 1 March 1603
   Father: William Wigan
   Indexing Batch number: C03990-2; England ODM; 548396

   Married Elizabeth and is found in the Coughton, Warwickshire, records. One known issue:

   - Richard Wiggin, b. 1635 in Coughton, Warwickshire

GENERATION TWO:

John, born 14 Feb 1592, married Elizabeth Unknown. They had issue:

- William, b. 1619 (see next generation)
- George, b. 22 April 1621 (prob. died young)
- John, b. 6 October 1622; m. Mary Unknown and had daughter, Mary, 1640
- Thomas, b. 6 May 1625; m. Alice Unknown and had George in Aldridge, Staffordshire
- Richard,[324] b. 3 February 1627
- Edward, b. 3 June 1632; d. 16 August 1631
- Haniball, b. 17 August 1634; d. 23 August 1634

GENERATION THREE:

William Wigan, b. 1619, remains on the family lands in Bishop's Itchington and raises a family. He married about 1640 to Mary Unknown.

Issue of William and Mary Wigan of Bishop's Itchington:
(ch.=christened)

- Mary Wiggan, ch.[325] 10 December 1643; m. Richard Poole 1 May 1691; m William Cornish 18 November 1688
- John Wiggan, ch.[326] 28 January 1645; m. Elizabeth (see next generation)
- Catharine Wiggan, ch. 24 April 1649
- Elizabeth Wiggan,[327] ch. 8 April 1652
- William Wiggin,[328] ch. 22 August 1652
- Hannah Wiggin, ch. 13 July 1658
- Edward Wiggan, ch. 11 April 1661
- Hannah Wigan, ch. 10 April 1663; m. Moses Griffin, 1 May 1694
- Thomas Wiggan, ch. 20 February 1665

---

[324] This could be the Richard who died in 1708. Bishop's Itchington, St. Michael Burials, 1698–1812; data supplied by Nigel Draper.

[325] "ch." always stands for christened

[326] Ch = christened

[327] This might be the Elizabeth who died in 1699. Source: Bishop's Itchington, St. Michael Burials from 1698 to 1812; data supplied by Nigel Draper.

[328] I believe this is the William Senior who died 12 Feb 1704 and had a son named William who paid the death duty. Source: Bishop's Itchington, St. Michael Burials from 1698 to 1812; data supplied by Nigel Draper.

GENERATION FOUR:

John Wiggin[329] (William>John> William) was christened in St. Michael's, Bishop's Itchington, on 28 January 1645. He married Elizabeth before 1679 and had issue:

- Mary Wiggan, ch. 22 January 1679
- William Wiggan, ch. 27 February 1681 (see next generation)
- Elizabeth (1) Wiggin, ch. 28 August 1684 (died young)
- John Wiggin, ch. 16 November 1686
- Richard Wiggin, ch. 17 September 1689
- Elizabeth (2) Wiggan, ch. 29 September 1691

NOTES:

- William, 29 September 1732, Wm Wigan of Lower Itchington, Parish of Bishop's Itchington, gent., lands and tenements at Wellesbourne, Mountford (ER 3/419-687).
- 29 September 1732, Wm. Gent. Counterpart of mortgage to secure repayment of 520BPS.
- 29 March 1734: Wm. Gent, Lease and release of above.

GENERATION FIVE:

William Wiggin, b. 1681, had an unknown wife.
Issue of William:

- Butler Wigan, ch. 24 January 1709; m. Mary Ladbroke (see next generation)
- Elizabeth Wigan, ch. 20 January 1712
- William Wigan, ch. 15 September 1714
- Sarah Wigan, ch. 12 December 1716; m. Unknown Stevens
- Richard Wigan, ch. 20 November 1719; m. Elizabeth Large
- Anne Wigan, ch. 15 February 1721; m. Charles Smith
- Alice Wigan, ch. 23 July 1725
- Jane Wigan, ch. 1 January 1727

(SOURCE: IGI C039903)

---

329 This might be the John who died in 1724. Source: Bishop's Itchington-St. Michael Burials from 1698 to 1812. Data supplied by Nigel Draper.

BUTLER WIGGIN/WIGAN: Lived on Kingston Farm[330] in Bishop's Itchington.[331] He died 3 June 1766 and is listed as "from Kingston."[332] He owned it in shares with two others, and when he died (29 June 1766), his son Robert sold it.

- Butler married Mary Ladbroke of London, sister of the mayor of London and daughter of a former mayor of London. Will dated 1766.
- Butler is the last of the firstborn sons to live in Bishop's Itchington, Warwickshire. His estate there, Kingston Farm, is today the family seat of the Wiggin Clan.

Groom: Butler Wigan
Bride: Mary Ladbrook (Ladbroke)
Date: 17 March 1734, St. Lawrence Jewry and St. Mary Magdalene of Milk Street, London, London, England
Indexing Batch number: Butler Wigan M00146-1; England ODM
Source film: 374468, 942 HAV. 70, 942 B4HA V. 71, 942 B4HA V. 72[333]

Issue of Butler and Mary Ladbrook Wigan:

1. William Wiggin
   Baptism: 29 July 1735, Chesterton, Warwickshire, England
   Father: Butler Wiggin
   Digital Folder number 4294819

   NOTE: The child WILLIAM disappears and is not in Butler's will; he probably died young. Probably in London.
2. Sara Wiggin, b. abt. 1730. No further information.
3. Elizabeth Wiggin baptized 16 September 1747 in Chesterton and died 1766. No further information.

[330] AKA Kingston Manor; King's Farm
[331] Will of William Gyles of London, distiller, 1758 (proved 1760): "Butler Wigan of Kingston in the County of Warwick, Gentleman, the sum of two hundred pounds."
[332] Butler is the last Wiggin listed in the Burials of Bishop's Itchington-St. Michael's registers.
[333] These numbers refer to sources found in the Repository at Salt Lake City, Utah known as the Mormon library.

4. Robert[334] Wiggin
   Baptism: 27 May 1743, Chesterton,[335] Warwickshire, England
   Father: Butler Wigan
   Mother: Mary Wigan
   Digital Folder number 4294819

Robert marries Elizabeth Eason, and they live in Abbots Bromley, Staffordshire. Their issue:

Arthur Ladbrook Wiggin (1785 Abbots Bromley, Staffordshire, England-1847 London, England) who marries Lydia Elisa Cleveland, daughter of William and Sara Cleveland.
Their issue:

- Arthur William Wiggin (1814 London–1814 Croydon) died in childbirth
- Arthur Cleveland Wiggin (1815 London–1847 London)
- Basil Wane Wiggin (26 June 1823 London–?)

NOTES: Arthur C. Wigin m. Rosamund Dorothea Unknown. They lived in Folkstone, Kent, and had five children.

Thus closes a hundred years of occupation in Bishop's Itchington–Chesterton area between Vicar William Wiggin and Butler Wigan. Son Robert is found in the deeds as selling off his interests in his father's estate.

There are more Wiggin family members listed in the burial records for Bishop's Itchington–St. Michael's, but I have not researched them to find out who they were.

Mary Wiggin, 10 Feb 1733/4
Alice Wiggin, 01 Feb 1739
Mrs. Eliz Wigan, 01 Jan 1754
Mrs. Mary Wiggan, 09 Apr 1755
Mrs. Jane Wiggan, 19 Aug 1757

---

334 Robert Wigan: *Freeholders of Warwickshire,* 1774; Bishop's Itchington; Knightlow Hundred; resides in Abbots. Bromley, Staffordshire. In this same book, there is a Henry Wiggin in Birmingham and a John in Coventry owning land.

335 Chesterton and Bishop's Itchington sit side by side, and the famous Chesterton Windmill is located just west of the Kingston Farm, where Butler Wiggin resided. So Robert—and perhaps Butler too—attended the Chesterton church.

Mayflower II[336]

[336] Photo by Joyce Elaine Wiggin-Robbins

THE ADMIRALTY[337]

The Admiralty was a diverse organization, and different areas had their own procedures. As an example, I felt it worth the time to check the Southampton area and wrote the city council and received a reply from the senior archivists—Joanne Smith (16 December 2004) was most helpful. Southampton was exempt from the Lord High Admiral's jurisdiction from 1445 and was placed under the mayor of Southampton, who held court as admiral from Portsmouth to Lymington. Because of my belief that Captain Thomas Wiggin had contact with John Mason in the Portsmouth port, I felt it prudent to check those records. Nothing was found.

In 2007, I searched the Admiralty[338] records at Kew, Richmond, England, for a period covering 1625 to 1629. The records are in chronological order, well written, documenting ship, munitions, owners, masters, and the like. These records only hold the information for letters granted and not for requests for letters of marque. After checking and rechecking these files,[339] I came to the conclusion Captain Thomas Wigan never got his letter of marque.

The Admiralty is a very complex organization to read. Trying to garnish information about its range of jurisdiction from 1600 to 1700 can be a rambling experience. The chance for corruption is rampant, and it always was in the Admiralty.

In 1625, Sir William Russell, the man thought to have named Stratham, New Hampshire, was the Treasurer of the Navy, simultaneously holding posts as

[337] Admiralty records at Kew are extensive. They are well written and fairly intact, from what I had seen. However, it would take an expert on them to engage in any warranted search for small bits of information. There are researchers who specialize in these records.

[338] SP 16/115: Register book of warrants for issuing letters of marque and commissions to take pirates, granted by the Duke of Buckingham during his lord admiralship; with letters relating to the revenues of the lord admiral, 1625–1628. Sp 16/130 Register book of warrants for issuing letters of marque, granted by the lords commissioners of the admiralty 1628–1637. Sp 99/28 Wake on letters of marque 1627 Sept. 17/27.

[339] The National Archives, Kew, Richmond, England, SP 16/47/50, searched in 2007 by the author.

custom farmer and collector of silk duties, which provided him with substantial balances on hand to use for navy business. To his credit, history records that Russell did his job efficiently and with honor. He was able to secure funding for the navy more easily than his predecessors, and he had close connections with navy commissioners, including Buckingham.

Beginning in the middle of the Elizabethan reign, fully manned, armed ships were sailing the trading routes while serving as fishing vessels and on standby for royal war fleets. In that capacity, the country was underwriting, to some extent, merchant shipping.

Wages always seemed to be in arrears, which affected morale. As a result, seamen would sell stores. One such case was a longtime master gunner who sold barrels of gunpowder for personal gain. Morale and wages were not always on top of the game. Ships were undermanned, especially in peacetime, and duties doubled. All that with no pay was begging for disaster.

Ordnance was tightly controlled, and even Sir John Coke was questioning the expenditures for it. Sir John Coke was the leading commissioner of the navy after 1618. He knew every ship and her guns and kept tabs on them. He even questioned when four cannon on board one ship burned out and others didn't.

The crisis for the Admiralty seemed to begin with the voyage to Spain when King Charles and Buckingham went to transport Henrietta Maria back to England. The fleet comprised of eleven of the king's ships, twenty-four merchant ships, costing above forty thousand pounds. Lord Willoughby's expenses came to over ninety thousand pounds. That's a lot of money to secure a bride.

Then the seamen began to demonstrate and petition for back pay, and you have the scenario for chaos. It was under all this scandal that captains like Thomas Wiggin began to question their choices in life. More and more of them were showing up on the New England coast as agents and settlers. They sought peace and distance from all the corruption and threats of more war at home.

Bristol

Shipping into and out of Bristol was tightly controlled. Merchandise didn't move in any direction without the authorities knowing exactly what it was. A student of Bristol needs to read *Society of Merchant Venturers of the City of Bristol*[340] for knowledge on just how powerful this organization was. There is no mention of Thomas Wiggin in this book.

Bristol and London had a lot in common, and both places considered the accumulation of money as a measure of wealth. Even if they owned land in the counties, money was still of prime importance. Thus, the Merchant Society regulated and governed all commerce.

In Bristol, a merchant apprentice's training took place during the actual course of the trade, and in due time, the apprentice was allowed to make judgments and decisions on his own in the marketplace. They could be sent to purchase raw materials, sell merchandise, settle debts, and manage a shop if need be. Such activities also provided an apprentice social networking to bolster his future livelihood and life. Bristol would have been a prime location for Thomas Wiggin to have done his apprenticeship since his grandfather, Thomas Gybbes, was a wool merchant. However, Thomas Gybbes is found in London, not Bristol. Still, it was worth the years spent investigating Bristol, just in case Gybbes decided to send Thomas Wiggin there.

Bristolians were granted a license if they wished to frequent New England, even for purposes other than fishing.[341] A flotilla of ships was granted a license under a lead ship such as " . . . is granted licenses with five ships to sail to New England . . ." and the five ships aren't named because they may not have been known when license was applied for. So if Thomas Wiggin was in one of those flotillas, he wasn't named. We know that in 1629, a lot of ships were showing up on the Maine to Massachusetts shoreline. It would have been rare for a ship to

---

340 Society of Merchant Venturers of the City of Bristol, With some Account of the Anterior Merchants' Guilds, John Latimer, 1903, J. W. Arrowsmith, Quay Street, Bristol, England.

341 *The Widening Gate: Bristol and the Atlantic Economy 1450-1700*; David Harris Sacks; University of CA Press; London, England, 1991; pg. 105. Croft, "Free Trade and the House of Commons," pp. 21–22 Croft, ed., *Spanish Company*, p. 78.

sail the ocean by itself. Smaller cargo ships were escorts of a sort, and the larger ship with ordnance was insurance for the smaller ship that had none or only a few. Once clear of the pirates' haunts off the west coast, the flotillas often broke up.

I was convinced for a long time Thomas Wiggin must have been in Bristol early on. However, I was so fortunate in having the archivists eagerly working with me as they were also attempting to put the records back together. The secretary[342] of the present Merchant Venturers[343] was "bringing the boxes of documents up from the cellar," so he too was eager to know what I was finding. We e-mailed back and forth for a long time and learned a lot from each other, but we never found a clue about Thomas Wiggin.

The Wiggin clan is documented in Bristol as far back as 1479, where a Thomas Wigan is found in the will of Joan Kempson, proved 5 October 1479, inheriting a loom "being near the Avon." This was an era of prosperous merchandising in Bristol that soon faded due to war, inflation, poor harvests, epidemic influenza, and civil unrest.[344]

Bristol was instrumental in the North American and Caribbean trades and settlements. Sir Robert Yeamans was sheriff, mayor, and chief magistrate of Bristol; and his brother John settled Barbados and later founded a slave colony in America now known as Charleston. Tobacco and sugar became the leading commodities by 1650. Since European ports were drying up for Bristol, they turned to the Caribbean and North America.

The best source for everything Bristol is found in *The Widening Gate.*[345] This book became my bible while researching the city. You cannot be a student of life and commerce in Bristol without this book. Aside from the archivists of Bristol, this book is the leading source of history for not only Bristol, but of the entire west coast. All roads in the West Country led to Bristol, along with every channel port. The wool industry was centered in Bristol, and suppliers in the West Country ferried their wares down the canal systems to Bristol.

Bristol Record Society in 1951 published a volume titled "Records Relating to the Society of Merchant Venturers of the City of Bristol in the Seventeenth Century," but no one surnamed *Wiggin, Wigan*, and the like, is listed.

In the end, I had to accept that Bristol was just a port of embarkation for Thomas Wiggin and home to his early backers in New Hampshire. He had frequented the city enough to make some sound connections.

---

342 Mr. Pat Denney, with whom I traded e-mails in 2004. Of special interest was a school to teach the skills of a mariner to poor children.

343 The Merchants of Bristol incorporated in 1552 and became known as the Merchant Venturers.

344 Documents Illustrating the Overseas Trade of Bristol in the Sixteenth Century; Jean Vanes; 1979, Bristol Record Society, p.

345 *The Widening Gate: Bristol and the Atlantic Economy, 1450—1700*; David Harris Sacks, 1991, University of California Press.

Bristol Merchant Venturers

The Society of Merchant Venturers[346] of Bristol is a group of businessmen today mainly concerned with charitable endeavors. Their beginnings go back to the fifteenth century. The group today is comprised of all men, but it did, at one time, include Margaret Thatcher as an honorary member. Prince Phillip, Prince Charles, George Carey, Lord Carey of Clifton and the ex-Archbishop of Canterbury, have been/are all members.

In the seventeenth century, individuals of the group maintained shares in shipS and cargoS. Monetary losses could be overwhelming when a ship went down, or was taken as prize by another country, or pirates who plagued the coast of England.

They were seeking quick profits and were more interested in acquiring their products than in producing them; in other words, they wanted to distribute their products with little or no investment in their production. So it was little wonder they sold the Dover patent to the lords in 1632, as it was probably producing little to no quick profits.

Take care not to confuse this group with the Merchant Venturers who operated from London and were mainly concerned with the Ulster plantation.

In the seventeenth century, the Bristol Merchant Venturers (BMV) maintained a school for poor mariners' children, teaching them navigational skills. Correspondence with both the Bristol Record Office (BRO) and the Merchant Venturers' secretary produced a myriad of information on this school, but there is no record of Captain Thomas Wiggin ever having attended. The records of the school that did survive the centuries hold only the name of the *master.* These records were found in the accounting records. At the time of my inquiry to the BRO, there wasn't even a ready record of this school. They consulted a book by P. McGrath titled *History of the Merchant Venturers,* which did confirm the existence of the school in the 1600s. My inquiry did serve a useful

[346] *The Society of Merchant Venturers of the City of Bristol,* author John Latimer, 1903; pub J.W.Arrowsmith of Bristol. An excellent history of the organization.

purpose in that the BMV secretary decided it was time to centralize all the old records, and this was accomplished in due course. They are now maintained at the BRO.

Some of the more notable members are as follows:

1. ROBERT ALDWORTH: b. 1561; member of a prominent Bristol merchant family; Burgess of Bristol in 1584; 1603 he joined with John Whitson in backing a voyage of exploration by Captain Martin Pring to New England. Robert is of particular interest as he was affiliated with several ships and owners discussed in this manuscript. In particular, he owned, in whole or part, the *Gabriel* (80 tons and co-owned with his uncle, Thomas Aldworth), the *White Angel* (100 tons), the *Falcon* (70 tons) and the *Angel Gabriel* (240 tons).

Aldworth was deeply involved with the BMV on the continent. He also apprenticed both Abraham Shurt and Giles Elbridge in 1608; both men would later play large roles in Aldworth's business. Elbridge owned ships with letters of marque in 1626–28. Abraham Shurt became a Bristol burgess in 1615. In 1626, Aldworth sent Abraham to New England to purchase an island called Monhegan off the Maine coast. It was to become a base for the BMV. He bought Monhegan from Abraham Jennings of Plymouth. In 1630–31, he acquired twelve thousand acres with his son-in-law, Giles Elbridge, at Pemaquid Peninsula. This—combined with his investments in Martin Pring's expeditions to find the Northwest Passage in 1602–03 and 1606—make him a major player in the New England venture. Aldworth kept ownership of the *White Angel* to his death. Under Isaac Allerton, this ship sailed to New England on a regular basis. She ultimately became the property of some Massachusetts settlers.

2. GILES ELBRIDGE: Elbridge, an Aldworth apprentice, was admitted as a Bristol burgess in 1615 and married Elizabeth Aldworth, daughter of Robert, brother to John Aldworth. Elbridge became a member of the Society of Merchant Venturers in 1618.

In 1625–26, he launched a 250-ton ship, *The Charles*, which did not show up on a list of ships with letters of marque. By 1628, Elbridge had shares in, or owned outright, five Bristol ported ships including the *Angel Gabriel* (240 tons) and the *Dolphin* (140 tons), both listed as built in 1614. Giles Elbridge married for a second time the daughter of Humphrey Hooke, owner of six ships with letters of marque in 1626–28.

3. Humphrey Hooke: 1629 mayor of Bristol; occupation shown as "merchant." During his term of office, fellow shipowners Elbridge and Thomas Colston served as sheriffs. Humphrey owned Frampton Manor, a large 700-acre estate in Gloucestershire. He lived in Bristol at Ashley Court Road, a road named after his mansion, which stood there.

Complete lists of the members during the first half of the seventeenth century are nonexistent, and we can only garnish names from tax lists. In 1631, the Society owed the Crown money, and the men on that list are as follows: Mr. Tomlinson (Master in 1628), Alexander James, Richard Holworthy, Abel Kitchin, Henry Gibbes, William Jones, Walter Ellis and Frances Creswick, Edward Peters, John Locke, and William Wyatt. William Colston (father of Edward) is also listed. Undoubtedly, there are many more members.

Back in 1617, this was the list of those paying a tax to the Crown: Edward Williams, Peter Miller, William Pratt, Arthur Hibbins, William Hicks, Thomas Colston, Giles Elbridge, Walter Ellis, N. Butcher, G. Butcher, Francis Creswick, Derrick Popley, Francis Derrick, John Locke, John Gardner, Philip Ellis, Miles Jackson, Thomas Clement, William Pitt, Richard Plea(?), Matthew Haviland, Alexander James, and Nicholas Meredity. The mayor was John Guy.

Most of the members in the early seventeenth century were domiciled somewhere other than Bristol, with the majority living in London.

Letters of Marque[347] and Bristol Merchants

In 1619, commerce of the Port of Bristol was carried out chiefly by Scottish and Flemish Ships, the city and its merchants were "very poor".[348] By 1626–1628, when the government granted letters of marque authorizing the capture of French and Spanish merchantmen, upward of sixty privateering ships were fitted out in Bristol, and nearly all the larger vessels belonged to the merchantmen of the society.[349] I never found one belonging to a Captain Wigan/Wiggin. However, it is noteworthy to show a list here as they were early associates of Captain Wigan in some manner.

Humphry Browne (etc.)	*George*...300 tons
John Barker (etc.)	*Charles*...300 tons
	Joseph...150 tons
	Mary Rose...200 tons

[347] All Letters of Marque came from the Admiralty. Application had to be made in format and through the Admiralty offices. Only the actual awarding of Letters was recorded and listings are at Kew, Richmond, Surrey, England. You might well find a recording of an application received in the Admiralty meeting minutes, if you are able to find them, but it would take a super-human effort to locate just one mention and it would likely lack any useful information other than the recording of an application being received. For our purposes here it was not time efficient to undertake such a search on behalf of Captain Thomas Wigan. If he had received his requested letter, it would have been recorded as approved with all the appropriate information. It was not.

[348] The History of the Society of Merchant Venturers of the City of Bristol, by John Latimer, 1903, J. W. Arrowsmith, Quay Street, Bristol, England, page 152

[349] Ibid.

Humphry Hooke (etc.)	*Abraham*...200 tons
	Eagle...140 tons
	James...100 tons
	Two smaller tonnage
Thomas Colston	*The Bristol Merchant*...200 tons
	Mary...60 tons
John Gonning (etc.)	*Lion*...220 tons
	Another of 100 tons
	Another of 50 tons
Giles Elbridge (etc.)	*Angel Gabriel*...300 tons
	(Thomas Nethaway, master)
	Four more of 150 tons
William Pitt (etc.)	three of 200 tons
C. Diver (etc.)	four of 200 tons
W. Ellis	one of 200 and one of 100 tons
Alderman Barker	*Charles* (Martin Pring,[351] master)

[350] In 1602, Bartholomew Gosnold was sponsored by the Merchants and sailed in the *Concord* with 32 men under master William Street. On board was Martin Pring, who the next year, 1603, would make a voyage of his own in two ships, the *Deliverance* and *Speedwell*, with 43 men to survey the Saco and Kennebunk, York, and Piscataqua Rivers.

Barnstaple

There's always one source of information that sticks with you. For me, that source on Barnstaple was a book called *Barnstaple, Town on the Taw.*[351]

Barnstaple was long noted as a port of successful privateers preying on Spanish shipping. Richard Dodderidge, mayor in 1589, brought in a prize from the Guinea coast valued at sixteen thousand pounds. There was dancing in the streets that day.

In the late sixteenth century, the port was noted as a staging place for troops pushing the Spanish out of Ireland. In 1601, the Spanish had landed at Kinsale, and a great battle ensued. Almost two thousand Spanish invaders were killed.

Port books between 1560 and 1603 show the merchant vessels were very small, with several at only four tons[352] and the largest only sixty tons. They were dealing in whale oil, fish from Newfoundland, wine, cheese, salt, sugar, pepper, spices, and soaps and some brass, pewter, pots, iron, and materials of calico, linen, canvas, and woolens.

In 1623, Barnstaple was rumored to have a proposal to settle a plantation in New England, and Francis Weekes promised to pay 250 pounds one pence for a grant from Sir Ferdinando Gorges's Council of New England on behalf of the Barnstaple merchants. No further details were forthcoming.

Barnstaple lost a lot of ships in the English Channel and the Bristol Channel. In 1636, a report was made showing no fewer than eighty-seven ships (of the value of 100,000 pounds) and upward of three thousand men were lost to foreign buccaneers.

Other than visiting Drake in Barnstaple in 1627 and again showing up in the city in 1632 regarding transfer of a land patent, I found nothing in the city.

Bristol merchants have been involved in voyages of discovery from very early on. In 1498, Sebastian Cabot (a Venetian) sailed from Bristol with five ships and three hundred men. In 1602, Bartholomew Gosnold was sponsored by the merchants and sailed in the *Concord* with thirty-two men under Master William Street.

---

[351] *Barnstaple, Town on the Taw*, Lois Lamplugh; Genealogical Department, Church of the Latter-day Saints; British 492.35/81; pub Phillimore; also available on Amazon.com.

[352] Tonnage always refers to the cargo capacity, not the ship itself.

Letters of Marque and Barnstaple, Devon

Barnstaple[353] was well represented with explorers on the New England coast.[354] Again, I never found a Captain Thomas Wigan/Wiggin among these men:

1623: Richard Whilkey.... *Rebecca*

John Witheridge.... *Eagle* (also in 1624 and 1625)
Christopher Browning (master)
James Cook (master)
Mark Cook (master)
John Hodge (master)
Adam Horden (master of the *John*)

1624: In addition to the above, we find the following masters and owners: John Lausey, John Lucks, Anthony Nichols, John Penrose

Barnstaple was frequented by Sir John Drake, representative of the Admiralty, the man Captain Thomas Wigan (sic) sought help from in obtaining a letter of marque against the French in 1627.

Barnstaple was the staging port for the military in their struggles with both France and Spain. It was more noted as a military port rather than a commerce port like Bristol.

---

353 A great source of information on Barnstaple's participation is also found in *Barnstaple, Town on the Taw,* Lois Lamplugh, Phillimore, (no date) 942.25/81 H2d.

354 *Pioneers on Maine Rivers,* W. D. Spencer, Lakeside Printing Co. Portland, Maine, 1930.

In the latter half of the sixteenth century, we find a very active group engaging in letters of marque.

SHIPS, MASTERS, AND OWNERS

White Hart
Unicorn (1589)
1591–1596: A pinnace called *Fortmouth*
Gift . . . owner W. Morcombe
Busse . . . owner John Delbridge

Perhaps the greatest of them all was RichardDodderidge, who was mayor in 1589 and owned a 100-ton ship named *Prudence*. This ship has two entries in the records of 1590, when she sailed with eighty men to the Guinea coast and brought back four chests of gold valued at 16,000 pounds, and other gold items weighing 320 pounds.[355] The same year, this ship brought in two more hauls.

In 1592, the *Prudence* brought in a prize haul of 10,000 pounds worth of goods. *Prudence* made Richard Doddridge a very wealthy man. By 1596, his ship *Prudence* was involved in action with three Spanish ships in the Irish Sea. And on 8 August, she arrives back in port after taking part in the "takynge of Cales (Cadiz)."[356]

By 1620, there is another ship in port named *Prudence* (100 tons) that is sailing under letters of marque. This is owned by William Lee and company with Thomas May as master.

The year 1596 found Barnstaple busy with the Crown's Irish conflict. With over three hundred troops in port and a food shortage, they were overly burdened just to feed everyone. Barnstaple's struggles as a military port were still ongoing in 1607.

The record book entries for sizes of ships engaged in these activities are surprising. They ranged from 3 to 4 tons to just 60 tons, coming from ports in Wales, Devon, and Cornwall, as well as the Barnstaple area. Barnstaple ships tended to have biblical names such as *Mary, Anne, Elizabeth, Peter,* etc.

When you read the history of the merchants and "shipowners" of Barnstaple, you get the impression they were not as cohesive as the Bristol merchants. They seem to be more individually inclined rather than as a cohesive group. Richard Dodderidge, a very rich man, was involved in a scheme to trade at the river of Senegal and Gambia in Guinea, but if it ever got off the ground is not known. By 1623, there was a move afoot to make a settlement in New England. State

---

355 *Barnstaple, Town on the Taw*, Lois Lamplugh, Phillimore press (no date), pp. 51–52.
356 Ibid, pg. 53.

Papers[357] show a Francis Weekes promising to pay 250 pounds for a grant to be obtained from Sir Ferdinando Gorges's Council of New England in the name of the merchants of Barnstaple[358]. However, when I tracked down this Francis Weeks, I find he went to New York on his own. Weeks was born in 1618 in Broadword, Devonshire, and died in 1689 in Oyster Bay, Nassau County, New York. He descends of the Weekes family of Honeychurch, Devonshire.[359]

The 1623 State Papers include a letter to John Delbridge showing he's actively trading with the Virginia plantation, and he's one of the early importers of tobacco. John was born in 1564 and was also deeply involved with passing on information regarding the Spanish news, plans, and war preparations to Queen Elizabeth's court. He died in 1636 at the age of 72.

The merchants of Barnstaple were not incorporated, and when they were asked in 1619 to contribute 500 pounds to help eradicate the pirates off their coastline, they could only raise 330 pounds. The following year, they were demanded to pay a further 250 pounds; they refused as they were denied tax relief for their goods at Exeter, Plymouth, and elsewhere.[360]

1625–1628: Letters of Marque

Deciding to act alone, eight Barnstaple owners received letters of marque for fourteen ships: *Prudence* (which I spoke of earlier); *Blessing* (40 tons and the smallest) was captured in 1632.

1634: The Crown's demands for ships and money continued, one for a 900-ton ship and as many as 100 armed men. The demands seemed to be unending. On top of material demands, the town had to support the families of prisoners taken during the assaults on the pirate strongholds.[361] The town was soon borrowing on bonds.

Considering the above history of Barnstaple alone, it is even more puzzling why Captain Thomas Wigan did not get his letter of marque against the French in this same time period. Everything from very small to very large ships was getting them, so ship size had nothing to do with it. This man—our ancestor or not—had to have owned his own ship (in whole or in part) to apply for this license. I think the only chance of finding this particular man and his ship will lie in the records of each individual port. I searched in both the Barnstaple and

---

357 Ibid, pg. 60.

358 The merchants of Barnstaple were not organized into a group like they were in Bristol.

359 There is an extensive site devoted to the Wykes family, located online at www.wykes.org.

360 *Barnstaple, Town on the Taw,* Lois Lamplugh. Phillmore press (no date), pg. 63.

361 See "Privateers" in this book.

Bristol port records on my 2007 trip to the National Archives at Kew, England, and found nothing.

Summary

I never found a record linking Captain Thomas Wiggin with either the Barnstaple or the Bristol merchants who had letters of marque. I totally believe that if he had been aligned with either group, he would have received his own letter of marque. Since he did not, I have concluded he was seeking such a letter in order to recoup losses sustained during the years of conflict between England, Spain, and France. A second possibility—and the more likely one, it seems—was he was planning to return to New England and knew the French in Canada could be a problem.

I also considered the chance of his being ported at Portsmouth, England, and soon ruled that out as a waste of time to research. If he had been at Portsmouth, he would have gone to Captain Mason for help in getting that letter of marque.[362] Instead, he shows up in Barnstaple.

[362] In which case Mason would have sent him to the Piscataqua River in 1629. It's a possibility and might account for the great animosity between the Wiggin and Mason families. We may be wrong in thinking that it was based solely on animosity toward the Masons.

Henry Kirke Map 1871[363]

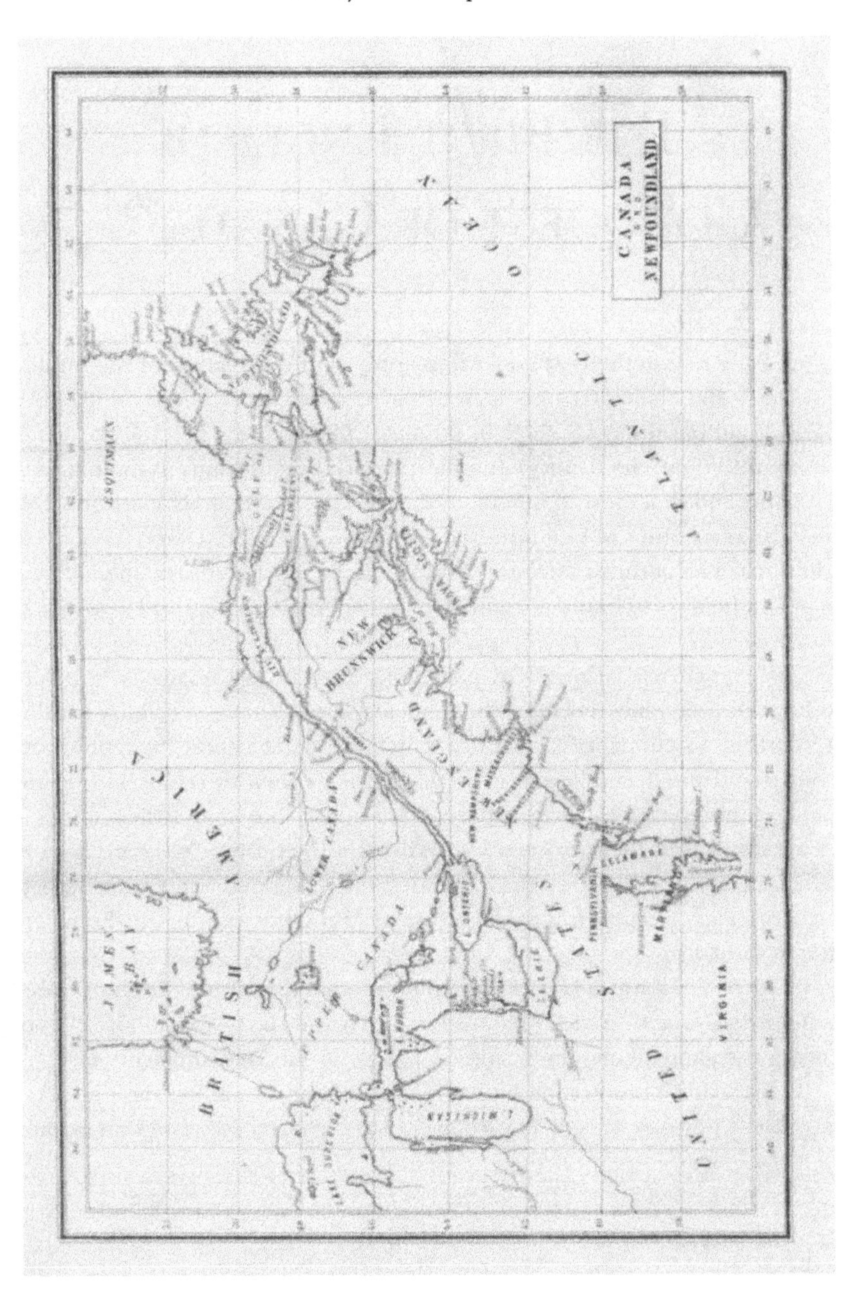

363 Conquest of Canada, *The earliest settlements in Nova Scotia and Newfoundland*, by Henry Kirke, pub. 1871, London, Bemrose & Sons, 21 Paternoster Row, London.

The First English Conquest of Canada[364]

This is one of the best books to read to acquire a picture of the English merchants and their attempts at settling America from about 1600, when England had but thirty-six ships in the navy. The author, Henry Kirke, states that up until then, the British left such territorial acquisitions in the hands of merchants and that most, if not all, of the ships were merchant class outfitted with ordnance. Ships of one-hundred cargo tonnages could carry as many as eight guns. The author's ancestor Gervase Kirke was one of the members of the patent holders to found a trading settlement on the rivers and seashore of Canada in 1627.

The French had a long and productive history in Canada long before the English ever ventured into the area. The French were very busy settling the coastline when, in 1613, a British ship[365] happened upon them at Mount Desert Island and declared war on them, capturing their two ships, killing one man, and taking the rest as prisoners. The English ship, under the command of Captain Argoll, then proceeded to Port Royal, and he continued his war against the French. These events happened when England and France were at peace with each other. It was purely a case of Argoll not wanting the French to settle in Canada.

In 1600, the naval forces of England amounted to thirty-six ships, all of small burden. One ship of 1,000 tons (30 guns) and the rest of about 100 tons (7 to 8 guns), and all merchant ships were hastily outfitted and armed.[366]

By April 1627, the French had at least two ships of war on the Canadian coast. The Company of New France had a royal charter to settle Canada and

[364] By Henry Kirke, 1842–1925; pub HardPress Pub in January 1913; ISBN 978-1313622523.

[365] Captain Argoll out of Virginia

[366] *The First English Conquest of Canada*; Henry Kirke; pub 1871, London, Bemrose & Sons, 21 Paternoster Row.

had shiploads of settlers eager to set sail. The territory of New France then included Florida.

England started taking greater note of both Canada and the New England territories, and anyone settling Nova Scotia was made a baron of Scotland.

During all this turmoil, Sir William Alexander outfitted a naval force in 1627, backed by the merchants of London.

With his two brothers, Captain David Kirke plundered and burned Port Royale, Nova Scotia, and other French ports. This one act was the powder keg that started the hostilities between the French and English settlers of North America.

In the spring of 1627, a small fleet of three ships (the largest 300 tons) under the command of Captain David Kirke set sail. In the same month, a very large fleet set sail from France laden with cannon for the French Canadian port, provisions, and settlers. They were not armed for war. The English three and the larger convoy of French ships would meet in Canada. The small English fleet, armed to the teeth for war, soon captured the 1,000-ton command ship of the French fleet.

Captain Kirke sent his captive elite French officers back to England along with the 138 cannon found in the holds of the French ships.

This history book is rich with descriptions of the conflicts between the French and the English in Canada in the year 1627.

In 1629, a fleet consisting of one 300-ton, two 200-tons, and two smaller ships with three pinnaces set sail for Canada, all armed to the teeth and with letters of marque and reprisal.

Could it be that Captain Wiggin's ship was to be part of this fleet?

Samuel Champlain surrendered Quebec to the English in August 1629. It had taken Captain Kirke but two months to capture all of Canada from the French. Little did Kirke know that peace had been reached between England and France, and all his work in Canada was for naught. The territories were to be returned to France.

Having read this history brings me full circle back to why Captain Thomas Wiggin wanted a *letter of marque and reprisal* against the French in 1627. Again, we can only speculate, but the conflicts with the French in Canada seems the more plausible reason to me. However, by 1629, peace with France was reached, and Wiggin had no need for a letter of marque against them. He sailed for New England without one.

North American Staple Trades

Merchants were driven by the staple trades of the British Empire all during the age of sailing ships. These staples were codfish, furs, timber (especially tall masts for ships), tobacco and cotton from Virginia territory, sugar from the Indies, sea-otter fur from the Pacific Ocean, indigo, cattle, wheat, flour, potash, wine, and of course, the wool trade. England tightly controlled where these products could be traded in order to collect excise taxes from them.

English cod fishing has been recorded as far back as the fifteenth century. It was a profitable venture as a ship of only 100 tons manned by forty men, with eight smaller boats on deck and a three-man crew for each, could process 200,000 pounds of dry fish and about 10,000 pounds of wet fish. Contact with the Native Americans on shore—when they were processing the fish for drying, acquiring water and wood, or catching bait for their fishing lines—provided the quickest and easiest opportunities for trading for furs. Cod fishing was the single biggest impetus for colonizing the northeastern areas of North America in the first place. Fishermen were not fighters, and their occupation meant they had to set up drying stages on land. Islands were the obvious choice, as they provided a buffer from marauding Indians. They could at least spot them coming across open water in their canoes. So it's no surprise to find drying stages on places such as the Isle of Shoals off the coasts of Maine and New Hampshire for decades prior to attempts at settling the mainlands.

So it's not a question of what drew the merchant adventurers to colonize North American shores; it was only a question of how to achieve it to get the quickest return on their investment. By the end of the fifteenth century, more Europeans were fishing for a living than any other occupation, other than farming. In 1497/8, John Cabot had discovered the fishing banks off Newfoundland. Just a hundred years later, in 1584, the London and Bristol Company, a joint stock company, informed the Crown they were going to form a permanent settlement in what is now Newfoundland.

By the time Thomas Wiggin was a child, there would be hundreds of opportunities to read of adventures by not only all these fishermen, merchants, and infant settlements, but of the many mariners seeking the Northwest Passage.

By the year of Thomas's birth, 1601, England was sending over 200 ships a year to the fishing banks off Canada. It was a huge undertaking just to satisfy the Catholic European population's desire for fish. In 1615, a Richard Whitbourne[367] estimated some 250 English vessels alone were off the Canadian banks, carrying over 5,000 men and processing over 120,000 pounds of codfish. That's a huge amount, but it didn't even equal what France was producing.

[367] Sir Richard Whitbourne was born 1579 and died 1628; a colonist, author, and mariner who sailed around Europe more than once and spent numerous years in Newfoundland in the cod-fishing industry. He published *A Discourse and Discovery of New-found-land* in an effort to promote colonization.

Shrewsbury Men

There was a group of men all too often called the "Shrewsbury Men" in the early history reports of New England. No one seems to call them by name, ever—just the "Shrewsbury Men." I found this very intriguing, so I searched for a list of these so-called adventurers. These merchants were drapers, and their prosperity lay in their role as "middlemen" in the woolen and cloth trade of north and central Wales as well as Shrewsbury. The lighter, coarse Welsh materials—known as cottons and friezes (later flannel)—found an export market through the Shrewsbury Drapers. [368]

The Welsh trade flourished from the middle of the sixteenth century until about 1660. The word "staple" was used to describe the official trading center for this woolen cloth, which was located about sixteen miles from Shrewsbury in the town of Oswestry, until it moved into Shrewsbury in 1620.

The Drapers bought cloth on a weekly basis in the Oswestry market, where they met at the "Old Three Pigeons Inn" at Nesscliffe. From there, they journeyed with each other over the dangerous roads to Shrewsbury, where the cloth was put out to be finished by shearsmen. Then it was sent weekly on packhorses to a London cloth market known as Blackwell Hall, whence the London merchants would export it to Rouen, Bay of Biscay, and the Iberian Peninsula.

The Drapers Hall, designed as a guildhall for business meetings, drew both wealthy and influential men from the ranks of burgesses, yeomen, and gentry alike. Some of the more prominent names were William Jones (died 1612), Thomas Jones (leading Draper in 1638), David Lloyd, Robert Ireland, Richard Owen, and William Rowley. These were members of the Drapers Company, and all built fine townhouses.[369]

William Rowley seems to be the foremost of the group. The Shrewsbury Museum and Art Gallery is now housed in what was his house; and in 2007, when we were in England, the building was closed for extensive renovations.

---

[368] An organized group made up of men from Shrewsbury and other places.

[369] Shrewsbury Drapers Guild Corp. records: Internet site http://www.shrewsburydrapers.org.uk/guild.

The best record I found for who these men were is the following:

> Citation: Charles I, 1640; an act for the relief of his Majesties Armie and the Northern Parts of the Kingdome'. Status of the Realm: v. 5: 1628–80 (1910) pp. 58–78: for the Towne of Shrewsbury: Unto Hugh Haris Esquire; Major Sir Richard Prince, knight; Timothy Turner; Thomas Jones Sr.; Esquires: Edward Jones, Thomas Owen, Humphrey Macworth, Esquires: William Rowley, Simon Eston, Charles Benyon, Robert Betton, Thomas Winfield, John Studley, Alderman. This listing gives us the upper merchant class of Shrewsbury c. 1628.

It is the only such listing I've ever encountered. The merchants would have had strong connections to both Bristol (the Bristol Merchant Ventures) and London.

The two groups (the Shrewsbury Merchants and the Bristol Merchant Ventures) are quoted only in those terms regarding Captain Thomas Wiggin's early employment interests in New England pre-1635.

It is difficult to imagine a group, let alone more than one group, singling out one man for employment, as it is likely each member of those groups would have a candidate for leadership of interest to themselves. Who decided on Captain Wiggin as their factor in each of these two groups? I cannot imagine the Captain being plucked off the deck of a ship to administer a patent for such a diverse group of individuals! Not a likely scenario. What set of circumstances placed the Captain in the right place at the right time to be chosen as administrator for such powerful groups of men?

By 1627, all these men had business interests and homes in London. It appears they knew William Whiting in London, and he is also involved with them in the Dover patent. I think it more likely Thomas Wiggin was placed in his position by William Whiting. William was also going to resettle in New England (and he and his new wife, Susanna Wiggin, sailed in 1633 with the newly married Thomas Wiggin couple) and was chosen to head up the groups' interests in Connecticut. I think it highly likely Thomas Wiggin (who was marrying William's sister Catherine) was William's choice to head up the New Hampshire settlement. All these London merchants, including the lords, would have been very pleased with this arrangement. It gave both William Whiting and Thomas Wiggin someone to fall back on if a time of need ever arose, and it gave the backers two men, who were well acquainted with each other, to serve their interests.

The Pioneers of Maine and New Hampshire[370] tells us the Shrewsbury men were in part:

1. William Walderne (1615–1689): Arrived in Dover, New Hampshire, in 1635; had mills on the Chocheco River.
2. Richard Percyvall: Draper who sold his share to Obadiah Bruen in 1640.
3. Obadiah Bruen (1606–bef. 1690): Draper; immigrated to Newark, New Jersey.
4. Richard Hunt (b. 1562 in Shrewsbury; d. 1656 in Shrewsbury): Father of Thomas, who immigrated to New York.
5. William Rowley: His house is now a museum. It's a stone-and-brick building built about 1618 and called the home of the Merchant William Rowley. He came to Shropshire some time before 1594, when he was made a burgess. A draper, brewer, and maltster. The buildings that now comprise the museum were the timber-framed buildings typical of the day and are said to be the finest in all of Shrewsbury. By 1618, he had made sufficient fortune to build an adjoining magnificent brick mansion.

Another man of early colonial importance from Shrewsbury was Thomas Lewis (1590–1640), who came to New England in 1628. He resided at Saco, Maine, and was a tavern keeper. He was, however, not a part of the Shrewsbury Men. He did have land transactions with Captain Thomas Wiggin.

[370] Charles Henry Pope; Boston, Mass., pub by Charles H. Pope, 1904; p189.

Mayflower II[371]

371 Photo by Joyce Elaine Wiggin-Robbins

Privateers and The Smuggling Trade

Of particular interest is the Isle of Lundy, an island rich in traditional history and myths. Lundy was the isle of choice for Lord Saye and Sele when he vacated England in self-exile after King Charles was beheaded. He did not come back until after the Cromwell ruling years. The island is rich in history of pirates and mystery. I spent a great deal of time researching this island's history, but could not find a connection to Captain Thomas Wiggin. Nothing in the Captain's life indicates he was involved in the smuggling business, although its history is a good read.[372]

The guidelines for privateers states they are to take any prizes to the nearest (English) port of authority; so if he was involved with such a prize on the west coast, between Ireland and west England, the Isle of Man would have been a proper port to enter. The Isle is self-governed, but a protectorate of England.

Privateering records go back to the fourteenth century. However, the "golden age of privateering" was under Queen Elizabeth I. She was trying to get a hand on the Crown's share of the captured wealth and was the first monarch to clamp down on the ships and owners.

The Calendar of State Papers at the National Archives is rich with reports on piracy. Petitions, complaints, compensations, requests for assistance, and the like—all are subjects cramming the State Papers.

If you want to pick out just one man to read about, then go for Martin Frobisher's biography. He typifies a man who goes from a common ship's captain to a Crown favorite through perseverance and piracy. He crosses swords with Sir Francis Drake during the Spanish Armada conflict. Although his career was not unique, it was brilliant as he played such a historical part of England's attempts at dominating the high seas.

---

[372] Read *The Widening Gate* for a good history on smuggling.

A "privateer" was not a man—it was a ship! One armed and commissioned with a letter of marque from the Crown could take a *prize* (ship) flying the flag of a country at odds with England. The first letter of marque was issued in the late thirteenth century, but it would take another two hundred years for restraints to be placed on these ships. When the Admiralty Court laid down the rules and regulations during the conflict with Spain, the rules changed dramatically. Letters of marque were issued by the High Court of the Admiralty to anyone wishing to take prizes and had the price of a commission.

This is what I believe qualified Captain Thomas Wigan/Wiggin to ask for a letter of marque in the first place: he had the "price of a commission." He seemed to fit all the qualifications until I researched the likely reasons why he didn't get one. The only thing I found was either his ship was not seaworthy (had not passed a seaworthy test of some sort) or he himself had not taken the mariner's exam. Anyone can purchase a ship. The third and most striking reason was infighting among the southwest Admiralty members, causing them to overlook the marginal request by Drake in 1627 on behalf of Captain Thomas Wigan.

The Royal Navy

I never found a list of men comprising the navy who were engaged in the conflicts between England, Spain, and France. There's a reason for that: England did not have a royal full-time navy.[373] Whenever the Crown needed ships and men to man them, it told the port cities what it wanted, and the ports supplied both ships and men. This is especially true of the Cinque Ports, which gained special compensations such as tax relief by supporting the Crown. The reason these ports were created in the first place was to supply ships and men when the Crown wanted/needed them. So records are to be found in each port's documents but nothing under the heading of "the Royal Navy" as one would hope.

The merchant citizens of each port footed the bill to outfit its ships. They did receive Crown funding for salaries and outfitting the ships with things like cording and maintenance once engaged. It's far more involved than I am relating here, but suffice to say, it was a strain on the ports of western England and their economy to supply these ships on demand.

I had to search each port city's records for ship owners and their records. This project took years to accomplish. In the end, I had to accept that I was

[373] I corresponded with several authorities in England on English history, and each of them gave me the same answer. Basically, there are no central records because there was no Royal Navy at that time. Each port maintained its own records during this era.

not going to find what I was seeking. Perhaps in years to come, someone will come across something to indicate what port city a Captain Thomas Wiggin was affiliated with, what his ship's name was, and who her owners were. The Port of Southampton cannot be overlooked, nor Plymouth. I thoroughly searched the Port of Bristol because of his connection to the Merchant Ventures, yet found nothing. Records are very good regarding ship owners, descriptions, and usage in the Bristol and Admiralty records.

My conclusion was that Captain Thomas Wiggin may have purchased his first ship about 1627 with the express desire to go to New England. He probably ported on the West Coast for two years, getting ready for his voyage. This may be one reason he's well-documented on the New England coast by 1629 but not listed on any ship as a passenger. It would also explain the grounding of his ship off Massachusetts in 1631.[374]

[374] History of Essex County, Massachusetts, Volume 2, Part 1: *Captain Wiggin ran a ship aground on Long Beach on 18 Feb 1631.*

The Devil and the Deep Blue Sea

Pirates, Privateers, and Islands

Dixey Bull

Probably born around 1600, the London native shows up in Boston Colony in 1631. In 1633, Bull became New England's first pirate. By 1634, he had vanished. No doubt, he left behind a legacy rich in stories for early mariners. Little is known of him, but there is a poem from the 1600s, which claims he died in a sword fight. He is thought to have been killed by natives in 1634 after a raid on Marblehead, Massachusetts.

Sir Francis Drake (1540–1596)

One of Queen Elizabeth's privateers. He was revered as the hero of the Spanish Armada's downfall, yet he had many enemies in the old nobility class. He was considered rapacious in his quest for Spanish treasures on the high seas as well as a man of vision, skill, and daring. Historians consider him to be the greatest of all English sea captains.

Sir John Hawkins (1532–1595)

Hawkins was a cousin to Sir Francis Drake, another of Elizabeth's privateers/ pirates who is credited with having an eye for profits akin to a merchant's skills. He was at sea early in his life and made his fortune trafficking in slaves. John Hawkins is considered the epitome of pirates. He not only commanded his own ships, he built them as well. Hawkins was rear admiral of the fleet during the battle with the Spanish Armada in 1588. He had redesigned the old English fleet of galleons with lower, sleeker, racing-type ships prior to the battle with the Spanish Armada. Hawkins financed his cousin Sir Francis Drake's voyages and made his last trip with Drake, dying at sea in 1595.

Sir Martin Frobisher (1535–1594)

Frobisher died from wounds suffered during a battle off the coast of Spain. He was born a Yorkshire man, spending his youth in London. Apprenticed as a cabin boy in 1544, he became a sea captain in 1565, an explorer whose quest for the Northwest Passage is so well-documented.

Sir Humphrey Gilbert (1539–1585)

Half-brother to Sir Walter Raleigh; educated at Eton and Oxford. In 1566, he authored *A Discourse of Discoveries for a New Passage to Catala* (China). He served under the Earl of Warwick at Le Havre and served in Munster, Ireland, where he was knighted in 1570. He was a great explorer and an inspiration to his two siblings, Walter and Carew Raleigh, in their endeavors to settle the New World. Humphrey, after refusing to board the *Golden Hind,* went down with his ship, the *Squirrel,* which was swallowed up by the sea.

Sir Richard Hawkins (1562–1622)

Son of Sir John Hawkins, Sir Richard was at sea early in life on board Drake's ships. He made the trip with Drake to bring the Roanoke, Virginia, settlers home. In one battle with the Spanish, he was outnumbered and taken prisoner. Some three or four years later, he was ransomed from prison and returned to Devon, where he was made vice admiral of Devon. He was to spend his time defending Devon's coastline from pirates. He spent 1604–05 writing *Observations of His Voyage into the South Seas, AD 1593.* Richard's close ties to Bristol and Barnstaple, combined with his literary skills, had to have had an impact on young Thomas Wiggin's life.

Martin Pring (1580–1646)

Pring is of special interest as he made the first voyage of significance to the seacoast of New England, spending time exploring the Great Bay region in which Captain Thomas Wiggin would eventually settle. Pring is buried in Bristol, St. Stephen's Church. He was made a captain by Richard Hakluyt and sailed as master for Captain Hanam's ship on his 1603 voyage to New England, sanctioned by Sir Walter Raleigh, the patentee holder. Martin Pring's flagship was the *Speedwell* and was accompanied by another barque called the *Discoverer* with master Edmund Johns. Pring's accounts of his voyage became an important factor in the stimulation of interest in the New England regions, and being domiciled in Bristol, a port very familiar to Captain Thomas Wiggin, had to have some significance in his life.

By 1625, Pring's papers had fallen into the hands of Samuel Purchas, who published them.

Sir Walter Raleigh (1544–1618, beheaded)

Sir Walter was a prolific writer, composing the *History of the World* while imprisoned in the Tower of London for thirteen years. The history books, Internet, and libraries are full of colorful life stories of this man. We can have no doubt Sir Walter played a strong part in Captain Wiggin's life at sea. One of the Elizabethan pirates, she threw him up and bounced him around until he fell into great riches. He had powerful enemies, however, and his life would end with a beheading in 1618.

Sir Robert Rich (1587–1685)

Rich was a privateer, a colonial administrator, and an admiral who became Captain General of the Parliament's Armies in opposition to the Crown. To the Crown's displeasure, he sent privateers to the West Indies, and on 17 April 1627, he sailed with other privateers to harass Spanish trade with the west.

Robert Rich took an early interest in colonial settlements, and in 1628, he managed to acquire the Massachusetts Patent. He had been a member of the Council of the New England Company since 1620 and of the Bermuda Company since 1614. He was a Puritan in sympathies, connections, and convictions; and he opposed the forced loan of 1626. The forced loan was a tax levied on maritime towns and shires to provide funding for ships of war.

In 1630, a Barque[375] called the *Warwick* arrived off the coast of Maine a day ahead of the Winthrop fleet. The *Warwick* was to have joined the Winthrop fleet out of England, but she sailed on ahead of the main fleet. On board was a man called "a soldier," sent by the Duke of Warwick to explore the area for settlement.

Rich's sea activities fit a timeline to have included Captain Thomas Wiggin, but the facts just don't fit. There are no records to tell us if Captain Wiggin was one of his sailors.

SUMMARY: Of all the above, the only one Captain Wiggin was likely involved with was Sir Robert Rich. I always had a suspicion that due to his father's love of history, Thomas Wiggin probably read a lot of renditions of the sea captains who came before him and thus had a love of adventure and the sea from a very young age.

ISLE OF LUNDY

The mystic Isle of Lundy is located in the mouth of Bristol Bay. During the period of our interest, it was owned by the Grenville family but occupied more

---

[375] Barque is a three or more masted sailing ship with rigged square mainmast and only the mizzen (the aftmost mast) rigged fore-and-aft.

often than not by the French pirates and the scum of the Spanish seas. They plagued shipping into and out of Bristol and Barnstaple for years, with their heyday being in the 1630s when the notorious Captain John Nutt occupied it. Lord Saye and Sele had a claim to the island, and it was surrendered to him about 1641.

Lundy is described as looking like a brick that has been pushed up out of the sea due to the cliffs all way around, towering 147 feet, which makes for a natural fortress. It is flat on top and with at least one cave that is accessible at high tide. It was a natural, profitable base for pirates of all sorts. Lundy is about 5 km long, but very narrow at 1.25 km at its widest point, containing about 1,000 acres on the top with 500 more on the south end that are tillable. Lundy is 13 miles off the North Devon coast.

Sir Bevil Granville, born in Cornwall in 1576, owned the island until his death at the battle of Lansdowne in June 1643. Early in the seventeenth century, complaints made to the government by Shipowners and local authorities concerning pirates in the Bristol Channel became so constant that a commission was issued in 1608 to the Earl of Bath to inquire into the matter. In 1618, the enemy at court of Sir Walter Raleigh, Sir Lewis Stukeley, Vice-Admiral of the Coasts of Devon, ended up on Lundy to die a poor distracted beggar having, for a bag of money, falsified his faith. Stukeley was a relative of Raleigh's and was involved in the debacle preceding Raleigh's arrest following his trip to Venezuela in search of a gold mine, where Raleigh's ship's crews had raided, sacked, and burned St. Thomé, which was in contradiction to the Crown's orders.

A body dug up by a tenant farmer named Hole, and said to be that of Lord Saye and Sele, may have been that of Sir Lewis Stukeley. Hole flung the bones over the wall, and that very night, he himself was killed by falling from the cliffs. He was buried the next day in the grave he had desecrated.

By 1625, the mayor of Bristol reported to the Council that three Turkish pirates had taken the Isle of Lundy with its inhabitants and were threatening to burn Ilframcombe (a city on the mainland). Depositions were taken from several merchant captains and sent to the Earl of Pembroke.

In 1628, Captain Fogg of HMS *James* sent a letter to the Admiralty saying that a French man-of-war had taken some vessels off Lundy and adding "Hope we shall meet with them."

On 30 June 1630, Captain Plumleigh, who was in command of a warship, wrote as follows to the Lord Treasurer: "Egypt was never more infested with caterpillars than the Channel with Biscayers. On the 23rd there came out of St. Sebastian twenty sail of sloops; some attempted to land on Lundy, but were repulsed by the inhabitants."

By 1632, Lundy had become the headquarters of the notorious buccaneer Captain Robert Nutt. He had more than one ship and gave himself the title of admiral. He occupied his ships chiefly in the pilfering of small traders.

The history of the Isle of Lundy paints a picture of Captain Thomas Wiggin's frustrations with perhaps being a sea captain and constantly having to battle pirates. Thus, his request for a letter of marque and not getting one in 1627 deepens with mystery.

To thine own self be true, and it must follow, as the night the day, thou canst not then be false to any man.[376]

—William Shakespeare

[376] The Wiggin motto

SECTION II

THOMAS WIGGIN

20 SEPT 1601

BISHOP'S ITCHINGTON, WARWICKSHIRE, ENGLAND

16 JUNE 1666

SQUAMSCOTT HOUSE[377], ROCKINGHAM, NEW HAMPSHIRE

377 AKA Quamscott house

SECTION II INTRODUCTION

Section I presented to you family pedigrees, associates and connections, wedding-ring connections, timelines, and histories that set the record to begin breathing life into a man called Captain/Governor Thomas Wiggin.

It is not the mission of this manuscript to document Captain Wiggin's actions after 1633 except as it pertains to his life prior to that year. I leave it to others to document and verify from his settling on Great Bay in 1633 to his death in 1666.

By 1629, Thomas Wiggin has a solid accumulation of education, merchandising, and farming, equipping him for the rigors of New England. Thomas became a man with a mission and the determination to make it work.

His knowledge of New England is vast, given the amount of books, maps, and reports at his disposal by explorers in the early sixteenth century. Combined with stories heard in the merchandising marketplaces of London, Bristol, Barnstaple, and other active ports along the English coast, there isn't much left to the imagination regarding what New England can offer someone of vision, determination, and a desire to achieve something denied him in old England—namely, wealth and property. That alone was impetus enough to leave the comforts of home for the wilderness of a land yet to be discovered.

So whether or not Captain Wiggin ever made a voyage of discovery to the New World is almost immaterial as he had easy access to a myriad of data.

In section II, we leave his family and connections and take a look at the man himself. How exactly did he acquire his knowledge and reputation? Having blood and wedding-ring ties is one matter, but establishing oneself as reliant, ambitious, controlled, and knowledgeable is another matter. To become a man whose very life exemplified the ambitions of a nation yet to be born, to be founded on the highest principles of mankind, sets him up as someone to take reckoning of.

London becomes one of the greatest experiences of his life and sets the stage for the last half of his life to be spent in New England. London was the most important city of his day—a city where contacts and contracts are made, a city where deals and wheels turn over with rapid speed, and a city that will make or break a man. It was the dominant city of commerce and immigration, and it was populated by men and women of means seeking ways to increase their powers and wealth.

Wiggin's successes in London will govern his successes on the western shores of England. His backers, domiciled in London, have a lot of pull on the west coast and, more importantly, in New England and other points across the ocean.

The year 1603 brought his brother Richard into the world and likely the loss of his mother, as she drops from the records. Two years old and no mother, Thomas Wiggin is still deeply loved by his father and older siblings. His sister has already become his "little mother" but is way too young to handle the responsibility all on her own. The church dominates his father's life, and he would have followed their wishes very closely regarding the raising and future mothering of his children, which required him to marry again rather quickly.

The vicar's occupation within the Church of England requires him to remarry; but that doesn't guarantee a happy atmosphere, and I can envision a home life that was, likely, strained. His stepmother is not young, having grown children of her own, and while she brings a daughter into the marriage with her, she still takes on an awesome burden by acquiring seven children under the age of 10. One wonders if there was strife between her daughter, Margaret, and the vicar's eldest child, his daughter, Katherine. If so, it would account for Katherine's marriage at such an early age.

If Thomas's mother, Anne Gybbes, suffered illness for any length of time before death, then, conceivably, the younger children were removed from the home by relatives. I never found any Wiggin family in the life of the vicar—meaning, if he had siblings, I never found any mention of them. This leaves us to think the Gybbes family members likely took over the younger children, if just until the vicar remarried. Besides Thomas Gybbes, father of Ann, there is a very large clan of Gybbes all around Bishop's Itchington. Also consider that the vicar had household servants and close friends as noted in his will, and they may have also helped out with the children. We will never know for sure.

However, they were cared for, and by whom, all of them seem to have fared well. We next hear of young Thomas in the will of his father, which was written right about the time Thomas began his apprenticeship. From age 14 to his majority at age 21, we hear nothing of Thomas. It's after the age of 21 we begin to acquire a peek into his life through marriage records and a handful of other records.

Someone taught Thomas the value of owning land and how to acquire money. His grandfather fit that bill very neatly. Through his grandfather, he will also learn of his cousins who are mariners. You will read a lot of records regarding a John Gybbes/Gibbs, mariner, making regular trips to the New

World as master of ships. The Gybbes clan of the southern counties of England were all mariners, farmers, and fishermen.

It will require a lot more research to make a connection for Thomas Wiggin within his Gybbes side of the family, and yet nothing more will likely be found. I dug deep into the English records trying to make the connections I did.

Let us now go forward with Captain Thomas Wiggin's life with the records I did find after he reached his majority of twenty-one years of age.

Time Line Regression
Back to the Future
1633 Back To 1616

We are going to work backward in time so we can make the connections between all the characters and the chronological influences:

1633: New England, July 11, the day Thomas Wiggin married Catherine Whiting.

1632: Bristol, England

> He's in the employ of the Bristol Merchant Ventures. No doubt, during these six months in Bristol, he also finds time to go home to Warwickshire. The two counties border each other. Although Captain Wiggin was not to realize it, the year 1632 was to provide a bounty of data on his character, beliefs, ethics, and ancestry. He would leave behind a solid record of handwriting samples and early associations that would tell us much about him. It was in this year the two letters credited to his pen were written in Bristol.
> One of the men Thomas Wiggin seems to know well is Richard Lane.[378] He speaks of Mr. Lane in one of his 1632 letters as being an old acquaintance.

1631: New Hampshire

> The plantation of New Hampshire was divided into two parts—with Captain Thomas WIGGIN appointed agent for the upper and Captain

[378] You will find the surname spelled "Lance" in several records, and this is just an incorrect interpretation of old English handwriting. It's actually "Lane."

Walter Neal for the lower. A house was erected at Strawberry Bank, called the Great House.[379]

1629: Maine

This is the year of the infamous forged Wheelwright deed, 17 May 1629.

1627–29: West coast of England

1624–1626: London

This is the era of Thomas Wiggin's first marriage; he's in the employ of his grandfather, Thomas Gybbes. His days are spent in the field of merchandising.

1629:

Isobel Wiggin[380,381] m. William Huntington in Stepney, St. Dunstan, Middlesex.

1626:

Thomas Wiggin m. Winifred Read (Reid/Reed) at Stoke Newington, St. Mary, Middlesex.

1626:

There is the death of a child[382] of a Thomas Wiggin listed in the St. Margaret, Westminster, records. This must be a child of Thomas and Isobel Baines Wiggin.

---

379 Some History from *GAZETTEER of the State of NEWHAMPSHIRE, Compiled from the Best Authorities by Eliphalet Merrill and the late Phinehas Merrill, Esq.*, Printed by C. Norris & Co., for the Authors – 1817.

380 London Marriage Licenses 1521–1869, 942.1/L1 K28F, p. 731: 30 April 1629, Isobel Wiggins m. Wm Huntingdon.

381 1591: Isobel Wiggin m. Edward More at St. Mary Strand, London (Boyd's MI 1500–1600, 942 K22 B Ser2 V46).

382 Sarah Wiggin, "a child of Thomas," 27 Nov 1626; burial records for St. Margaret, Westminster, London, 908, 519, Memorials 1539–1660; Burials. Same source for the marriage of Thomas and Isobel. Also, there is a Margaret Barefoote who d. 18 July 1626.

1625: Cadiz, Spain

On 5 October 1625, a fleet of eighty English and sixteen Dutch vessels sailed against the Spanish fleet off the coast of Cadiz.

1624:

A Thomas Wiggon (sic) m. Isobel Banes (Baines) at Westminster, St. Margaret's, Middlesex.

NOTES: These are the heaviest of plague years in London. I have never been able to prove either of the marriages above were Captain Thomas's as there was more than one Thomas Wiggin in London. However, since he declares he's a widower in 1633, I highly suspect one of the above was his first marriage.

1615–1623:

Apprenticeship years with his grandfather, Thomas Gybbes.

1605–1615:

His mother has died and he's likely learning lessons from his stepmother (and her daughter), who has already raised five children of her own.

1603–1605:

His mother has died, and he is probably in the home of a relative—perhaps his grandfather, Thomas Gybbes.

1601–1603: A toddler.

Time Line Of Historical Events for Captain Thomas Wiggin

Anyone who believes that they belong to one race, or that their ancestors were fine people, haven't done enough genealogy.
—Mark Humphrys[383]

1601:

Captain Thomas Wiggin is born in Bishop's Itchington, Warwickshire. The Poor Law of England is passed.

1603:

This is most likely the year of his mother's death; probably because of childbirth complications. Elizabeth, Queen of England, dies. James I becomes king; 1603–1713. The Stuarts rule.

1601–1614/15:

Captain Wiggin is on his father's farm, King's Farm, Bishop's Itchington, Warwickshire.

[383] See http://humphrysfamilytree.com/meaning.html for a very humorous read on researching family trees. Visit the site of a friend, Mark Humphreys.

1605:

On 11 November, Guy Fawkes and associates were revealed in the *Gunpowder Plot* to blow up Parliament.

1606:

The London Company sponsors a colonizing expedition to Virginia.

1607:

Colonists of the London Company found Jamestown, Virginia. By the end of the year, starvation and disease reduce the original 105 settlers to just 32. Captain John Smith is captured by Native American, Chief Powhatan, and saved from death by the chief's daughter, Pocahontas.

1609–1613:

The Plantation of Ulster, Ireland, was being settled. The Douay Old Testament is added to the Rheims New Testament (1582), making the first complete English Catholic Bible. Henry Hudson takes a seven-month voyage to North America sailing up the Hudson River; native tobacco is planted and harvested in Virginia.

1611:

The King James Bible version is published—originally, all 80 books. The Apocrypha was officially removed in 1885, leaving 66 books.

1613:

A Dutch trading post is set up on lower Manhattan Island.

1615–1622:

Captain Thomas Wiggin's apprenticeship years in London and elsewhere.

1616–1620:

Vicar William Wiggin's death; probate 1620/21 by son John; the smallpox epidemic decimates the Native American population of New England.

1618:

George Villiers was appointed first Lord High Admiral by King James II.

1619:

The first session of the first legislative assembly in America occurs as the Virginia House of Burgesses convenes in Jamestown with 22 burgesses representing 11 plantations. Twenty Africans are brought by a Dutch ship to Jamestown for sale as indentured servants, marking the beginning of slavery in Colonial America.

1620:

On November 9, the *Mayflower* lands at Cape Cod, Massachusetts, with 101 colonists; On November 11, the Mayflower Compact was signed by 41 men, establishing a form of local government in which the colonists agree to abide by majority rule.

1621:

One of the first treaties between the colonists and Native Americans is signed as Pilgrims enact a peace pact with the Wampanoag Tribe with the aid of Squanto, an English-speaking native.

1622–1626:

The period of Captain Thomas Wiggin's first marriage.

1622–1627:

Captain Wiggins was in London and the west coast as a freelancing merchant; probably still with Grandfather Gybbes.

1624:

Thirty families of Dutch colonists arrive in New York.

1624:

The Statute of Monopolies makes monopolies illegal in England.

1625:

This was probably the death of his first wife by the devastating London plague. James I, King of England, dies; Charles I becomes king (1625–1640). The bubonic plague decimates London's population.

1626:

Peter Minuit, Dutch colonists, buys Manhattan Island from Native Americans for 60 guilders (about $24) and names it New Amsterdam.

1627:

Captain Thomas Wiggin applied for a letter of marque against the French. An English trading post was established on Palmer's Island, now called Garrett's Island, near Havre de Grace on the Susquehanna River.

1627–29:

Captain Thomas Wiggin travels from Bristol to Maine. This was the time of war between Louis XIII, King of France, and the Huguenots of La Rochelle (1627–28).

1628:

George Villiers, Duke of Buckingham, is assassinated at the home of Captain John Mason in Portsmouth, England.

1629–1632:

Captain Thomas Wiggin is in New England.

1629–1640:

Eleven years of tyranny when Charles I rules without Parliament, spurring many to leave for the American colonies.

1630–1640:

The time of the Great Migration into New England.

1632:

Captain Thomas Wiggin is in Bristol, Barnstaple, and London.

1633:

On 11 July, Thomas marries Catherine Whiting in London. First town government is organized in Dorchester, Massachusetts; settled on Great Bay, New Hampshire.

The Hat[384]

[384] Plymouth Colony reenactor; photo by Joyce Elaine Wiggin-Robbins.

Another Hat[385]

[385] Plymouth Colony reenactor; photo by Joyce Elaine Wiggin-Robbins.

Period Clothing[386]

[386] Plymouth Colony reenactor; photo by Joyce Elaine Wiggin-Robbins.

Gardening[387]

387 Plymouth Colony reenactor; photo by Joyce Elaine Wiggin-Robbins.

Clothes Make The Man[388]

We know clothing was important and a status symbol to Captain Wiggin due to the importance he placed on his own clothing in his will. Clothing is found in nearly all wills of the era because it was made to last and would not be thrown aside as worthless items. Clothing was respected and tended to with care in all regards.

When the 1623 settlers arrived at Cape Ann, Massachusetts, backed by the Company called the Massachusetts Bay Company (MBC), each settler had suitable outfits consisting of four pairs of shoes and stockings, gaiters, four shirts, two doublets, a hose of leather lined with oilskin, a woolen suit lined with leather, a green cotton waistcoat, a variety of caps and belts, two pairs of gloves, a *mandilion* (cloak) lined with cotton, and an extra pair of breeches. Their outfits were designed to be worn in layers as needed against the weather of New England.

A year after Thomas Wiggin settled permanently on Great Bay, New Hampshire, the MBC court passed a law forbidding even the purchase of "any apparel, either wollen, silke, or lynnen with any lace on it, silver, golde, silke or thread" and that they shall not even make clothing with slashes in the items other than "one slashe in each sleeve and another in the back." Even needlework (embroidery) was forbidden in gold or silver on any item. By 1636, even lace was forbidden, excepting for a small edging on linen.

There is a Puritan mandilion on display in London, England, at the South Kensington Museum. It's made of black silk with tiny embroidered buttons, a very drab garment.

In 1638, the MBC court passed an order stating that "no garment shall be made with short sleeves, and such as have garments already made with short sleeves shall not wear the same unless the arm is covered to the wrist," and even the width of the sleeve is governed. The records in Salem are jammed with offences against these laws.

388 All photos in this chapter by Joyce Elaine Wiggin-Robbins of *Mayflower II* reenactors.

In 1643, a book was published titled *Theatrum Mulierum*,[389] whose author is looked to today as the authority for dress in Europe. I once saw this book in the British Museum in London, England, back in the 1970s and have no idea if it's still available for viewing. It's an extremely rare book and the only one I've ever found on the subject. No doubt there may be copies in private libraries somewhere in Europe. It would appear the women of the Pilgrim settlement copied the Dutch styles described by Hollar in his book.

The Pilgrims were far stricter than the Puritans and even regarded long hair as a sin, issuing a manifesto against it.

Since Thomas Wiggin was not only dealing with the MBC but aligning himself with them, he would have also adopted their way of dress. So it's the Puritans that draw our interest.

We are told that Puritans expressed their piety in somber hues and simple cut of cloth. It's not uncommon to find quotations from the Bible sewn into the garments, or even historical facts.

By 1655, the courts of Massachusetts passed a law calling for the repression of spending too much of one's income on wardrobe. The court was constantly involving itself in correcting morals and placing restrictions on dress that one wonders how they ever got anything else accomplished.

These early Puritans looked at clothing the same way they did their caste system of social ranking. Only the rich dressed in expensive clothing, and the lower classes dressed according to their labors. Even rank and breeding figured into the style worn. Any citizen worth less than two hundred pounds had the strictest of dress codes—especially women, who paid a penalty if found wearing silk and tiffany hoods. Women often hid the finer materials under their skirts but had better take care for fear that it be seen.

The wardrobe of a deceased person was treated with all the respect accorded the person before the funeral ceremony was even completed. Items of clothing are found in nearly all the wills of New England's settlers. Fabrics were made to last in their day, and the best of them cost no more than the cheapest of them. Thus, velvet would have been the choice over a "cotton" material, even for a petticoat.

We even read of stockings in the early wills. These garments were not like our socks of today but were made from material and very warm. Shoes were dressed up with rosettes, and gloves were embroidered.

In the colony, men never went about without their armor. Swords were more often than not suspended from shoulder belts that could be highly embroidered. Even silver and gold lace were used for trimming, which seems

---

389 Wenceslaus Hollar (Bohemian [active in Germany, Netherlands, England], 1607–1677)

to belie the edicts against its use in clothing. You will find the records filled with mentions of bandoliers, flasks, corselets, and pikes.

Study the portraits of Sir John Leverett, governor of Massachusetts. You will find him in all the regalia I've described and then some. Even his gloves are described as being trimmed in gold. Major Thomas Savage, in 1676, is pictured in so many layers of clothing and ornamentation one wonders how he even moved, much less remain capable of fighting Indians. Note his shoulder-hung sword.

THE SCARLET SUIT[390]

[390] Photo by Joyce ElaineWiggin-Robbins, static display at *Mayflower II.*

Suit and Robe of Scarlet

We read of scarlet robes going back as far as Jesus when, in Matthew 17:28, they describe the Romans stripping Jesus of his clothing and placing about him a robe of scarlet. The Romans were mocking Jesus as being a "King of the Jews."

The scarlet color has always been associated with royalty, the ruling class, and a sign of authority. Henry VIII is pictured in a very ornate robe of scarlet trimmed in gold. Judge Jonathan Curwen of the infamous Salem Witch Trials is described as wearing a scarlet robe. Sir John Popham, Lord Chief Justice of England (1531–1607), is shown with an ermine-lined scarlet robe. Sir Christopher Wray,[391] judge and Chief Justice of the King's Bench (1524–1592) is likewise shown in an elaborate robe of scarlet trimmed in gold.

The color scarlet, almost without exception, was associated with power and breeding. Royal blood went a long way in the acceptance of wearing the color.

Apart from the authority associated with the color, it was just a favorite color of men in the Bay Colony. Perhaps they were also establishing themselves as authorities by wearing this shade. Governor Bradford is said to have worn a scarlet cloak while out riding.

Captain/Governor Thomas Wiggin possessed a suit and robe of scarlet he put great store by and willed it to his wife, signifying he knew she understood the importance of that suit. He was not willing to give it outright to his heir and eldest son, Andrew. He made his son earn that suit by paying his mother for it and thus ensuring the suit would always be accorded the respect Wiggin felt it signified.

I firmly believe the suit was a gift from the Lanes (in particular, Richard Lane), who not only grew madder but were involved in the merchandising of red dye procured in the Caribbean. Thomas Wiggin and Richard's relationship went way back to their youths in London and remained intact when, in 1632, Wiggin secured employment for Lane with the Lords Saye and Brook. The scarlet suit and robe were a gift of gratitude.

Did Wiggin wear the suit? Most likely he did; he would have worn it during court sessions, on visits to Winthrop, and on other special occasions. That suit signified that he had attained the ranking he sought and so highly prized by settling in New Hampshire. It signified acceptance, authority, and stability in a life that had started out with none of it.

Clothes make the man.

---

[391] Patron of Vicar William Wiggin, father of Captain Thomas Wiggin.

Equipment and Hair

We also know Captain Wiggin possessed a fighting sword, as he nearly came to blows with it over a piece of land on the Piscataqua River. Swords would have been highly prized, and either of his sons could have come into possession of it long before the Captain died. If that sword could be found, it would prove very valuable in more ways than just monetary.

Men always wore hats befitting the occasion they found themselves in for the day. It may only be a woolen or knit cap, but something was on that man's head. Caps would have been popular on open water with the wind blowing about their ears.

Being around swampy land and the water constantly dictated they wear well-oiled leather boots. Saltwater is particularly rough on leather of any sort, so all their gear from sword scabbards to boots would have been well-oiled.

Hairstyles for grown men ranged from short, loose hair to longer braided or ponytailed gatherings at the back of the neck, tied with a ribbon. Men of authority usually had hair pulled close to the scalp and tied at the back of the neck.

We should not forget to at least acknowledge that womenfolk had different outfits for each occasion too. A Sunday best dress and petticoats, outfits for indoor work and others for outdoor work. Seasons of the year also dictated what outfit should be worn.

Woman at Work[392]

[392] Photo by Joyce ElaineWiggin-Robbins

Education

I wrote to every institution of higher learning in England that existed in Thomas Wiggin's young life. All of them replied to me, and none of them had a record under any variant surname spelling for him.

Apprenticeships, more often than not, took the place of higher education, with the exception of the wealthiest of families. However, with an apprenticeship completion, the apprentice is usually recognized in a guild of one sort or another. I never found Thomas Wiggin listed in them either.

The Drapers' Company/Guild seemed to be the most likely, given his grandfather's occupation. Yet Thomas Wiggin is not listed there either.

The lack of education records for Thomas does not surprise me, and the tradition seems to have carried on with his own children. Harvard was founded in Massachusetts in 1636, yet he did not send his sons there, indicating he considered apprenticeships an appropriate education. What they didn't learn at their mother's knee, they learned at his side.

The picture presents a dilemma. Where did he learn to sail a ship? Some sea captains started as cabin boys at a young age and worked their way up through the system. This could not have been the case for Thomas Wiggin or he would not have a history in London, he would not have known Richard Lane, and he wouldn't have had the contacts to become an agent in 1629. His life would have taken a far different path.

If he had his own ship—which I surmise is true—who sailed it? He had to have a crew of some sort. No one seems to have come to New England with him on his own ship as, surely, it would have been recorded somewhere.

Every indication is he was a loner on the sea, at least by 1629. His is but one of hundreds of ships plying the Canadian and New England fishing communities engaged in merchandising, not warfare. Nothing happened in his sea life to warrant recording by someone.

Or he was a part of someone's fleet—like Sir Rich, who had a flotilla of his own. In such a grouping, he would not have been singled out unless he had done something very heroic while in service, or something horrific had happened to his ship. Obviously, that's not the story.

Since no records have surfaced in my research (or, apparently, anyone else's either) regarding sea service of some kind, he probably wasn't at it for long. I could be comfortable with thinking he may have made one trip to the fishing banks, one season, and decided he would rather colonize than cross that ocean one more time! I can even stretch that scenario and say he may have sailed to the Caribbean and then up along the American coast from Mexico to New England before returning to England, as is claimed by some historians. However, he didn't do it alone.

His inheritance from the death of his father would have been enough to purchase a ship of about thirty to sixty tons cargo weight. Suppose he purchased it in 1621; we have the record of 1631 where he grounded a ship off the coast of Massachusetts in that year. That ship was probably ten or more years old when he bought it. By 1631, it was leaking and rotting out from under him and ready for scuttling. What better place to do it than off the Massachusetts coast, where he was assured of finding transportation back to New Hampshire, or walking across that sandbar to dry land.

Again, I don't want to cut my toes off to make the story fit, so I leave you with the urge to research that aspect more. I can even give you advice on where to start research: Massachusetts Archives, Trinity House archives in London, Kew in Richmond, and private collections of colonial records. Not an easy task.

His education regarding sailing ships came in handy when he was required to lay out towns on the Piscataqua and mark the boundaries of land. The same tools would have been used on land as he used on the open seas—a great example of where learning a technique on water works on land too and vice versa.

The versatility of his learning years seems to have served him well as he aged. There is no indication that he forsook the aspects of one occupation to engage in another; he just incorporated previous learnings into new adventures. Versatility was one of Captain Wiggin's strongest suits.

1666 FIRE MONUMENT[2]

WESTMINSTER HOUSES OF PARLIAMENT[3]

---

393 Photo by Arthur R. Mullis. Top of 1666 Fire Monument marks where the church stood and where the 1666 fire started, on New Fish Street, London, England. Captain Thomas Wiggin and Katherine Whiting were married in that church.

394 Photo by Arthur R. Mullis. Westminster Houses of Parliament, London, England.

LONDON 1615–1627

Social groups of this era were largely kin-based occupational. In other words, if Thomas Wiggin was to be found in London prior to about 1625, he would have kin there as well. Such was the case as we find his grandfather Thomas Gybbes domiciled in the city. Having also found Wiggin's brother Hanibal in London, and possessing the manuscript from Fred Schultz on Richard Lane, provided good reasons to look for Thomas Wiggin in the city.

Before my research was finished, I had searched such a wide variety of records it would take another book to list them all. I missed nothing that I am aware of. Guilds, churches (all of them in London), a large variety of assessment records, parish records, parish clerk's records, merchant records, subsidies levied on the citizens of London, Trinity House[395]—and the list goes on.

Every fact about London, every person associated with London and Westminster as recorded in the survey of the city's books[396] was carefully researched more than once. No clue relating to Thomas Wiggin was found.

Hannibal Wiggin: The name was one of a kind,[397] and the trail was easy to follow because of that. Hannibal married Ann Cater/Cator 14 September 1627[398] in St. Swithuns, Sandy, Bedford,[399] England, and they are found in London-Cripplegate church records. However, by this date, Thomas Wiggin was on the west coast of England. He would have been with his brother in London before sailing to New England in 1629 and again in 1633.

---

[395] Founded in 1514 by Royal Charter. The records are mostly gone with the 1666 fire and 1940s bombings. Before 1845, a separate register of Master Mariners was not kept.

[396] A Survey of the Cities of London and Westminster, borough of Southward and Parts Adjacent, Vol. II; by Robert Symore, Esq., London, J. Read in White-Fryars, Fleet Street, M,DCC,XXXV.

[397] If you don't count his nephew, who almost died at birth, carrying the name *Hannibal Wiggin*.

[398] LDS no. 826,481

[399] There were so many Wiggin entries for Bedford that it took a great deal of time to chart them all.

I never found a death record for Hannibal[400] Wiggin. Ann shows up back in her birth home in Bedfordshire following the deaths of her children, as recorded in the Cripplegate parish records. She is mentioned in her brother Andrew's will.

What were they doing in Cripplegate? Following Hannibal, I found that Bernard Cater and his son Andrew owned houses in Cripplegate but lived on Coleman Street. They were merchants. It stood to reason that Anne and Hannibal were living in one of the Cripplegate houses. Hannibal and Ann had three children baptized in the church, and all three children died and are recorded in those same church records. That's quite a history.

With the exception of John, the eldest son, all Vicar William Wiggin's sons' names are found together in the Cripplegate, London, records: Hannibal, Richard, Edward, William, and Thomas. But again, I caution that these given names are common and found in every Wiggin line, with the exception of Hannibal. They may just as easily be from the London Wiggin clan who carried all the same given names as Captain Wiggin's family clan.

So next, I searched for all marriage records for any Thomas Wiggin in London. When I say London, I include the surrounding areas, such as Westminster. A lot of wealthy merchants lived outside of London. Westminster has a Wiggin family domiciled there with a son named Thomas and a lot of siblings.

BAKERS AND BANKERS

Another London Thomas[401] (born 1592) is the son of the baker William Wiggin,[402] and they descend of a long line of bankers.[403] At one time, their ancestors owned Wiggin's Quay.[404] An ancestor, William Wiggin (the "money man"), is so well-documented because so many men of importance owed him money. His dealings are recorded in the court records. His ancestral trail leads back to Lancashire. Knowing he owned Wiggin's Quay (dock), I spent some time in the London Port Records[405] seeking any ships owned by this family descending from him. I found none. William Wiggin of Wiggin's Quay was dealing in tin (storing it in his quay). A lot of his activities are found in the

---

400 There was only one Hannibal Wiggin to reach the age of majority in England. A nephew carrying the name died in the year of his birth, 1638.

401 Wigan/Wygan, Tho, Citizen and Baker, St. Mary, Vol 86; Reg 9 Folio 181V; and Reg 7 35V, 36V. Leaves a will.

402 He also owns Wiggin's Quay.

403 Also called "money men."

404 A quay is a dock with storage capacity.

405 PRO, records of the Exchequer and Customs Accounts. They list ship, owners, merchants involved and cargos in a lot of detail.

Chancery records held at Kew (National Archives of England), Richmond, England.

The London sixteenth-century records reveal both Thomas and father, William of London, were bakers.[406] Neither one had ever lived in the country, much less farmed. This Thomas simply did not have the skills displayed by Captain Wiggin or, apparently, the education since he followed in his father's footsteps as a baker.

The Thomas of this family does not seem to have gone anywhere, and after years of research, I abandoned him as a prospect for Captain Thomas Wiggin, who died in New Hampshire in 1666. He simply does not have the qualifications to fulfill that role.

London will become the dictionary and library of Captain Thomas's learning. Here he will learn the value of networking, how laws are made and by whom, and the benefits of versatility, merchandising, and so much more.

The surname *Wiggin* is found in London in all its popular forms, including—but not limited to—*Wiggen, Wigon, Wigan, Wiggan, Wigaine,* and the like. All with or without the final *s*.

HANSEATIC LEAGUE: About 1303–1598, London

Although the official closing of the League in London was 1598, they were essentially finished by 1500. I won't cover the entire history of the League in London, but let it suffice here to say it was a rocky relationship that led to the Anglo-Hanseatic War of 1470–74.

It has been stated more than once that Thomas Wiggin could have come from this merchant league. It simply isn't possible given the dates. By the time Thomas was born in 1601, the League was long gone. However, I do believe the League brought the spelling of *Wiggen* into London.

The Hanseatic League was quartered in an area of London called "the Stilyard" (Steelyard), which is upriver from London Bridge. The merchants of Almaine (Germany) used to bring in products such as wheat, rye, cables, masts, pitch, tar, hemp, cloth, wainscots, and steel. In 1157, King Henry II granted the merchants of Almaine free usage throughout his realm, meaning they paid no taxes and held other privileges. The League's freedom from taxes did not sit well with other English merchants who were taxed every way possible.

During the time of their flourishing trade, it is said the Thames River was choked with ships, and one could walk across the river from ship deck to ship deck.

---

[406] C1/578/42 Smyth of London, baker, late servant to Thomas Wygan of London, Baker; subject: action of debt by William Wygan, clerk, executor of the said Thomas Wygan, 1518–1529; Kew, The National Archives.

By 1551, Edward VI honored the complaints of the English merchants, and the liberties of the Steelyard merchants were seized by the Crown. The Hanseatic League was in decline, and while falling to pieces, generally, the cities of Lubeck, Hamburg, and Bremen continued to acknowledge the authority of the League.

APPRENTICESHIP 1615–1621

Looking for likely men to have *mastered* his apprenticeship, the most salient one was his grandfather, Thomas Gybbes (a.k.a. Gibbes). We cover the history of Thomas Gybbes elsewhere, so let's progress from there to his relationship with his grandson.

Young Thomas Wiggin arrives in the city in his teen years with his grandfather, Thomas Gybbes. Gybbes maintains a residence in London, and it is there I found his death record.[407] Thomas has a wide-open door with not only the association with his grandfather Gybbes, but because his own father had been employed by Sir Christopher Wray,[408] and networking is the name of the game. He would prove an asset to his grandfather.

Thomas and his brother Rychard come into their apprenticeship years about the same time their father is showing signs of illness (1615–16). The vicar is very concerned for their welfare, knowing they must do apprenticeships in order to have a good vocation. Once again, he's on the networking system in order to put his last two sons in the right hands in London before his illness overcomes him.[409]

In 1563, *The Statute of Artificers*[410] was introduced, and under this law, no English citizen could enter into a trade without serving a term of seven years as an apprentice. No centralized records were kept until 1710, so research had to be conducted at the local level rather than civil records. These contracts are between the "master" and the apprentice and will typically name the apprentice's father and his residence, terms of service, endowments at the successful termination of the apprenticeship, and cost, which typically was

---

[407] See his biography elsewhere.

[408] 1524-1592, Chief Justice of the King's Bench; buried in St. Michael's Church, Glentworth, Lincolnshire.

[409] In 1617, when Vicar William wrote his will, he leaves each of his children thirty pounds. Coincidentally, that's the price of an apprenticeship.

[410] The Statute of Artificers 1563 (5 Eliz. 1 c. 4) was an Act of Parliament of England, under Queen Elizabeth I, which sought to fix prices, impose maximum wages, restrict workers' freedom of movement, and regulate training. Local magistrates had responsibility for regulating wages in agriculture. Guilds regulated wages of the urban trades. Effectively, it transferred to the newly forming English state the functions previously held by the feudal craft guilds.

Source: http://en.wikipedia.org/wiki/Statute_of_Artificers_1562.

thirty pounds.[411] Surviving records of guilds, businesses, charities, parish collections (court records, church records, etc.), and family records are all sources for these records. Borough records are excellent sources for these records, but small farming villages like Bishop's Itchington are not likely to have such records. I never found any. Quarter Session records and Poor Law records are also good sources.

London Livery Company apprenticeship registers are also in a variety of places, and a good starting place was found in the Society of Genealogists, London archives.[412] I spent a lot of time over the years in these sources to no event. *The London Apprenticeship Abstracts* of 1531–1850 also produced nothing for Thomas Wiggin.

Since the vicar was affiliated with at least four churches, I searched them all for clues to no avail.

It is my best summation, based on the missing records in Vicar William Wiggin's church at his death, that the good vicar maintained his own library and his own records, which were probably destroyed by time or lack of interest in following generations. The vicar's eldest son, John, inherited his farms and lands and likely his library too. If it was intact when his great-grandson (Butler Wiggin's son) sold the farm, they were likely destroyed as just some old unwanted records.

One Gibbes researcher told me she had found both Thomas Gibbes and Thomas Wiggin in France. That's a distinct possibility, but I am not an authority on French records. She would not give me a reference point, so take this as you will. I don't find it unusual that a master would take his apprentice on a trip with him to teach him the occupation. Thomas Gybbes was aging, and no doubt, he wanted his grandson to know how to manage his affairs in other countries. What I do find unusual about this is that France and England were not on good terms, and I'm not at all sure they were trading at that time. The point being, I cannot disprove what this researcher told me.

Another shadow being cast is why did his second marriage take place in a church on New Fish Street if he was in the Cripplegate parish and Catherine Whiting was in the St. Stephen Coleman Street parish? I think that one is easier to figure out. In all likelihood, even though they certainly knew each other, this was an arranged marriage of sorts. William Whiting, brother to Catherine, was a backer of Thomas and the plantation in New England. He was a close associate of the lords as well. No doubt, he wanted his sister to go to New England with him, and being about thirty-two years of age, her marriage opportunities were running out. Knowing Thomas Wiggin had no wife, William would have stepped right in to champion his sister as a wife. Since he was

---

411 Ibid. In 1617 as in number 1.

412 LDS has one book 942.1/L U25w v.1–4.

also a backer of the plantation, how could Thomas refuse? Marrying William Whiting's sister was also a great networking maneuver in more ways than one. It assured a close tie between governors of two separate New England settlements, and Catherine Whiting had just come into her inheritance from her father's estate—that would be an asset to Thomas in his new home on Great Bay. St. Margaret[413] New Fish Street was located in the marketplace near London Bridge. It was made up of a lot of wealthy merchants and well-to-do tradesmen. Getting married in this church was one of convenience and was expeditious, considering they were shipping out.

I did not find a marriage record in the church records, but I did find an entry of a donation to the poor of the church by Thomas Wiggin.

London Connections: 1615–1627

No one came alone to New England, and so many of the men and women who migrated had strong ties to London, even if that city was not their family seat. London became the hub for merchants of all sorts after England and Spain started their feuds, and once France entered the fray, the merchant ports in those western countries dried up for commercial shipping. Barnstaple, Devonshire, became a military staging port and declined in wealth with the loss of merchant trades. Gloucester became a trade port to the North American fishing grounds and exploration of the Caribbean Isles. Gloucester also became a strong home port for ships holding *letters of marque and reprisal.*[414]

In 1610, Ireland was the main interest for English royalty. Colonization was underway, and naturally, the western ports figured strongly in that activity. With the western ports out of the merchandising picture for Eastern Europe, that activity shifted to London. London was also a strong staging port for the American colonies.

So, although New England settlers were from counties all over England, they knew each other either through London contacts or their military service. Military service connections are covered elsewhere.

LONDON LANDMARKS

Blackwell Hall, London, was the hub of the English merchant trade in the seventeenth century. The woolen goods, both raw materials and finished products, were the main commodity passing through the hall. Here the Whitings, Cators, Gybbes, the men we know as the lords—anyone who was

---

413 Record found in the Bishop's Transcripts sated 11 July 1633.

414 LoM were assigned to ships, not people. More on this subject in *1627.*

in the cloth merchant trade would gather here. It was located next to the Guildhall.

Guildhall has always been the site of London government of one sort or another and is thought to have originally been a place where taxes were paid. There has been something on the site since the Roman occupation era. It was here that the ruling merchant class of London held court and many famous trials took place. The Guild made laws governing trade and accumulated London's wealth. The Guildhall is located in the very heart of London.

Wiggin's Quay,[415] one of the legal storage docks/quays, was located on land now occupied by the Custom House. Trading mostly in tin from the midlands, it was owned by William Wiggin of London, a banker (or "money man") who lived in the sixteenth century. By the late seventeenth century, wheat was a big seasonal export from the quay. Wiggin's Quay was the main shipping wharf for this commodity.[416] The London docks were a lively place, with ships jockeying for berths to unload cargos, a deafening level of voices and machinery, horses and mules with the odd dog running around—it was a scene of organized chaos.

Coffeehouses[417] were a mecca for traders of all sorts. There were probably a thousand or more coffeehouses in London during the seventeenth century, and each one was unique unto itself. Some were noted for drawing customers who were bent toward one trade over another, but all of them were meccas for gossip, politics, overseas news, and religious issues of the day, just for starters.

London: Richard Lane[418] and the Lane Family: 1615–1633

In one of the infamous 1632 letters accredited to the pen of Thomas Wiggin, we come across an interesting association. Thomas mentions a man named Lane[419] has been with him in Gloucester and is in need of employment.

---

415 *Wiggin's Quay* in *London*, which was presumably *named* after '*wyggen the warfyn-* ger' who testified in the Mayor's Court in 1586.

416 Excellent sources for the study of shipping are Henry Roseveare, *Wiggin's Key Revisited: Trade and Shipping in the later Seventeenth-Century Port of London*; *The Widening Gate*; The Oxford History of the British Empire; Vol. I; the Origins of an Empire.

417 The coffeehouse society, so described by Dr. S. Inwood in a lecture, 2004, New York University, London. *The Social Life of Coffee: The Emergence of the British Coffeehouse.* Brian Cowan, 1969; c/r Yale University.

418 These documents are held at the Oxford University, Bodleian Library, Special Collections and Western Manuscripts; 22 Oct 1640 of note. Also see Connections for more on the Lanes.

419 Early historians report this surname as being LANCE. It is LANE as a true copy of the original 1632 letter in the hands of the author reveals.

Lane has been in the Caribbean and has found a crop[420] of interest to the New England settlers, Thomas writes.[421]

Mr. Lane becomes one of the "shadows" in Thomas's life that will lead me down a path filled with clues as to who both of them were. Lane is none other than Richard Lane. Most of the Lane records are found in St. Peter's Church,[422] Cornhill, London, and there are still more in St. Margaret Moses of Friday Street.[423] However, like all families of the merchant class, they have ancestral lands elsewhere. In the case of the Lanes, it's a farm in Gloucestershire, western England, which produces madder,[424] a root used to produce a shade of red dye. Richard Lane has been extensively documented by Fred Schultz,[425] and we have corresponded over the years. I came across Fred Schultz's manuscript quite by accident, and it immediately grabbed my attention when he links Captain Thomas Wiggin to Richard Lane in London. Schultz also claims both Lane and Wiggin were in the Caribbean together prior to 1632, but further research negates that claim. The dates just don't mesh. I am going to discuss more of this subject in another chapter, so I will digress no further and return to the current subject.

Richard Lane did his apprenticeship under a merchant of London. Following the completion of his apprenticeship, he married and had children in London. However, he was not only a proponent of Puritanism, but he was far too vocal for his own good; and by 1627/28, he was on his way to the Caribbean to escape imprisonment. He left his wife and children in London until he took permanent assignment of a plantation in the Islands to grow his crops in 1632. His backers were Lord Saye and Sele and Lord Brooke, among others. He would ultimately lose his life by drowning in the Caribbean.

Thomas Gybbes undoubtedly had a strong merchant relationship with the Lanes. Gybbes, primarily a wool merchant with trading interests in France and elsewhere, likely bartered for madder. Madder was tightly regulated as it rendered the color of royalty.

Thomas Wiggin had a long and enduring relationship with the Lanes of New England too. In 1643, Ambrose Lane[426] and Thomas Wiggin were judges

---

[420] I thought this crop might be the potato, which would have been easily grown in the New England soils, but it turned out to be a dried-up bug that, when crushed, produced a crimson red dye. More on this in the chapter titled "Associates."

[421] Cal of State Papers Colonial: V1; author W. Noel Sainsbury (editor); pub 1860; p. 155; West Indies: 31 August 1632, p.155.

[422] St. Peter's is said to be the oldest Christian church in England, with records going back to the fourth century.

[423] I also found Edward Lane living on Friday Street in 1638.

[424] Madder is tightly regulated by the Crown as it's used in dyeing fabrics for the royals.

[425] See acknowledgments

[426] Ambrose had a sawmill at Sagamores Creek.

and associates of "Norfolk County," New Hampshire, when it was acquired by Massachusetts. Ambrose and Sampson Lane[427] of Maine-New Hampshire were brothers and associates. Ambrose Lane, of Tingmouth, Cornwall, England, was a merchant. All these men were directly related to Richard Lane, friend of Thomas Wiggin.

Both Thomas and Richard Lane were deeply interested in the opportunities presented by exploration and immigration. Both men were thoroughly indoctrinated in the past and present voyages and possessed books written by previous explorers. While Richard wanted to go to New England, the door to the Caribbean had been opened to him. I do not believe Richard and Thomas Wiggin had direct contact after 1632–33.

Whitings of Coleman Street London[428]

Coleman Street was famous as a gathering place and refuge for those with a Puritan leaning and for merchants seeking business deals.

Thomas's second wife, Catherine Whiting, was the sister of William Whiting[429] of Coleman Street. Just prior to her marriage to Thomas, Catherine, along with her siblings, is found in a court judgment case to settle her father William Whiting Sr.'s estate. Thomas and Catherine are about the same age and have undoubtedly known each other for years. She was *about* thirty-two when they married—*a spinster.*[430]

William Whiting married Susan/Susanna Wiggins and brought her to New England in 1633 on the same ship as his sister Catherine and Thomas Wiggin. I found a Susan Wiggins christened 29 March 1597 in St. Andrew, Holborn, and daughter of a Robert Wiggins. She is the only Susan I found in the London area in the time span needed. I could not rule out her being a cousin through Vicar William Wiggin's family.

There are two William Whitings of Kent. One has a wife named Margaret Peterson, and they come from Mersham. They have issue: Margaret, b. 1599; William, b. 1607; John, b. 1608; Francis, b. 1615; and Jane, b. 1618.

---

427 Steward at Strawberry Bank for three years ending in 1644. Returned to England and left brother Ambrose in charge of his New Hampshire affairs; lived in Mason's Great House at Strawberry Bank, NH.

428 Coleman Street, London, was famous as the street of Puritans—a place where they took refuge when in trouble, where they gathered for meetings and prepared for their immigration to New England.

429 I speak of him extensively in other chapters. He was the governor of Connecticut, where he chose to settle.

430 Bondsman Lole's statement of age and testimony to Catherine's being single, but of marriageable age, and a *spinster.*

Another William Whiting is of Canterbury, Kent, and has issue: John, b. 1607; Katherine, b. 1608 and d. 1610; Martha, b. 1610 and d. 1610; James, b. 1616 and d. 1616; Martha, b. 1617; Katherine, b. 1619; and Ingie, b. 1620.

If you find your calling to research this Whiting family you will need the above information as it is claimed by many that he came from Lincolnshire without any source materials that verify it. You will find the London Whitings came from Kent.

Peter Lowle

I never found a connection between Peter Lowle and Thomas Wiggin other than as bondsman to second marriage of Thomas Wiggin to Catherine Whiting. The Lowle surname is also found as Lowe and appears in the London records, during the time period of my research, about three or four times. Contact with Lole/Lowle researchers further cemented the non-relationship suspicions as they had nothing linking the two men either. Lowle was the bondsman who submitted the marriage intention application[431] along with a twenty-pound fee that would be forfeited if the marriage was found to be in violation of the laws. Twenty pounds was no small amount, so I felt sure Lowle either knew Thomas or someone very close to him. He would want to know he wasn't going to lose his money. They may have been connected through a mutual friend.

There is a Captain John Low, master of the ship *Ambrose* and vice admiral of the fleet that brought over Governor Winthrop's colony in 1630. Thomas Low, his son, was of Chebacco, Ipswich (now Essex).

Thomas Wiggin of London, Notary

While I never could confirm it with records, I always felt there was a connection between Thomas Gybbes and the Duke of Buckingham, thus the assignment as a notary for the Countess of Derby as follows. In his capacity as a clerk for his grandfather, Thomas was a notary, as he had to record ship cargos and taxes.

The following records are from the Calendar of State Papers:[432]

> 121 In October 1623, Certificate of Thos Wigan Public Notary appears in the Admiralty records stating that a ship belonging to Simon Nevilla, Robt Hue and others laden with sugars and from Portugal was captured by a Dutch pirate, brought to the

[431] A true copy is in the hands of the author.

[432] Calendar of State Papers, Domestic Series, of the Reigns of Edward VI, and Mary; pg 366; by Great Britain, PRO, M. Green, Editor.

> Isle of Man and there seized by the officers of the Countess of Derby.[433]
>
> 121 In Petition of Ant. (probably Antonio) Roderigo, Simon Neville and Company merchants of Rouen[434] to the King detailing the capture of the above ship in May 1623. They sued the Admiralty Court and had a commission of restitution but the Isle of Man being an exempt jurisdiction[435] beseeches His Majesty to command to the Countess of Derby to restore their goods.

Whoever this Thomas Wiggin was, he was recognized by the Admiralty as a notary, or he was in the employ of the Countess of Derby on the Isle of Man. The countess did reside in London, but not until later than 1623. That does not mean she wasn't in London in 1623.

No further records were found on this incident with Thomas Wigan/ Wiggin's name on them, or any others where he is the notary. I present this record here as it is impossible to know if it was taken by Captain Thomas Wiggin or the Thomas Wiggin, baker of London, or if it was taken on the Isle of Man. It is very easy to mix records relating to these two men. You have to consider occupations in deciding which record belongs to whom; and even then, there are borderline records like this one. I find it odd that a baker would also be a notary, so you know in which direction I am leaning on this one.

I never found another Thomas Wiggin who could fulfill this scenario. He may have been on the Isle of Man in 1623 with (or for) his grandfather Gybbes or with the countess. We have no way of verifying that.

Duke of Buckingham, George Villiers,[436] favorite of James I of England:

Lord Buckingham purchased a mansion in London, commonly called Wallingford House, paying three thousand pounds for it. He had been living in the mansion for quite some time when he prepared it in August of 1626 to accommodate the Duchesse de Tremouille,[437] a.k.a. the Countess of Derby, who lived there until the following February. During her stay at Wallingford House, the duke resided at York House. On January 30, 1627–28, the duke's second

---

433 *The Life Story of Charlotte de la Tremouille, Countess of Derby*, Mary C. Rowsell; Kegan Paul, Trench, Trubner & Co. Ltd., 1905, London.

434 Located on the Seine River in France; capital city of Normandy.

435 Isle of Man was a protectorate only and was self-governing.

436 1592–1628

437 a.k.a. Countess of Derby

son, George, was born at Wallingford House.[438] In August 1628, the duke was stabbed to death in the home of Captain John Mason by a disgruntled unpaid soldier named John Felton.

The duchess was politically nnon grata in London after her husband's death, so her stay was short. She returned to the Isle of Man.

POSSIBLE FIRST LONDON MARRIAGE

1625: Thomas Wiggin marries Isobel Baines on 22 December 1625, Saint Margaret, Westminster, London, England,[439] and they lose their first child, a daughter, in the following year.[440] I never found a death record on Isobel or Thomas, but they disappear from these church records. The dates fit to make Isobel Baines the first wife of Thomas Wiggin, and if she and child both died, the scenario becomes almost irrefutable. Proving this without records, which I never found, is tricky.

1626: There is the death of a child[441] of Thomas Wiggin listed in the Westminster, St. Margaret records.[442]

1629: Isobel Wiggin[443,444] m. William Huntington in Stepney, St. Dunstan, Middlesex . . . is this the Isobel of 1624? If so, the Thomas of 1624 is deceased. The name *Isobel Wiggin* goes back to 1591 with the marriage of Edward More and Isabel Wiggin in Westminster, St. Mary Le Strand, Middlesex. (This is not the same church as Westminster St. Margaret's. So here again, we can't be sure if this is the same woman as in 1624.) This could be the Isobel of the Wiggin family domiciled in Westminster and not the wife of Thomas Wiggin of Warwickshire.

Because of its relevance, I must make mention here of another marriage. In 1626, Thomas Wiggin m. Winifred Read (Reid/Reed) at Stoke Newington, St. Mary, Middlesex. I can find no further records on this couple. However, in the Testamentary in the Archdeaconry Court of London (942. B4b V89, p 499) is

---

438 The Admiralty, Survey of London; v 16; St. Martin-in-the-Fields I; Charing Cross (1935), pp. 45-70; http://www.british-history.ac.uk/report.aspx?compid=68108

439 London marriages; 1521-1869; 942.1/11 K28f, p731.

440 M001601 Salt lake City, Utah, Mormon repository

441 Sarah Wiggin, "a child of Thomas," 27 Nov 1626; burial records for St. Margaret Westminster, London, burial records 908,519, Memorials 1539-1660; Burials. Same source for the marriage of Thomas and Isobel. Also, there is a Margaret Barefoote who d. 18 July 1626.

442 Sara Wiggins, St. Margaret Westminster, London 0,908,519

443 London Marriage Licenses 1521–1869, 942.1/L1 K28F, p 731: 30 Apr 1629, Isobel Wiggins m. Wm Huntingdon

444 1591: Isobel Wiggin m. Edward More at St. Mary Strand, London (Boyd's MI 1500–1600, 942 K22 B Ser2 V46)

the following entry: *Wiggin, Winifred, H. T. Min, Adm. 1646; Reg 8, Folio 8, "widow of Thomas Wiggin."* So this Thomas Wiggin was deceased by 1646.

Something happened in London to cause Thomas Wiggin to leave, and I strongly believe the death of his first wife could have been the catalyst. His grandfather Gybbes is in declining health and would die in 1631 in London.

Portion of Drake's Letter of 1627[445]

[445] National Archives, Kew, Richmond, England SP 16/47/50

1627 Letter of Marque and Reprisal

January 6, Barnstaple, 1627
Sir John Drake[446] to (Secretary) Nicholas:[447]
He (Drake) *has been at Barnstaple to take examination respecting a ship of Flushing*[448] *driven ashore at Appledore. She was taken by the Spaniards and remained in the service of the King of Spain for six months when the original crew revolted and carried off the ship. Drake's men took possession of the goods cast ashore from the wreck, but Kifte, the Judge of the Admiralty, ordered them to be restored, which Drake complains of and wishes Kifte to be dismissed. Capt. Tho Wigan desires a letter of marque.*[449]

Mike Day[450] had gone down to Kew, Richmond, to search for a 1627 letter written by Sir John Drake. Mike mailed me an exact copy of the letter. The letter itself is an interesting rendition of the taking of a Flushing ship and the disbursement of the goods on board. But what I was after was found in the lower left margin of the letter, written almost as an afterthought. It read, "One

---

446 Sir John Drake was an arm of the Admiralty who resided in Devonshire. He was the son of Sir Francis Drake, who had circumnavigated the globe.
447 At this time, he was secretary of the Admiralty under the Duke of Buckingham.
448 Netherlands
449 Source: Calendar of State Papers/Domestic Series/Reign of Charles I, V21627-1628; John Bruce, William Douglas Hamilton, Sophia C. Lomas; pub London by Longman, Brown, Green, & Roberts, 1858.
450 Mike Day, Mayday Genealogy, Twickenham, London, England.

Captain Thomas Wigan has asked a letter of marque and reprisal[451] be granted against the French and found to be in favor, will wait out you for it."[452]

I made a trip to the British National Archives and spent an entire day searching the Admiralty records from 1625 to 1629 in hope of finding that Captain Wigan had been granted that letter of marque. He had not. The Admiralty records are well organized, easy to read, and contain a lot of information on ships that were granted letters of marque.

In December 1626, a royal order was made to seize all French ships in English waters. Just a month previously, France had seized the English and Scottish wine fleets with a year's supply of wine on board. By January 1627, war with France was inevitable.[453] Was this what precipitated Wiggin filing for a letter of marque? It could have been. It's just not provable. If this were the incident and why Wiggin didn't get his letter, then he probably made the decision to go to New England out of sheer frustration with the system.

There is another scenario we have to consider. Sir John Pennington, Admiral,[454] Treasurer of His Majesty's Fleet, was knighted for his service to the Crown during the French and Spanish Wars. The Penningtons were fishmongers and mercers in London, Wigan, Lancashire, and elsewhere. Sir Isaac Pennington was Lord Mayor of London in 1645. So Captain Wiggin had every reason to have known the Penningtons. Just being on the west coast of England would have put him in the sphere of Captain Pennington in 1627. Wiggin may have even been sailing with Pennington's fleet. Sir John Pennington had two sisters who married into the King family, which Captain Wiggin had a connection to through his grandfather Thomas Gybbes. So there's that wedding-ring scenario again.

In March 1627, Captain Pennington was sent against the French shipping with a lot of success. Pennington and his captured ships were earning the Crown more money for war chests than the forced loans[455] were. The Duke of Buckingham and King Charles were determined to rid the seas of both the Spanish and French ships. Buckingham "issued instructions to Edward

---

451 Letters of marque and reprisal were issued to ships in times of conflict and amounted to granting permission to seize ships flying flags of the enemy. The cargos, or value of the ship itself, were divided amongst the crew, owner(s), master, officers, and the Crown, with each getting a share based on their importance.

452 National Archives, Kew, Richmond, England SP 16/47/50

453 Source: *Mr. Secretary Nicholas (1593-1669), His Life and Letters,* 1955, Bodley Head, London; copyright 1911; by Donald Nicholas, pgs. 54–55; Nicholas was secretary to the Duke of Buckingham and the Admiralty.

454 C. 1646; A Royalist and champion of the King; *The History and Antiquities of Allerdale Ward, above Derwent,* by Samuel Jefferson, 23 entries in the book, pub 1862 Carlisle, by Nicholas and Son.

455 "The Forced Loan"

Nicholas to give out letters of marque,"[456] so why didn't Captain Thomas Wigan secure one?

Three reasons why Captain Wigan/Wiggin did not get a letter of marque:

1. His failure to take the master mariner's exam
2. Infighting in the Admiralty; upheaval of the Admiralty
3. His ship couldn't pass a seaworthy test

Master indicates an accomplished/apprenticed craftsman in any trade, such as master craftsman. *Master mariner* is the term in use since the thirteenth century to define someone in charge of a ship and its crew members, who have passed the Admiralty's exam process. *Master,* in this case, means there are no limitations placed on his skills, and he can captain a ship of any size. A lot of men who never took this exam owned ships. For example, ships running between Ireland and England didn't even have ordnance on board and were typically small-tonnage crafts. They more often than not leaked badly and were not seaworthy ships. Anyone who has commanded a ship can be called captain. This does not define him as a master mariner.

All the letters granted to mariners on the west coast of England at that time had very recognizable names, with the merchants of Bristol and Barnstaple being heavily favored. They included the Wright brothers, who figure into New England's settlement and explorations and will become Thomas Wiggin's bosses.

On 7 May 1627, Captain John Mason wrote to Secretary Nicholas that the men were about to mutiny for want of pay.[457] Even before this, in January of 1627, Sir Ferdinando Gorges wrote that the garrison of Plymouth had not been paid for three years, and many of them, and their families, were starving to death.[458]

Captain Walter Neale[459] wrote a petition to the Council of War stating he had served in the expedition with Count Mansfeldt[460]and had not been paid. He's but one of the captains seeking back pay for services to the Crown. Captain Neale ends up in New England from 1630 to 1633, working for Captain John Mason as an agent.

---

[456] Ibid, pg. 57.
[457] Ibid, pg. 57.
[458] Calendar of State Papers; Vol. L: January 17 to 21, 1627
[459] More on the Captains in New England later.
[460] Battle of Dessau, April 15, 1626, between the German Protestants under Count von Mansfeldt and the Imperialists.

Thomas Wiggin had to know about this situation, and this was another reason he didn't want to get drawn into military action.

The key to why our good captain didn't get that letter of marque lies in the infrastructure fighting among members of the Admiralty. Our list of characters begins with the Duke of Buckingham.

> January 6 Barnstaple 1627: Sir John Drake[461] to (Secretary) Nicholas: (Drake) *Has been at Barnstaple to take examination respecting a ship of Flushing driven ashore at Appledore. She was taken by the Spaniards and remained in the service of the King of Spain for six months when the original crew revolted and carried off the ship. Drake's men took possession of the goods cast ashore from the wreck but Kist, the Judge of the Admiralty, ordered them to be restored which Drake complains of and wishes Kist to be dismissed.* Capt. Tho Wigan desires a letter of marque.
> (Source: Calendar of State Papers/Domestic Series/Reign of Charles I, V2 1627–1628; John Bruce, William Douglas Hamilton, Sophia C. Lomas; pub London by Longman, Brown, Green, and Roberts, 1858)

Let's put this in perspective and correctness because it impacts the life of Captain Thomas Wiggin in a profound way. William Kifte (sic . . . "Kiste/Kist"), Deputy Judge of the Admiralty for Devonshire, and Sir John Drake[462] did not get along at all. A ship had been driven ashore at Appledurcombe (the south shore of the Isle of Wight), and the Admiralty (the Duke of Buckingham) wanted to know why the ship was under arrest. Kifte[463] told the Admiralty Sir John Drake had detained the ship and nailed down the hatch, removed her sails, and placed guards about it after Sir John Eliot, the vice admiral, had released the ship. Sir John Drake had command to take the actions he did, according to Buckingham. Drake is calling for the removal of Kiste over this incident.

Apart from the fact that Captain Thomas Wiggin is included in this letter, it clearly demonstrates the infighting in the Admiralty and struggle for power. This case would have ended up in court, except Sir John Eliot was thrown in prison for other offenses. This incident was his last official act.

---

[461] Sir John Drake was an arm of the Admiralty who resided in Devonshire. He was the son of Sir Francis Drake, who had circumnavigated the globe.

[462] Born 1591 in Ashe, Devonshire; died 1636 in Ashe, Devonshire; married Helen Boteler (Buttler) dau. of Sir Henry Butler and Katherine Waller. The Butler clan were from Warwickshire.

[463] Sic; Kist.

Sir John Eliot[464] was the youthful traveling companion to George Villiers, the Duke of Buckingham, and he went with Villiers on his first European tour as a young man. Eliot was born in Cornwall in 1546, the same year Villars was born, and imprisoned in the Tower of London many times for his support of Parliament (Puritans). Eliot contracted tuberculosis and died in 1632 at age 40 while imprisoned in the Tower. Eliot was not Puritan himself, but defended the right of anyone to pray in his own way.

The Duke of Buckingham, the king's *favorite*, rose rapidly into power, from poverty of birth to head of the Admiralty. Once he attained that power, he appointed his old friend, John Eliot, vice admiral of Devonshire. It was a duty that demanded honesty, tenacity, and trust as the safety of commercial ships depended on him. The Devon coast was rife with pirates, and even the inhabitants of the coastline depended on the vice admiral for their safety. The vice admiral's duties included boarding ships to determine the lawfulness of cargo or prize ships and adjudicating salvage and payments.

George Villiers, the Duke of Buckingham, was at the home of Captain John Mason in Portsmouth, Devonshire, in October of 1628, engaged in negotiations to settle the claims of the military ship's captains and crews who had not been paid in three years. He was also preparing to make another assault on the French port of La Rochelle, France. A disgruntled former officer of the previous La Rochelle assault, Lt. John Felton, decided to put an end to his own mental anguish and the life of Buckingham with a knife. Buckingham's death drove the king into deep depression and the country into upheaval. Buckingham was hated by the population, loved by the king, and the glue that was holding a fragile Admiralty together while it was trying to figure out how to finance the king's wars and maintain solvency.

Felton was hanged for his deed while London rejoiced in the streets over Buckingham's demise. Shortly after Felton's hanging, his only son immigrated to the American colonies.

The duke's death was probably the last straw for Captain Wiggin. He had waited a year to hear something on his request for a letter of marque, and with the duke's death, his hopes were dashed. Wiggin probably felt the Admiralty would be in disarray for some time to come.

Drake's handwriting on the letter itself shows a lot of stress, with inconsistent penmanship. Putting Captain Wiggin's request in the margin of the letter and haphazardly signing his own name by squeezing it in the lower left corner, clearly demonstrates his emphasis on the political nature of this letter and the stress it's causing him.

---

464 Eliot was a close friend of Sir Richard Knightly, a Puritan leader of Northamptonshire, whose family owned Offchurch Bury, Warwickshire, which is adjacent to the Offchurch church where William Wiggin, father of Thomas, is buried.

Was Captain Wiggin's request for a reminder to the Admiralty about his letter of marque an afterthought? Yes. Clearly, it was. It appears Wiggin was right there with Drake, reminding him to mention the situation. Why was Wiggin important enough to Drake for him to even do this? Wiggin could have been sailing in Drake's personal fleet. No port records under Wiggin's name will come to light if that was the case. His ship would have been noted as a Drake ship in port records. Then, of course, there is the wedding-ring connection (see "Pedigrees").

It is also highly likely Captain Wiggin had never taken the master mariner's exam, and thus he was not being recognized by the Admiralty in his request for a letter of marque against the French. It may also be a fact that his ship was aging and was the same one grounded in 1631 off Massachusetts. That ship had seen better days. Or perhaps this 1631 ship was one made for him by the Hiltons upon his arrival and had some sort of collision, causing Captain Wiggin to ground it?

> History of Essex County, Massachusetts, Volume 2, Part 1: *Captain Wiggin ran a ship aground on Long Beach on 18 February 1631.*[465]
>
> This would not be the last ship he ran aground on this same sandbar:
>
> History of Lynn: *A vessel owned by Captain Thomas Wiggin, of Portsmouth, was wrecked on the Long Beach, and the sails, masts, anchor, etc., purchased by Thomas Wheeler, on the third of June 1657.*[466]

If this "ship" was a coastal craft that became so popular on the Piscataqua, then what was he doing with it on the ocean? If it was a larger seagoing craft, why would he ground it and leave it? That sandbar—while probably not visible at high tide—was at low tide, and he certainly knew it was there with the second ship grounding. At low tide, in good weather, you could probably walk in shallow water to shore. Couldn't he have just waited for the tide to float him off that sandbar? Neither record gives us that craft's name or if there was a crew of any sort. We are left with a lot of unanswerable questions.

There is one more scenario you should consider. The Royal Navy was comprised of merchant ships outfitted with ordnance (if they didn't already

---

[465] History of Essex Co., MA, pg 1430, Vol 2, pt 1; edited by Duane Hamilton Hurd.

[466] History of Lynn, MA, by Alonzo Lewis and James R. Newhall; pg. 242; pub Boston, 1844, pg. 146.

have it). Could it be that the Admiralty, knowing Captain Thomas Wiggin had a ship, wanted him to patrol the New England coastline? He had left, he thought, such things behind him, but just maybe it was catching up with him again. Or was pressure coming his way via Winthrop to guard the coastline? That clearly was not the life he chose by coming to New Hampshire. Grounding that vessel in 1631 would take care of any threats of pressing him into service as a New England patrol vessel.

Captain Wiggin's acquaintance and working relationship with Drake would have held tremendous weight with merchants of the West Coast of England. It would have opened many doors to Wiggin, which an ordinary captain would not have been able to walk through. The fact that Wiggin had an ancestral tie to the Drakes would certainly help his cause.[467]

The years 1627 and 1628 became the pivotal points for Captain Thomas Wiggin. His country is a political mess, and his world is falling apart. Sir John Eliot is in jail, the Duke of Buckingham has been murdered in the home of Captain John Mason (proprietor of New Hampshire), Sir John Drake and Judge Kifte[468] are at each other's throats, and Wiggin is not hearing anything on his request for a letter of marque due to the political atmosphere and for the reasons previously mentioned.

There is one more person in all this we need to address as he was lighting some fires of his own, and that is Sir James Bagg (born 1592 and died 1638). Bagg was a man who had a bad reputation and has been completely destroyed by historians. He was Comptroller of Customs for Plymouth and Fowey, Cornwall, from 1614 to 1621. In 1626, he was Commissioner for Martial Law in Devon and Cornwall; in 1626–28, he was investigating Sir John Eliot. You name it and he had about all the offices a man of his time could hold, most of them having to do with revenues of one sort or another. During the 1630s,[469] he would be exposed in Star Chamber for all his fraudulent deals. His nickname became "the bottomless bag"—an extorting, arrogant, foul-mouthed, and sweet-as-honey man to anyone whose favor he needed.

By the time Drake and Kifte were deep into their conflict, Bagg wrote to Secretary Nicholas, professing to be his true friend, stating that Drake should not be allowed to share in all his ship seizures and insinuating Drake was not a faithful servant of the Crown.

---

467 See "Pedigrees."

468 This name is pronounced "Kist," but I use the spelling of record here.

469 In 1634, his former ally, John Mohun, now a peer, accused him of having embezzled much of the £80,000 he had received during the war years for victualing the fleet, and of providing "stinky and unwholesome victuals such as dogs would not eat," which had caused 4,000 men to die.

That triangle—Drake, Kifte, and Bagg, with poor Secretary Nicholas caught in the middle—reads like a soap opera. What a great movie that set of characters would make. The only way they hurt Captain Thomas Wiggin/ Wigan (and probably others too) was their focus was on each other and not on business for/and to benefit the Admiralty.

This is a 1627 letter penned by John Drake[470] wherein he says, *"One Captain Thomas Wigan has asked a letter of marque and reprisal*[471] *be granted against the French and found to be in favor will wait out you for it."*[472]

Captain Thomas Wiggin does not appear in the port lists of Barnstaple, Devonshire, or Bristol, Gloucestershire, as having a ship ported there. The lists of grants for letters of marque and reprisal for both ports are rather extensive and appear to be complete in the National Archives at Kew. Many of the Bristol Merchant Ventures had letters on their ships making regular ocean crossings between England and New England and through the English Channel. Many of them were also very successful at taking prize French ships.

> Here are the connections for Captain Wiggin having been with Sir John Drake's fleet:
>
> 1. Captain Thomas Wiggin's mother was Anne Gybbes, daughter of Thomas Gybbes of Honington, Warwickshire.
> 2. Thomas Gybbes was a brother of Robert Gybbes, who married Margery Prideaux, daughter of Humphrey Prideaux.
> 3. Margery Prideaux had a half-sister named Elizabeth, who married Robert Drake.

The Gybbes of Devonshire:

> Henry Gybbes of Woodbury died in 1549; George Gybbe of Clist Saint George died in 1562; and John Gibbe of the same parish and who was probably the purchaser of Pytt in 1573. Two years previously, the Rectory of Clist Saint George, the patronage of which was in the *family of Prideaux of Nutwcll*

---

[470] SP 16/47/50; The British National Archives, Kew, Richmond, England.

[471] Letters of marque and reprisal were issued to ships in times of conflict and amounted to granting permission to seize ships flying flags of the enemy. The cargos, or value of the ship itself, were divided amongst the crew, owner(s), master, officers and the Crown, with each getting a share based on their importance.

[472] National Archives, Kew, Richmond, England SP 16/47/50

> *Woodbury*, had become vacant by the death of the Rev. William Gybbe, and it is again noteworthy that Margery, daughter of Humphrey Prideaux of Theuborough, who died 8th May 1550, was the wife of *Robert Gibbes*[473] *of Honington County, Warwick.*[474]

The marriage connection is this: Robert Gibbes, who married Margery Prideaux, is Captain Thomas Wiggin's great-uncle, brother of his mother's father, Thomas Gybbes.

The Gibbs, as shipmasters, are found in numerous listings for both Virginia and Barbados in the 1620 decade. Next, they are found in the 1630–1660 mariner records for both Virginia and New England.

> 16 August 1627: Mr. Thomas Gibbs, bound from London to Virginia (PRO:E190/31/1)
>
> 20 August 1627: Mr. John Gibbs, bound from London to New England (PRO:E190/31/1)
>
> December 1632: Mr. John Gibbs, to Virginia with 4 passengers and return with 4. (EAE)[475]

1627 becomes a very informative year for who Thomas Wiggin was. The life of a sea captain had not been an easy one for either merchant seamen or the Royal Navy.

On 7 May 1627, Captain John Mason wrote to Secretary Nicholas that the men were about to mutiny for want of pay.[476] Even before this, back in January of 1627, Sir Ferdinando Gorges wrote that the garrison of Plymouth had not been paid for three years, and many of them, and their families, were starving to death.[477]

Captain Walter Neale[478] wrote a petition to the Council of War stating he had served in the expedition with Count Mansfeldt[479] and had not been

473 Robert is my tenth great-granduncle, brother of Thomas of Honington, Warwickshire, father of Anne, mother of Captain Thomas Wiggin.

474 Devonshire wills: by Charles Worthy; pg. 488; pub 1896, London, Bemrose & Sons.

475 *The Complete Book of Emigrants, 1607—1660* by Peter W. Coldham, 1998 by Genealogical Pub. Co., Baltimore, MD; various pages.

476 Ibid, pg. 57.

477 Calendar of State Papers;Vol. L: January 17 to 21, 1627

478 More on the captains in New England later.

479 Battle of Dessau (April 15, 1626) between the German Protestants under Count von Mansfeldt, and the Imperialists.

paid. He is but one of the captains seeking back pay for services to the Crown. Captain Neale ends up in New England from 1630 to 1633, working for Captain John Mason as his agent.

By 1629–33, a great many of the military captains are to be found in New England working for Captain John Mason as agents and overseers. They were seeking employment—some temporary and some permanent—to recoup from the Crown's wars with European countries. They may also have been trying to get away from England, knowing a new La Rochelle attack was about to take place, and they wanted no part of more senseless wars and no pay. A lot of them had gone to Newfoundland in the 1620s to escape conscription.

With so many ships' crews unpaid, they were engaged in mass exiting and revolt. The Crown needed these men and ships for its ongoing conflicts with France and Spain.

The Crown had assessed each port of England to furnish ships, crews, and ordnance to build up a navy. A lot of these were converted merchant ships. All were owned in shares by the local merchants, who could ill afford taking ships out of merchant shipping and sending them off to war. The ports of Western England were in dire straits due to loss of trade ports in Europe and could not meet their assessments for funds or ships.

Most of the early North American settlers came from the "west country" for good reason. Going to Newfoundland and New England—not to mention Virginia and Barbados—was a way to recuperate their lost revenues and get out of the endless cycle of Crown wars that had all but shut down the western trade ports.

All the sailors leaving England were not honorable and would turn to piracy to make their fortunes. No sea so full of trade ships was free of pirates and privateers in the seventeenth century. Great convoys of ships left harbor together to try and break through the pirate fleets. As only one example, take the case of the pirate George Nutt. Nutt was born in Devonshire, but in 1620, he arrived in Torbay, Newfoundland, and liked it so much he moved his family there. He almost immediately began piracy, taking a French, a Flemish, and an English ship into his fleet, which he manned with unemployed sailors and disgruntled press-gang conscripts from the English ships. By 1621, he was off to the west coast of England, where he preyed on shipping between England and Ireland. In one week, he took a dozen ships. While Nutt was off the seas by the time Captain Wiggin was sailing about, he is still an example of the troubles men like him presented to honest shipping.

Sir George Calvert, Lord Baltimore, obtained a patent covering fishing rights in the surrounding waters and established a settlement near the southern end of the peninsula in Newfoundland. He built a handsome mansion there, where he resided with his family for years. By 1626, more than 150 vessels were dispatched annually from Devonshire to Newfoundland. The fish caught were salted and dried on the Newfoundland shores, and on the approach of winter, those engaged in the fisheries returned to England with the products of their enterprise.[480] Vessels engaged in the Newfoundland trade sometimes went to the Isle of Shoals and New England before returning to England. Thomas Wiggin could have been involved with this trade route to and from the fishing banks.

While we will never know for sure, due to a lack of records, which of the events related engaged Captain Thomas Wiggin, I think you can see any of them would have resulted in the same actions by Wiggin: immigration to an area where he might find some peace to raise a family. And it would give him safety and the opportunity to make his fortune, not to mention a decent life.

---

480 Hakluyt's Chronicles; Pedley's History Newfoundland; Encyc. Brit. "Newfoundland."

Wheelwright Deed, 17 May 1629

On the above date, the Sagamores[481] of New England granted unto John Wheelwright a parcel of land before quite a large gathering of settlers, which included Richard Vines, Richard Bonithon, Edward Hilton, Walter Neale, George Vaughan, Ambrose Gibbins, and Thomas Wiggin.

This deed was declared a forgery by James Savage[482] of Boston, early historian of New England. I have been unable to find out if anyone has ever seen this deed. If so, it would be easy enough to ascertain if it's a forgery just by comparing signatures. We have Thomas Wiggin's signature on his will.

However, if we think outside the box here, then we'd have to consider this: Exeter was being developed during Thomas Wiggin's time. There are no records in protest to this settlement that I've ever found. If it was not acceptable to Thomas Wiggin, we are sure to have heard of it, if from no other source than John Winthrop. Since he had jurisdiction over this area, he would have been vociferous about its establishment.

If Thomas Wiggin had never signed this deed, he too would have had a voice in the matter. When Wheelwright presented this deed to anyone seeking a reason why this settlement was coming into existence, they would have noted the witnesses' signatures and questioned someone about them. There is no record of any such protests.

When Wheelwright got into trouble in Massachusetts about 1638, he proceeded to move to this land with some followers. This would have been the time for protests to surface. I could find none.

The dilemma comes about because of the names used in the 1629 deed. The name "North-ham" was not known until about 1636, "Portsmouth" about

---

481 Sagamores are tribal chiefs among the Algonquin tribes.

482 Original data: Savage, James. *A Genealogical Dictionary of the First Settlers of New England Showing Three Generations of Those Who Came Before May 1692. Vol. I—IV.* Boston, MA, USA: 1860–1862.

1650, and "Hampton" about 1635. So how could they have been used in this deed scribed in 1629?

The stage has been set for someone to investigate this bit of history in minute detail and with a lot of research. I did not take it further than those questions arising in my own head, just because the answers would not have taken me back into England, which is where my research and interests were focused regarding who Captain Thomas Wiggin was.

What this deed does do is establish the presence of Captain Thomas Wiggin on the Piscataqua by May of 1629, providing it was not a forgery.

BLOODY POINT MAP[483]

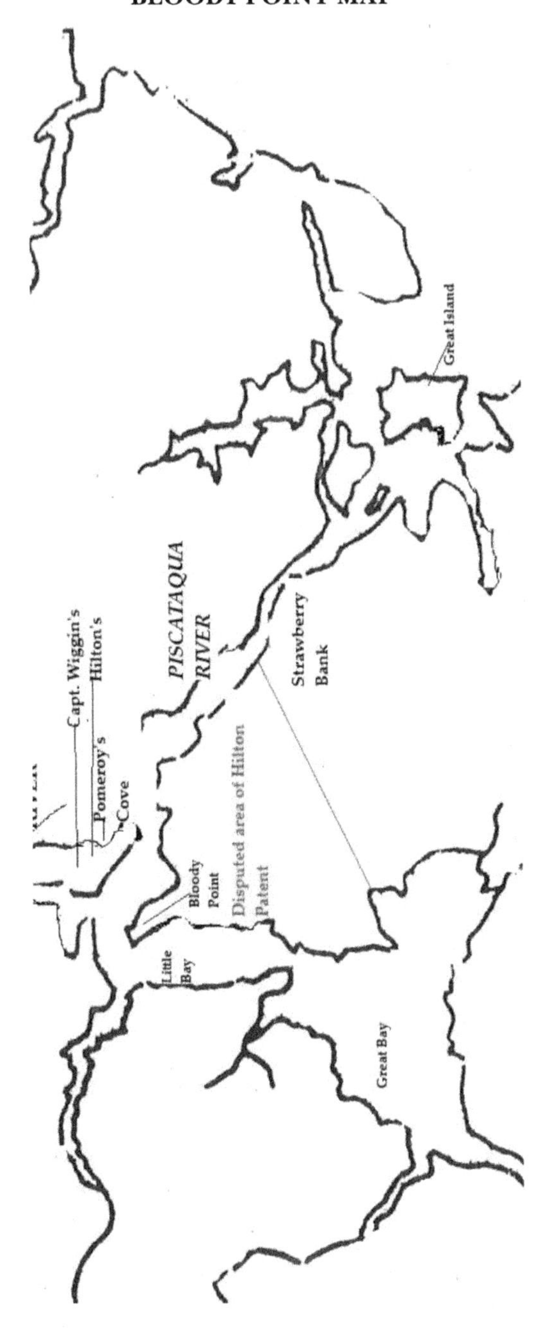

483 Drawn By Joyce Elaine Wiggin-Robbins

Bloody Point

BIO: Captain Walter Neale[484] was born about 1595, the son of Captain Walter Neale, and died after 1639. A soldier under Count Mansfeldt in the French and Spanish wars, 1629 finds him in financial straits. In the spring of 1630, he traveled on board the bark *Warwick*[485] to the Piscataqua. Built fortifications on the Piscataqua, granted lands to settlers, and for three years, was the chief man on that river.

Hilton's patent was granted on 12 March 1629–30 and placed in his hands on 7 July 1631. Shortly thereafter, Captain Wiggin was spearheading some improvements to some of the land that would become known as Bloody Point. It would have been good land to run cattle on, with water on three sides as natural fences.

Neale told Wiggin to stop and leave, but Wiggin was ready to defend his right at the point of a sword.

Captain Neale has a solid history of being a soldier, and the last thing military leaders do is put themselves in jeopardy at the enemy's hands to achieve a goal. They will seek an alternative route. Also, Captain Wiggin did not come this far to end it all at the point of a sword over land he did not own.

These men have been working together, surveying and seeking the best place to mount cannon for defense of the river, plus everyday encounters wheeling and dealing for the good of their communities. Killing one another was never going to make sense. Captain Wiggin knew Captain Neale was only going to be there for three years, so why make an enemy of the man?

The historian Jenness believed the incident at Bloody Point occurred after the arrival of the patent of the Laconia partners, which was granted in November of 1631, and that the title Captain Wiggin was defending was that of Massachusetts Bay under their Great Charter of 1628–29 as there is no documentation that Wiggin was interested in the Hilton Patent until 1632.

---

484 *Captain John Mason*, by Charles W. Tuttle, edited by John W. Dean, pub. Of Prince Society by John Wilson & son, 1887, Boston.

485 You will find many references to there being a "soldier for discovery" on board the Warwick without an actual name being used. It's Captain Neale they are referring to.

What I would like to see from this encounter is the sword(s)! What happened to Captain Wiggin's sword(s)? That metal would not melt, so where did they go? There is no mention of them in his will, so he must have given them to his son(s) before he died. He would have valued them if he owned them for any length of time. I always wondered why he valued a scarlet suit, taking such great care of what happened to it via his will, and no mention of a sword or armor of any sort in his will. I'm curious.

The Caribbean

"Lying in the heart of the Indies and the mouth of the Spaniards."[486]

> 4 December 1629, *Company of Adventurers* for the Plantation of the Islands of Providence, Henrietta and adjacent Islands with Earl of Holland, Governor, and John Dike, London merchant, Deputy Governor: Robert, Earl of Warwick; Henry, Earl of Holland; William, Lord Saye and Sele; Robert, Lord Brooke; John Roberts, Sir Benjamin Rudyerd; Sir Gilbert Gerrard; Sir Edward Harwood; Sir Nathanial Rich; Sir Edmond Mountford; John Pym; Richard Knightley; Christopher Sherland; Oliver St. John; John Gourden; Gregory Cawsell; John Dike; John Grant; and others hereafter to be joined with them.[487]

While it would later be claimed the lords and their partners had always intended to inhabit these islands, I do not believe it. I wholeheartedly believe their intentions were solely to harass the Spanish shipping lanes and to fill their coffers with plunder from those ships. These men were all laying out huge sums to finance their New England settlements, their island adventurers, and the English Civil War. Some of them were going to die very broke.

I accept they wanted to leave England and take all their titles and privileges with them prior to the first English Civil War, but not to such a dangerous place as the Caribbean islands. I think perhaps this became their second choice when they realized the authorities of the Massachusetts Bay Colony did not want titles and privileges thereof to be brought to New England. Once that became clear to them, they not only turned their backs on their investments in New

[486] Philip Bell, governor of Bermuda, used the phrase in a letter to Sir Nathaniel Rich about 1629, calling Bermuda the perfect base to privateer against the Spaniards. The Earl of Warwick, who presented a proposal for colonizing the island, also used the phrase.

[487] Source: Calendar of State papers Colonial: v 1; pub 1860, 1574–1660; pp 123–124; Dec. 1630-036.

England, but began to encourage other settlers in New England to proceed to Providence. Some of them did and would live to regret their decision when the island fell into the Spanish domain in 1641.

The Caribbean story is fascinating and so well-documented. I found a lot of relatives of New England settlers in the Caribbean. A fellow researcher told me that he thought families split up and settled in different areas of the world to hedge their fortunes and guarantee success somewhere. I'm not sure they deliberately planned doing that, but that's probably what happened in the end.

None of the lords ventured into the Caribbean themselves. When their ships came back with such tales of piracy and danger, no lord in his right mind was going to attempt such a voyage. Their sole goal was to make money, not risk their lives.

Captain Thomas Wiggin was not seeking adventure either. He was seeking a home. There was no comparison for him between New Hampshire and the Caribbean.

The Caribbean became an area of many discoveries. The potato, for example, a staple of the Caribbean diet, was not eaten in the European countries (including England) in any of its varieties. Still, its discovery didn't go without notice. It would become accepted in Europe long before the English would touch it. Gold was being found from South America up to Mexico, and sugar was a great favorite. The discovery of cochineal would set the red dye industry on its ear.

During the seventeenth century, the islands were occupied by just about every European nation with ships plying the waters, with all of them seeking trades and riches. Piracy was rampant as each nation tried to establish themselves as the dominant occupier preying on shipping lanes.

The Caribbean wasn't a place to hold the attention of men like Captain Thomas Wiggin for very long. It was a transient lifestyle, and he wasn't after that.

The Caribbean had nothing to equal the Piscataqua River area. The lifestyle of the natives, the crops grown, and the everyday way of life was completely different from that of New England. Captain Wiggin was not turning his back on the familiar life of ole England. He just wanted to improve on it, and he wanted a measure of wealth for himself.

Land. Land was the greatest draw for Wiggin—land he could make pay handsomely.

Sea Business

They that go down to the sea in ships that do business in great waters; these see the works of the Lord, and his wonders in the deep.
—Psalm 107: 23, 24

Sir Francis Drake's[488] Prayer
1577

Disturb us, Lord, when we are too pleased with ourselves; when our dreams have come true because we dreamed too little; when we arrived safely because we sailed too close to the shore.

Disturb us, Lord, when with the abundance of things we possess, we have lost our thirst for waters of life; having fallen in love with life, we have ceased to dream of eternity; and in our efforts to build a new earth, we have allowed our vision of the new Heaven to dim.

Disturb us, Lord, to dare more boldly, to venture on wilder seas where storms will show your mastery; where losing sight of land we shall find the stars.

We ask you to push back the horizons of our hopes; and to push back the future in strength, courage, hope, and love.

This we ask in the name of our Captain, who is Jesus Christ.

488 1540–1596; vice admiral, privateer who circumnavigated the globe, securing half a million pounds sterling in booty. No children, so his titles and lands passed to his nephew, also named Francis.

So why is it we find a man grounded in farming and merchandising looking toward ships? I'm presenting here a scenario that was most likely Thomas Wiggin's mind-set, and you can be the judge if the records bear my vision out.

Thomas Wiggin has done his apprenticeship years (1615–1622) in merchandise and marketing with his grandfather, Thomas Gybbes. He's done his work well and has added to his education with learning the value of networking and family connections. By 1626, Thomas has lost his wife and any children of that marriage and is once again on his own. Considering that the life span of a seventeenth-century man is about thirty-eight years, Thomas is taking view of what he wants to do with the rest of his life. Farming has long been on the back burner and all the facets of merchandising on the front burner of his life. Marketing is what he knows best. Keep in mind that even when he becomes established in New Hampshire, his skills lie in marketing what he produces, and he knows what to produce for the English. There is also every indication he was trading with the native population and putting his marketing skills to work, targeting mainly furs, which he knew were in great demand in England and Europe.

The strongest apparent connection Thomas Wiggin had to the world of shipping was Sir John Drake and the mariners of the Gybbes family—such as Thomas Gibbs, the mariner[489] out of London. Captain Gybbes and others of London received a letter of marque on 30 May 1627 for the ship *True Love* out of London. He is listed as captain. Another ship he owned (named *Thomas*) also had a letter of marque, but the captain isn't listed.

English tradition runs deep when it comes to networking and family ties. Ties that are strong and reliable, and Thomas was about to try the system out. He's an adventurous man, as evidenced by his carving a life out of the New England wilderness, and not afraid of a challenge. In the terms of Sir Francis Drake, Thomas will not sail *too close to shore.*

When Wiggin visited Drake in 1627 regarding his request for a letter of marque, he got an earful and an eyeful of what was going on in the sea business of the day. Right there—and maybe he didn't realize it just then—his mind was turning away from his country, which was on the brink of yet another war at sea. He had to examine his heart and decide if he wanted to get involved, yet again, with war.

Opportunity had to open its door to Thomas for him to progress. He is cognizant of the west coast of England getting the most letters of marque and

[489] Not his grandfather of the same name. This Thomas Gibbs is found in a lot of mariner records connected with the entire area from the Caribbean to New England.

reprisal against the Spanish and French; he knows the door should be wide open for a letter against the French due to the conflicts at La Rochelle, France.

He would apply for his letter of marque and reprisal from the West Coast in hopes his connections would work in his favor. Getting a merchant ship wasn't difficult for Wiggin with his Gybbes/Gibbs family connections. A small-tonnage merchant ship could be purchased for thirty pounds, the amount of his inheritance from his father. He also must have accumulated some funds during his apprenticeship and in the ensuing five or so years. Thomas Gibbs, the mariner, may well have helped him along the way as he had letters of marque on his ships out of London. While laying the groundwork for immigration, he may have been running the trade route between England and Ireland. That ship was not lying idle at some dock, but earning a living for the Captain.

In order for my suppositions to work, I have to assume Thomas has made trips of discovery to both the Caribbean and the Americas and, more than likely, on the triangle shipping route of the Caribbean to Virginia to New England and Canadian English settlements and then back to England (or in reverse, according to the cargo being transported). We have to take license here to assume as there are no records of who was sailing this route, only scant individual records that mostly surround some event involving a ship and crew. So it's not much of a stretch to figure out Thomas has sailed this route. There are those who claim Thomas and Richard Lane, together, ventured into the Caribbean.

Thomas has had enough of strife and warlike struggles. Even though he will continue to find himself in the middle of strife in New England, nowhere do you find a record of his causing strife. He really wants a more stable life somewhere away from England, which he strongly feels is headed for political conflict within, combined with more wars.

The records over time bear out that New England had to defend itself against any invaders, especially of the French version, and pirates. Never at any time did New England enjoy an English armada off its coastline as a line of defense. It makes sense that Wiggin wanted a letter of marque and reprisal against the French. If trouble came, it would be from the French to the north in Canada. With the Massachusetts Bay Colony having a self-rule charter, it fell to them for self-defense as well—another reason why Thomas Wiggin wanted to align with the Puritans of that settlement. He knew full well all of New England had to band together for defensive reasons, if for no other.

So why didn't he get that letter of marque? Researchers have assumed that because the year was 1627, it had a tie-in to the conflicts at La Rochelle, France. I don't think the facts bear that out. First off, if he's sailing under one of the English fleets engaged in that combat, he would not need a letter of marque.[490]

[490] Remember, letters of marque were awarded to ships, not men.

Ships associated with both the ports of Barnstaple and Bristol received letters against the French. Some of those ships were small merchant ships traveling in flotillas to ports of trade.

One salient reason still sticks in my mind as to why Wiggin never got his letter: he must not have taken the mariner's exam. Combine that with him not wanting to turn the captain's duties over to someone else, considering where he was going. He wanted full command of that ship. Really, that letter of marque and reprisal against the French wasn't going to change a thing, one way or the other. He was going to New England.

Read on for more records, connections, and conditions surrounding what I've just told you.

1626: Although Thomas Wiggin was not associated with the French of Canada, we must and should make note that on 15 April 1626, Champlain[491] sailed from Dieppe for New France, reaching Quebec in July. A year later, the winter of 1627, Champlain wrote that 55 people (men, women, and children) were domiciled there. Just the fact that Champlain was moving into Canada had to create some concern for the English already in New England, and for the backers cutting settlements out of the wilderness.

The Dutch are 270 strong in New Netherland by 1628, which can't make the English all that happy as they essentially cut the northern and southern English settlements in two. Virginia was 1,275 strong, with 22 African slaves by 1624.

Another man to address was Robert Rich, 2nd Earl of Warwick (1587–1658). Rich was a friend and cohort of Lord Saye and Sele and a staunch Puritan. His activities at sea were against the Spanish, not the French. Rich's second wife was Frances Wray, daughter of Sir Christopher Wray,[492] Chief Justice to Queen Elizabeth I. In 1628, Rich obtained the patent for the Massachusetts Bay Colony, and in 1632, he was granted the patent for Saybrook, Connecticut. Rich even tried to secure religious freedoms for the English colonies. With such a varied field of interests, I was sure I'd find some direct connection for Thomas Wiggin to this man, but I never did.

1627: Buckingham and King Charles were determined to rid the seas of both the Spanish and French ships. Buckingham issued instructions to Secretary Edward Nicholas to give out letters of marque.[493]

---

[491] *Champlain's Dream,* David Hackett Fischer, Random 2008, pgs. 397–404.

[492] Patron of Vicar William Wiggin, Captain Thomas Wiggin's father.

[493] *Mr. Secretary Nicholas (1593—1669); His Life and Letters,* 1955, Bodley Head, London, 1911; by Donald Nicholas, pg. 57.

In 1627, another debacle under the tutelage of George Villiers was underway regarding France.[494]

6 January 1627: Sir John Drake writes his letter[495] with the notation of Captain Thomas Wigan desiring to hear something regarding a request for a letter of marque against the French. This would indicate Wigan has applied for his letter in 1626. I diligently searched (going over the records twice) for two years in each direction from 1626 for something regarding this request and found nothing. However, only actual letters of marque granted are recorded in the Admiralty[496] files, not the actual requests themselves. This indicates one of two things to me: (1) Wiggin has encountered hostilities with the French off the New England Coast; or (2) he is deeply concerned about the rumors of problems coming at the French port of La Rochelle. I can see why Wiggin was not granted his marque in early 1627 (or late 1626), and even why he was not granted one by July 1627. But was he with the Duke of Buckingham's flotilla in July? There are no surviving records of the ships and captains (or owners) in that armed flotilla.

December 1626: The order is given for all French and Spanish ships to be seized.

In January 1627, Sir Ferdinando Gorges wrote that the garrison of Plymouth had not been paid for three years, and many of them—and their families—were starving to death.[497]

On 7 May 1627, Captain John Mason wrote to Secretary Nicholas of the Admiralty that the men were about to mutiny for want of pay.

On 10 July 1627, an English fleet under Villiers reaches La Rochelle, France, where the French Huguenots are under siege.

10 August 1627, Cardinal Richelieu begins the siege of La Rochelle, and the Huguenots would hold out for fourteen months.

---

494 The irony here is in Jan 1630, "Pretensions of the King of France to Canada and all Acadia, including New England and New Scotland, that King assumes the sole privilege of fishing in those parts, whereby in a few years, he will be able to raise a nursery of sailors better than any in the world. In Captain Daniell's letters: Daniell has publicly confessed that the French King's intention this year to supplant the English in all those colonies and make prize of the English ships going thither; that the King of France only intended the peace with England to last two years, until he had secured America. Had the Admiralty known this, they may have granted Captain Thomas Wigan his request for a letter of marque against the French! (Source: Calendar of State Papers Colonial: Vol I; pub 1860; "America and West Indies: January 1630"; pp. 105–107).

495 The author has a copy of this letter secured in 2007, PRO, Kew, Richmond.

496 High Court Admiralty; The National Archives; Kew.

497 Calendar of State Papers; Vol L; January 17 to 21, 1627; Kew, England.

27 October 1627, George Villiers, 1st Duke of Buckingham, has 8,000 men and some 80 to 100 ships under his command. When he finds entry into the Port of La Rochelle barred, he attacks Ile de Ré, suffering a shattering defeat over a four-month period. King Charles, knowing full well his troops were on the verge of starvation, diverts funds for the expedition at La Rochelle to buy works of art!

8 November 1627, running out of money and with some 4,000 men dead, Buckingham returns to England.

La Rochelle, under the leadership of its mayor, held out for fourteen months and saw a decrease in population from 27,000 to 5,000 from casualties, famine, and disease. On April 1628, the Earl of Denbigh sets sail for La Rochelle and found the French defenses into the harbor impenetrable and the Huguenots under siege. Faced with sickness, lack of supplies, and a general lack of enthusiasm, he sailed right back to England.

England's populace was tired of wars that were very costly to a nation already hurting from a long series of conflicts and a lack of food supply due to poor growing conditions brought on by the Little Ice Age.[498] Buckingham is blamed for all the country's problems, domestic and foreign, and even London's citizens were demonstrating against him. On 23 August 1628, Buckingham is attacked and killed by a disgruntled former lieutenant of his Isle of Ré expedition, John Felton, who was shortly thereafter hanged. Felton's son immigrates to America soon after his father's ill-fated deed.

The question was do you think Thomas Wiggin was involved in this conflict? I don't.

1. He's not a master mariner, and his ship doesn't have ordnance.[499]
2. 1625: His first marriage probably ended.
3. 1625–1626: He's plying the waters off the west of England, perhaps to New England fishing grounds and even the Caribbean at least once.
4. 1626: He applies for a letter of marque against the French, which could mean he's tangled with them off the New England coast at worst, or just because he has decided to immigrate to the Piscataqua River.
5. 1627 January: He's with John Drake in Barnstaple.
6. 1627–28: He's in Gloucester seeking adventure/employment and, through John Drake, ends up with the Merchants of Bristol.

[498] 1607 was so cold in England, and the Thames River froze so solid, they held an ice fair. Scientists do not agree on a start and finish date for the LIA, but history is full of records of its effects on crops and life in general. The LIA is an event that could take a whole chapter, but I chose to just acknowledge its influence in each subject as this book is written.

[499] The Admiralty controlled ordnance and ships with permission to carry them.

7. 1628: He's preparing for travel to New England; this typically takes a year.
8. 1629: He's in Maine.

Where is there time, in this timeline, for conflict participation such as the Isle of Ré? You don't just pop a ship into a flotilla and back out again.

The Merchant Ventures of Bristol are deeply involved already in trips to both New England and the Caribbean. Spearheaded by the Wright brothers, who are seeking a patent to a section of the New England coastline, and who are backers of settlers already on the Piscataqua River, Bristol is not standing still during the Crown's wars with France and Spain. The Merchants of Bristol know where their fortunes lie and are moving forward at a rapid pace. They are looking for men just like Thomas Wiggin to oversee their interests abroad.

John Mason, a New England patent holder, is in a prime position as commander of the fort at Plymouth, England, to employ military men as agents in New England. He's another man well known to Thomas as he has likely been in the port controlled by Mason, at Portsmouth, Hampshire, England.

There were more than adequate opportune contacts on the West Coast of England to entice men like Thomas Wiggin to take a chance on the New England wilderness.

SEAMAN'S SECRETS
NAVIGATION AND SURVEYING[500]

THE SEAMANS SE CRETS.

Deuided into 2.partes,wherein is taught the *three kindes of Sayling, Horizontall,Paradoxicall,and fayling vpon a great* Circle: also an Horizontal Tyde Table for the eafie finding of *the ebbing and flowing of the Tydes, with a Regiment newly calcula-*ted for the finding of the Declination of the Sunne and many *other most necessary rules and information, not heretofore set fourth by any.*

Newly corrected by the author *John Davis* of *Sandridge*, neere *Dartmouth*, in the Countie of *Devon.* Gent.

Imprinted at London by Thomas Dawfon, dwelling neere the three Cranes in the Vinetree, *and there to be solde.* 1607.

[FACSIMILE OF THE 1607 FRONTISPIECE]

500 Cover of *Seaman's Secrets* manual owned by the author

On a visit to the Plymouth Colony, we also spent time on board the *Mayflower II*, which was docked at the State Pier. We seemed to be the only tourists on board that morning, and we took our time inspecting this wonderful replica of the original *Mayflower*. While inside an upper room, talking to a reenactor all decked out in a seaman's attire of the time, I spotted a very old book sitting on a bench. When I read the title, my jaw must have dropped clean to my chest. This was the exact book I had been trying to find a copy of for years, even though I didn't know its title or even if it existed. I just felt there had to be this sort of book available to men like Captain Thomas Wiggin.

The *Seaman's Secrets* was published in 1607, and every ship's captain would have had a copy. It was truly a seaman's bible. There are two volumes, and both are quite thick. The books describe everything from instruments used, navigation guides, terminology, how to calculate the hour of the day, and every phase of the moon is described, the tides, the cross staff and its use, and so much more. I cannot begin to relate to you all the subjects covered in these two books.

I always knew there had to exist something like this book, and when I saw it lying on that bench, my joy knew no boundaries. I spent a good bit of our time on that ship just reading this edition. He allowed me to photograph what I wanted to, and I used that information when I got back home to find my own copies.

One of the things that set me to trying to figure out what they used for navigation was wondering how they possibly knew how many miles they were traveling upriver in a boat, how many miles it was from one point of land to another—things like that. In my naivety of nautical things, I still had an idea they used the same instruments for surveying on land.

For land surveying, the staff was used. It was a straight rod with a pointed end that was stuck into the ground. A compass or transit was then mounted on the rod.

The staff was used at sea as a navigational tool to ascertain the position of a ship in relation to the sun. An accurate attitude of the sun was difficult, and the staff was replaced by the octant and the sextant. If the reader wishes to go deeper into the use of these instruments, look for "Jacob's Staff" and a book by John Sellers titled *Practical Navigation*.

1632–33 LAND SURVEYING

Both Captain Walter Neal and Captain Wiggin would have known how to use ship's navigation devices and adapt them to the surveying of land. There's no doubt they would have made a good pair of men to do such work.

There were two letters written in either 1632 or 1633 involving Thomas Wiggin. There are several versions of just which year they were written in, and one antiquarian stated, "It looks as if the '2' has been altered from the '3'."

Captain Wiggin and Captain Walter Neale, according to this letter, have surveyed out the Mason-held patent to try and create four towns on the Piscataqua and can't seem to accomplish that. Making three and setting their boundaries, they then comment on Exeter, which is founded by Wheelwright[501] (the "Wheelwright Deed").

The second letter was written in August of 1633 and concerns the placement of cannon at the mouth of the Piscataqua River to defend it from enemies. An invasion by the French in Canada was always a concern, as were the acts of pirates. Captain Wiggin and Captain Neal[502] were charged with selecting a site to mount the cannon—which they did, choosing Great Island.

Since Captain Wiggin did not get his letter of marque and reprisal in 1627, having that cannon at the mouth of the Piscataqua River was even more important to the security of the land he has selected to settle upriver, on Great Bay. If trouble was to come to the river, he felt strongly it would be the French in Canada behind it.

---

[501] John Wheelwright, 1592–1679, Puritan clergyman; 1638 established the town of Exeter in NH. Originally from Lincolnshire, England.

[502] Captain Walter Neal came to New England for Captain John Mason as his agent for three years, and once that tenure was up, he left, never to return.

Setting the Stage

What does it mean to remember? It is to live in more than one world, to prevent the past from fading and to call upon the future to illuminate it. It is to revive fragments of existence, to rescue lost beings, to cast harsh light on faces and events, to drive back the sands that cover the surface of things, to combat oblivion and to reject death.[503]

Captain Thomas Wiggin's activities in colonial New Hampshire all point directly backward to a life of farming, for that's what he did with his life in New Hampshire—farm (including salt-marsh farming), in every aspect of it. He also had mills on rivers, just like those he knew in Warwickshire, England. Not only did he have a business head on his shoulders, but also a head for well-organized farming. He knew what it took to bring in a good crop, as well as what it took to run a mill. Excavations at the Wiggin home site on Sandy Point[504] indicate knowledge of the finer things in life, such as china, silver, pewter, and most likely, fine furniture too. No, not only a knowledge of them, but a strong desire to surround himself with them!

As Peter Wiggin put it, "Someone had to teach him salt-hay harvesting."[505] Since this was not an activity he learned in England, we both believe he learned it from the natives who lived on his land at Sandy Point every summer. There's no reason to believe he did not have a good relationship with these natives and would have exchanged farming techniques, hunting, fishing, and so forth, with them. Though nothing has surfaced regarding a deed between Wiggin and the

[503] Elie Weisel, *All Rivers Run to the Sea: Memoirs*, 1955, Schocken Books, NY.

[504] Appears to have been the home of Thomas Wiggin Jr. and is unclear if Captain Wiggin ever lived there.

[505] Salt hay came out of salt marshland that lay between the ocean mud flats and grassy uplands. The marshland was subject to tidal flooding. Salt hay was not as nutritious as dry land hay, but it was needed to winter over live stock. It was often mixed with dry land hay. The salt hay was harvested and stacked on wooden frames, called staddles, to dry. These haystacks resemble giant grass-topped huts.

natives, it was the custom of the day. The Wheelwright deed is a good example of such a conveyance wherein the natives relinquished land to an Englishman but retained rights to use that land for hunting, fishing, and the like.

It took not only knowledge like farming, fishing, and hunting to survive in the wilderness; it also took certain strength in character. Thomas Wiggin grew up on agricultural land located just west of Bishop's Itchington, Warwickshire, in a district called Kingston—King Farms, to be exact. His family continued on that land for generations. Two of his brothers, John and William Junior, would stay in Bishop's Itchington and their sons after them. Thomas, Hanibal, Edward, and Rychard all left to make lives of their own elsewhere.[506]

Wiggin was an achiever and strove for perfection. He was not timid, but he was not overbearing either. He seems to have stood his ground well and he knew how to draw favorable attention toward himself; was not confrontational and very diplomatic in his approaches to people and the natives.

Thomas Wiggin, well versed in agriculture and merchandising, was sent to New England in 1633, under the employment of Lord Saye and Sele, Lord Brooke, Mr. Willis, Mr. Whiting, and the Shrewsbury Men[507] as an administrator for the next seven years.[508] The lords and company purchased the patent from the Bristol Merchant Venturers who had no interests in settlements and never did accomplish one. All they wanted was contact for commerce—a faster return on their investment than a settlement would provide—and they were probably happy to sell their interests to the lords and company. While two of the Bristol group[509] did engage in a settlement in Maine, they seem to have done it entirely on their own and not in the name of the BMV.

In 1604, the French had established a fur trading post at Quebec. England wanted to establish a colony as far north as possible in order to stake their claim to this new land. Jamestown taught them in 1607 that they needed a disciplined community structured on religion and sound commercial practices. The English investors wanted people who could live off land and sea, with a faith-based society to ensure a Christian community.

---

506 We will cover the family more thoroughly elsewhere in this manuscript.

507 The Shrewsbury Men were, in part: William Walderne, Richard Percyvail (draper who sold his share to Obadiah Bruen on 4 May 1640), Richard Hunt, William Rowley, and the Rev. George Burdett was at least employed by them. Source: Pioneers on ME & NY, Pope, p. 198.

508 There is significance in this "seven-year term." Seven years is the standard "indentured" time a man had to spend in exchange for something else . . . like land, passage, supplies, and so forth.

509 Robert Aldsworth and Giles Elbridge, merchants from Bristol, 12,000 acres of land in New England and an additional 100 acres for every person transported; laid out near the river Pemaquid, 4 Nov 1631 Patent; Calendar of State papers Colonial: V 1; pub 1860; pgs. 139–141.

Who else fit the bill for the English nobles more than sons of the clergy and well-honed, agriculturally knowledgeable people? Toss in some military experience and you have perfection. When you find a man with all three backgrounds, you've found the perfect colonizing man.

Thomas Wiggin was uniquely equipped for his role in New Hampshire.

WHY HE CAME

1776: *A witty Frenchman observed that the people of England reminded him of a barrel of their own beer: Froth on the top, dregs at the bottom, but clear and sound in the middle*[510].

—author unknown

The Church

By the early seventeenth century, Europe[511] as a whole has become destabilized on several fronts, but the most devastating blow to its society was the Protestant Reformation. Up until this time, there was no religious freedom anywhere in the world, and there wasn't going to be religious freedom in early New England either. King Henry VIII's separation from the Catholic Church and creation of the Church of England did little to change people's behavior. Even though church attendance was required by law, eventually—in New England[512] as well as Old England—the records were filled with charges against citizens who did not attend church.[513] Some were even burned at the stake as heretics in England for not adhering to the edicts of the church. The whole religious upheaval by Henry VIII was never meant to release his subjects

---

[510] The only time I have seen this quote is in "The 13 Colonies." It put a giggle on my smile, so decided to include it here: http://www.earlyamerica.com/earlyamerica/maps/13colonies/

[511] While a lot of reading went into the research of European and English history, my favorite authority has become the work of Anthony F. Upton, and I'm a huge fan of his book Europe, 1600–1789, which he wrote while emeritus professor of modern history, University of St. Andrews, Scotland, 2001; ISBN 0 340 66337 5 (bb); Oxford University Press Inc. NY, NY.

[512] Court records are full of early New England men who were working; "tipping" (drinking), or just not attending church. It was a serious offense to skip church three Sundays in a row.

[513] Read the *Book of Martyrs* for a shocking record of the trials of "heretics" written by John Foxx (1517–1587).

from church control, but the movement of reform and separation from the church had begun. The rise of the Puritan movement (those who wanted change within the church) would create a whole new society and add support for migration to America that had already begun for economic reasons.

Puritanism was a huge risk—a risk in ways modern man cannot even fathom. Today we are free to choose whatever church we care to patronize, or we can attend none. Today you can be religious without church affiliation, or you can be agnostic, and know you will not burn at the stake as a heretic.

For centuries, the populations of Europe had allowed the Catholic Church to be the authority on every single matter in their lives. These were basically uneducated peasants who were not stupid, just not formally educated or "thinkers." They were followers for good reason. If things went wrong in their world, crops failed, or loved ones died, then it was God's will and did not result from anything they themselves had done. By not making decisions, or being free-thinkers, they were able to place the blame on the Catholic Church (or God) for any disasters that befell them. It was never their fault crops failed or someone died; it was the will of God. Life was much simpler that way. These seventeenth-century people are not to be blamed for their way of life. They were controlled by an elite class who controlled them through the use of religion.[514]

Religion and marriage ties were ties that bound European nations together and identified them as the core of Christendom. Royalty married royalty, and the crown heads had strong family ties. Even while England warred with Spain and France, King James was seeking a wife for his son among their royal families. Not until 1648 would Europe move toward a diversity of religions that would become irreversible.[515] Until the continent of Europe became stable, England wouldn't either.

Great Britain would eventually lead the way into a capitalistic-generated world economy that would be so powerful it would sustain losing the American colonies, but losing those colonies would be for the same reasons the English settlers came to America in the first place. Some things just never change, because from century to century, generation to generation, people do not change enough.

The impetus to move into a capitalistic society was a combination of internal strife leading to English Civil War, heavy taxation of its people and cities to pay for conflicts with Europe, a population of people struggling on a day-to-day basis to make a living, crop failures due in part to the Little Ice

---

[514] Leviathan: or, The matter, forme & power of a commonwealth, ecclesiastical . . . by Thomas Hobbes, 1651, revised and reprinted in 1904, Cambridge University Press, England; available on Google digital books. If you wish to study the church, then this is an excellent resource.

[515] The Peace accords of 1648 in Westphalia, Germany.

Age, and the plagues. Earning power had dropped substantially by 1645, and a country populated with ambitious people had to make a recovery. History has taught us that when heads of state put all their attention into their military efforts, the general population cannot sustain the supportive load. All of Great Britain's history, even before Roman occupation, was one of conflict with its neighbors, both inside and outside its own borders. Conflict for the sake of greed, especially by heads of state, cannot sustain itself. The general population will not support it unless basic human needs are being met. It all seems to be a never-ending circle of events.

England's economy in the early seventeenth century was struggling. Ports on the west coast saw their commercial markets in France and Spain disappear due to military conflicts and were relying on being used as ports for staging the Royal fleet for attacks on enemy shipping, or were being used to send out fleets to the fishing banks of North America. All other trade had dried up. The economy of both Barnstaple (Devon) and Bristol (Gloucester) were plummeting to the point they could not meet the royal demands for ships, men, and ordnance for its wars, nor even find the funds to repair docks and ports. Bristol at one time had rivaled London in commercial port activity, but by the late sixteenth century, the foreign trade had shifted to Eastern European countries and the Port of London. Even the Welsh and Midland's woolen trades had shifted from Bristol to London.

This sort of economy has a rolling effect. Oddly enough, birthrates go up because marriage age drops. I suspect parents needed to relocate their children as soon as they were old enough because they could not feed them. In Europe, food prices in the early seventeenth century were rising by as much as 15 percent a year. Because of crop failure, more people were moving to cities in hope of finding employment, and death by diseases was on the increase. Plagues and other illnesses were taking as much as one-third of the population in a single year.

When basic needs are not being met, people become despondent, and the first thing that comes to mind is "flight"—"get away from this . . . turn our backs on this and start over. However, after the Great Migration of 1630–1640, immigration would be shut down by a king who suddenly realized he was losing his tax base. After 1640, for the most part, English subjects were going to remain in England.

Today we do not have the choices that seventeenth-century England had. There will be no new Great Migration, and there are no new continents on planet earth to discover.

Was not getting that letter of marque and reprisal a mitigating factor for leaving England? No. It would just have made leaving a little easier. If he had taken a French ship under a Letter he could have lined his pocket book. That was all that was about.

Applying for that letter of marque was another indicator of how well he planned his life and then stuck to the plan. He always seemed to have a back-up to everything he attempted so not getting that letter was not the end blow, just another corner to be turned and a new route to be followed.

Having lost his parents and his first wife, and with an aging grandfather, Thomas Wiggin was seeking a breath of fresh air, as the saying goes. With a little money in his pockets and nothing to keep him from leaving England, he was the perfect immigrant. Once he planted his feet on New England soil he wasn't likely to leave when a little adversity came his way.

WHY NOT SACO OR CASCO

Captain Thomas Wiggin was at both Saco and Casco on his initial trip to New England in 1629/30. I was curious why he was there but wouldn't have my answers for years. Even so, I began my investigation into everyone who could have been there.

Finally, when I found the names of the Bristol Merchant Venturers, I knew he was acting for the Wright brothers.

SACO

The Biddeford/Saco Patent was granted to Vines and Oldham on 1 February 1630, and formal possession was taken by Vines—before nine witnesses (including Thomas Wiggin)—on 23 June 1630. A copy of this patent can be found in the Avalon Project.[516]

It is said[517] that Thomas Wiggin arrived on the Maine coast in 1630 on board the sailing ship *Swift of Bristol* in the company of settlers for the two Maine colonies of Saco and Casco.[518] On board are two more military captains seeking not only land they can have title to, but compensation for service rendered to the Crown of England in its many conflicts with the Palatine (now Germany) and war with both France and Spain. These military men had not been paid in at least three years and were being offered land grants and patents by absentee proprietors. However, keep in mind he could also have arrived on his own ship. Since there are no passenger manifests for these early ships into New England, we can only draw a likely scenario.

All these captains would become leaders in their chosen settlements and lifelong friends of Captain Thomas Wiggin.

---

516 Yale Law School, Lillian Goldman Law Library, 127 Wall Street, New Haven, CT 00511; accessible online.

517 There is no proof of this, and it is my own belief he came in his own ship.

518 An unprovable statement; no records. Also consider he had his own ship that he grounded on a sandbar off the coast of Massachusetts in 1631. See chapter "Sea Business."

The settlers who came to Saco with Vines in 1630 appear to have been the following:

- Ambrose Berry
- Henry Boade
- George Cleave
- John Cousins
- Theophilus Davis
- George Frost
- Thomas Purchase
- John Parker
- William Scadlock
- John Wadley

Some of these were assigned lots of 100 acres each on the western bank of the river above Biddeford Pool, and others settled subserviently in Casco Bay. Two removed, seven years later, to Cape Porpoise.[519]

- Berry, Ambrose: In 1636, he's shown as a "planter" at Saco; married Ann Bully in 1654. Ambrose died in 1661. Issue: Ambrose Junior of Boston in 1686, who married Hannah Chase.
- Boade, Henry: Henry was a cousin of John Winthrop, Puritan leader in Massachusetts. A "planter" at Saco in 1636, he moved to Kennebunk by 1637 and died in 1657. Henry was not in sympathy with the Puritans and was a follower of Reverend Wheelwright.
- Bonython, Richard, Captain: Baptized at St. Columb Minor, Cornwall, 3 April 1580. Son of John Bonython (Richard>Ralph) and Eleanor Myllayton of Pengerswick Castle, heir to William Myllayton. Richard Bonython's sister, Elizabeth, married Henry Pomeroy, the mayor of Tregony, 15 April 1600. Captain Bonython's widow, "Ann," died 1650 in Saco, Maine. Son John died about 1684. Daughter Susannah married Richard Foxwell, and Elizabeth Bonython married Richard Cumming.

While researching flagons and voiders for Captain Thomas Wiggin's will, I came across a flagon that belonged to the Bonython family. It's inscribed with the date *1598*, brown stoneware, with three military medallions and probably of Dutch origin. It was used at a 1598 banquet officiated by a Bonython to

[519] Source: *Pioneers on Maine Rivers*; pp. 165–190; Saco River.

celebrate the coronation of James I and 6th of England/Scotland.[520] In the late 1800s, it was owned by Langdon Bonithon of Australia.[521]

- Pomeroy's Cove, Hilton's Point, NH:
  The manor of Tregony was very extensive, and the ancient family of the Pomeroys acquired it by the marriage of Joel, son of Ralph de Pomeroy, to an illegitimate daughter of Henry I, sister of Reginald, Earl of Cornwall.

  Contents: Marriage settlement[522]
  Thomas Pomeroy of Berry Pomeroy, Esq.

  Covenants: Hugh Pomeroy, brother of Thomas, is to marry Johan Borman, one of the daughters of Nicholas Bormann, Esq., and niece of Sir John Russell[523] and Thomas Pomeroy is to grant to Hugh and Johan his manor of Stockleigh Pomeroy, to be held by them and the heirs male of Hugh, also the manor of Tregony in Cornwall to be held by Hugh and his heirs male after the death of Thomas Pomeroy, who is also to grant to Hugh and Johan an annuity of £4. If Thomas Pomeroy dies without heirs—male of his body—then all his manors and lands are to remain to Hugh and his heirs—male of the body and for default of heirs, to William Pomeroy, another brother of Thomas Pomeroy.
  Sir John Russell has paid £100 and is to pay £50 on Hugh and Johan's wedding day and a further £50 at the following Michaelmas.

Richard's brother, Reskymer, was heir to the family's estates and Sheriff of Cornwall in 1619. Brother John was Captain of Pendennis Castle; his brother Hannibal was Captain of St. Mawes Castle; Sister Elizabeth married Henry Pomeroy (in 1600), mayor of Tregony, Cornwall; and he had two more brothers,

---

520 King James VI was King of Scotland from 24 July 1567 and known as King James I, King of England and Ireland, when the union of the Scottish and English crowns commenced on 24 March 1603.

521 The flagon was displayed in The Western Antiquary of Devon and Cornwall; Vol. 1; March 1881 to March 1882; pub. Latimer & Son, 1882.

522 3799M-0/T/11/2 1539 documents are held at Devon Record Office

523 Sir John Russell, 3rd Baronet Russell, was involved with the Hiltons and Pomeroy in settling on the Piscataqua. It is thought this Sir Russell named Stratham, NH. Russell died on 24 March 1672. He married Frances Cromwell, daughter of Oliver Cromwell and Elizabeth Boucier, on 7 May 1663 and had one daughter, Elizabeth.

Edmond and William, and another sister named Anne, who married Walter Rosenrock.

Staunch Church of England (Churchman) supporter; closely associated with Dr. Vines and Sir Ferdinando Gorges; an original patentee of Saco in 1631.

Richard married Lucretia Leigh with a son, John, born about 1648 (married Susanna Foxwell[524]) and daughter Elizabeth (married Richard Cumming[525]). Richard Bonython died 1653, in Saco, Maine.

NATIONAL ARCHIVES, KEW, ENGLAND, DOMESTIC PAPERS; JAMES I, 1603–1610:

1) Dated 20 August 1603: Grant to Richard Bonithon on surrender by his father of the Comptrollership of the Stannaries in Cornwall, and Keepership of the Goal of Lostwithiel.
2) Dated 27 February 1604: Grant to Richard Bonithon of the Comptrollership of the Coinage of the Stannary in Cornwall and Devon.
3) Dated 25 January 1605: Grant to Nicholas Fortescue and Michael Vivian of sixty pounds of the goods, &c, of John Bonithon, deceased, forfeit by outlawry.

Sources:

1) The Western Antiquary, V. 1; by W. H. Kearley Wright; pub Latimer & Sons, 1882;
2) Western Antiquary, Supplement; Devon and Cornwall Notebook, V. 1, 1882, pg. 201;
3) For a true and reliable source on the Pomeroys, see the work of Charles Arthur Hoppin, London, 1915, who refutes the work of the NEHGS articles on this family.

- Cleeve, George: "The founder of Portland"; Arrived in 1630 and became a planter at Spurwink from 1631–34; Casco in 1633–34; married to Joan who died in 1666 and his only child was Elizabeth (married a Mitten). George is much in early Maine records in regards to court cases. See George Cleeve of Casco Bay: 1630–1667, with

[524] Foxwell, Richard: Was in Saco by 1633–34; Died 1677; Married Susanna Bonython, daughter of Richard.

[525] Richard Cumming was the young man who missed jury duty because he was assisting "Worshipful Governor Wiggin to the ordinary."

collateral documents; by James P. Baxter, pub 1885; online at Google Books.

- Cousins, John: Born about 1596. He made two affidavits, the last one in 1683 at age 87, stating he had been living 56 years at Saco (two years; 1630–32) and Casco (1634), making his original arrival in 1627. He was one of two settlers to remain in Saco in 1628 when all but one other left and went back to England. Employee of Brown and Mackworth. Removed to Cousin's Island in 1639; died 1685.
- Davis, Theophilus: Planter by profession; not a lot is known of him. He was constable by 1636.
- Duncan, Joseph: Joseph Duncan would eventually become a servant of Captain Thomas Wiggin and would drown in 1648.
- Frost, George: Resident of Winter Harbor, Saco.
- Gee, Ralph: In New Hampshire by 1623. Probably part of the Levett settlement. There appears to be four branches of this surname in Early American Colonies from New Hampshire to Virginia.
- Gibbons, William: 1623. Agent of Levett, who was reported by his principal to have been resident in New England in 1627. He also appears to have been the brother of Edward Gibbons of Boston, whose administrators subsequently disposed of the Saco estate.
- Lewis, Thomas, Gentleman: Lewis was born about 1590 in Shrewsbury, Shropshire. He is first known of in New England in 1628 at Little Harbor, Pannaway, Piscataqua River.
- Oldham, John, Captain: Ejected from the Pilgrim colony of Plymouth in 1625. Oldham was a very successful Indian trader. Oldham's temper probably got the best of him when a group of Penobscot Indians murdered him in 1636. Captain John Oldham; born 1592 in Derbyshire, died 1636 at the hands of the Pequot Indians, starting the Pequot War of 1636–37. He was Puritan, captain, merchant, and Indian trader living in Massachusetts by 1623; on the third boat of the Pilgrims with his wife, Lucretia, and daughter, Lucretia.
- Parker, John: 1629–30, on Erascohegan Island (Parker's Island) in the mouth of the Sagadahock River; purchased it from a native in 1643. He died before the first Indian war, and his descendants held the lands for generations.
- Purchase, Thomas, an original settler of Saco, Maine, of 1626; removed to Casco in 1628.

- Reekes, Stephen, Master of the *Swift*: From Poole; his ship was taken as an English prize on its return trip to the Azores as it was flying the Spanish flag in an attempt to avoid pirates.
- Robinson, Francis: Unknown.
- Scadlock, William: Not a lot is known about William, but he raised a family of three sons (Samuel, John, and William) and two daughters (Rebecca and Susannah).
- Southcoate, Thomas, Captain: "List of freemen of Mass. 1630–1691" by Lucius Paige, and it states: Boston, 19 October 1630: list of those desired to be made freemen: Mr. Thomas Southcoate. Captain Southcoate had a military career in the Palatine and arrived in Massachusetts in 1629. He led an exploration up the Charles River in search of a sight for the colony of Dorchester. He may well have been an associate of Captain Richard Bonython.
- Tucker, Richard: Richard probably came over with Vines on his first voyage in 1607 and was found in the Bay area before 1630.
- Vines, Richard, Doctor: In 1607, Vines—with his fourteen-year-old apothecary apprentice, David Thomson—sailed on the *Mary and John*, a ship owned by Sir John Popham[526] and Sir Ferdinando Gorges, to erect a fort called St. Gorges on the Kennebec River, Maine. There were a total of 100 passengers on two boats, the second being a fishing vessel, including some native Indians previously captured by Captain George Weymouth.[527] This settlement became known as the "Popham Settlement" and would fail. Lewis and Thomson returned to England in the spring of 1608.

1. On the Saco again by 1618 as a servant of Sir Ferdinando Gorges.
2. Was with the Indians during their plague years of 1617–1619.

---

[526] Sir John Popham: b. 1531; d. 10 June 1607; m. Amy Games and had seven children. He was imprisoned in the Tower of London but rescued by Sir Ferdinando Gorges and rowed to safety. Speaker of the House of Commons and attorney-general. Succeeded Sir Christopher Wray as Chief Justice of the Queen's Bench.

[527] Captain George Weymouth: Sir Ferdinando Gorges sent Weymouth to Maine in 1605 with a group of settlers. Landing at Monhegan, one of the passengers wrote: "woody, growen with Firre, Birch, Oke and Beech, as farre as we say along the shore; and so likely to be within. On the verge grow Gooseberries, Strawberries, Wild pease, and Wilde rose bushes."
"Rosier's Relation of George Weymouth's 1605 Voyage,' in Ronald F. Banks, Ed., 1969, A History of Maine: A Collection of Readings on the History of Maine 1600–1974, Third Edition, scanned online by Davistown Museum, accessed 20 Oct 2009; *Wikipedia*.

3. Spring of 1620 returned to England; back in Saco again by 1626.
4. Occupation in Maine: Tavern keeper.

- Wadley, John: Sullivan's *History of the District of Maine* lists John Wadley as an original settler of Maine. Governor James Sullivan, author, published 1795.
- Warwick, Henry: Died about 1672. Not often in the early records of Maine; raised a family with a son named John Warwick. His widow is found living with a daughter in Massachusetts by 1690.
- Waters, Nathaniel, Captain: Master of the *Return* with a letter of marque and reprisal; of Millbrook, Hampshire, England. Fished and traded on the New England coast since 1627; instrumental in securing fisherman from the Millbrook area for John Winter of Richmond's Island. He was known on the coast up to 1647. Waters, a witness to the *Vines and Oldham 1630 Patent* with Wiggin, and the *Return* could have been sailing with the *Swift*.
- Wright, John, Captain: Had applied for a *letter of marque and reprisal in 1629 (Calendar of State Papers Domestic, Charles I)*. Brother of Thomas Wright, merchant living in Bristol, England, who owned the *Swift*. The two brothers were called the "Merchant Venturers of Bristol."

Men in Maine in 1630 included:

- Allerton, Isaac: Born 1586 and died 1658; was elected as Governor Bradford's assistant in 1621–1630. He was in England 1627, negotiating a buyout of the Plymouth Colony's debts; he betrayed them, and the Pilgrims found themselves in greater debt. He removed to New Haven Colony in 1634. In 1630, he was on his way back to Plymouth and then appears in Virginia for a short while.
- Bradshaw, Richard, Captain: Evidence of his early arrival at Saco comes in the grant of 1,500 acres in 1631, which states he had been there for several years prior.
- Garland, Peter: One of two settlers in Saco who stayed when nearly all the rest left in 1628.
- Levett, Christopher: In 1624, Christopher Levett discovered two rivers at Saco, which he believed had never been seen by any Englishman. He was not at Saco when Wiggin arrived, but was at Boston, Massachusetts, when Winthrop arrived in July 1630. He died at sea the same year on his way back to England. Levett was instrumental in starting the colony

at Casco. He sold his interests in Casco to Thomas Wright, Merchant of Bristol.

- Mills, John: A witness of illicit trade between one of Thomas Wright's agents and the natives, which took place before 1630.
- Mackworth, Arthur: Supposedly he came with Richard Vines in 1630, but he shows up at Presumpscot with Cleave and Tucker and gets a grant there by Vines, on behalf of Gorges; and by 1635, had erected a house there. Married and raised a large family; he died in 1657. He left his entire estate to his wife, Jane Andrews (widow of Samuel Andrews, citizen of London), a most unusual act. Jane died in 1676 in Boston, where she had gone to escape the Indian Wars.

Wiggin was in the employ of the following Bristol Merchant Ventures in 1629/30 to 1632:

A conglomerate of merchants based in Bristol, Gloucestershire, England: Seventeenth-century Bristol was motivated by high profit margins, with little to no labor output. Bypassing Spain and Portugal and finding a trading route to the spice-rich Orient was of primary importance. That elusive Northwest Passage was more of a goal for Bristol than colonizing New England. Their last voyage into the Arctic Ocean seeking the elusive route was in 1632. They wanted to tie up the headwaters of the Piscataqua River via Great Bay and Little Bay patents . . . especially the north to southwest side, where the rivers entered the bays. Bristol believed (as did Mason, who was tying up the mouth of the Piscataqua River with grants, patents, and towns) Piscataqua would lead them to the Great Lakes region.

The Bristol Merchant Venturers was a stock-owned company, just like they did everything. By owning stock in each ship (they chose to be), a merchant was cutting his losses and further guaranteeing an income. Their attempts at settlements in Maine and New Hampshire were undertaken in the same manner. However, there were two men who seemed to be the head/principal owners of the ventures, and they were the brothers Wright:

- Wright, Thomas: holder of a patent on the Piscataqua; Bristol merchant with ships holding letters of marque and reprisal.
- Thomas Wright sent his brother, Captain John Wright, to Maine in 1630 to govern Casco, and he lived on Monhegan Island off the coast of Maine. Captain Wiggin was closely aligned with these two brothers.

THE PATENTS:

- Grant of Land (North)* of the Saco River to Thomas Lewis and Richard Bonython by the Council for New England; February 12, 1629; by R. Warwick and Edward Gorges; Possession and Livery on 28 June 1631 in presence of Edward Hilton, Thomas Wiggin, James Parker, Henry Watts, George Vaughan. Their first colony came from Bristol on the *White Angel* in 1631.
- The Vine's patent was on the western side of the Saco, opposite the Lewis and Bonython patent, and carried the same dates, February 22, 1629–30 (Source: Collections of the MA Historical Soc., V 7, pg. 340) but was delivered on the 25 of June 1630 by Thomas Wiggin in Saco. Lewis and Bonython didn't get delivery of their patent for another year even though it carried the same date.

THE TOPOGRAPHY:

- Far off to the north, yet visible by ships approaching Saco, is *The Crystal Hill.* The mountain was sacred to the Abenaki Indians, who never climbed it. *Mount Washington,* as it is known today, is capped by snow almost year round and climbs 6,288 feet toward the sky; the fastest sustained winds on the face of the earth was recorded on this summit. It is the source of the Saco River. Darby Fields would be the first man of European descent to scale the mountain in 1642.
- Saco River is not navigable by large sailing ships. Its entrance is difficult to navigate and strewn with rocks and outcroppings of land and islands.
- Monhegan Island: Twelve nautical miles out to sea from the mainland. It was visited by

  1603: Martin Ping
  1604: Samuel de Champlain
  1605: George Weymouth
  1614: Captain John Smith
  1630: Merchant Ventures of Bristol

  Monhegan was used for decades by seasonal English fishermen.

Casco

Casco Bay was an area long known to seasonal fishermen. They traded with the natives in the Bay area for decades before Christopher Levett[528] arrived on "House Island." Born in York City, York, England, and christened on 5 April 1586, Levett would die on board ship in 1630 returning to England. Levett was the pioneer settler of Casco Bay.

In the British Museum, London, there is a book Levett wrote titled *An Abstract of Timber Measures*, printed by William Jones 1618. It is a pioneering work and an astonishing insight into the desires of English merchants for timber for all purposes. Levett lays out a convincing argument for the merchants to become actively involved in settling New England.

> *A Toone of Timber doth containe 40 square foot. In a foot square is 1,728 Inches. In three quarters of a foot is 1,296 Inches. In halfe a foot is 0864 Inches. In a quarter of a foot is 432 Inches.*

On 5 May 1623, the Council for New England granted Levett 6,000 acres of land with only one restriction: *it had to be within the limits of the Council's jurisdiction.* He chose Casco Bay.

Without men like Levett, Wiggin may never have ventured into New England in the first place. Such men wrote descriptive and alluring portraits of the New England wilderness.

The first pioneers into New England secured for themselves the prime locations in land and commerce. Those who followed were to become servants of the pioneering settlers like Captain Thomas Wiggin.

Captain Wiggin was clearly displaying the desire to own his own land, free and clear, and he steadily worked toward that end.

---

528 Levett's story is contained in a work titled *Christopher Levett, of York: The Pioneer Colonist in Casco Bay* by James Phinney Baxter, printed for the Gorges Society in 1893.

1. Thomas Alger: Thomas was on House Island in Casco Bay from 1624, a part of Christopher Levett's original ten settlers. With him was *Andrew Alger*, probably a brother.
2. Captain John Wright: Admitted to the freedom as a merchant 5 December 1642; sheriff 1662–1663. On 4 December 1627, Wright was given space to build a key (wharf) over against the Launcellott Hudson's House to make a building there serviceable for the building of ships. He was to employ six able shipwrights to work there. Another six were to be employed in the repair of ships brought in. *Thomas Wright*, his brother, was treasurer of the Merchant Venturers from 1619–1620; master from 1628–29.
3. Penobscot Natives: The Penawapskewi/Penobscot Native Americans of Maine are part of a confederacy with the Abenaki, Passamaquoddy, Maliseet, and Mi'kmaq nations. A First Nation Band of the Maritime Provinces of Canada.
4. Wolves and Coyote: In 1991, as Robby and I were driving across the Kancamaugus Highway near Conway, New Hampshire, what appeared to be a large German shepherd type of dog was loping down the highway in front of us. He seemed intent on tracking something, with his nose close to the highway. Suddenly, he sensed us trailing him and swung his head around, and I gasped with recognition. "That's not a dog, that's a coyote. Look at that head. How did the coyotes get so big here?" I'd only seen the smaller versions in the Southwestern United States. This animal was as big as a wolf. When we arrived at Cousin Brian Wiggin's[529] house in Center Conway, I told him about our road companion, and he was alarmed it was so close to a popular camping site. Brian said he was going to report the animal to the proper authorities because they were so dangerous. So, even today, the coyote is a feared and respected animal. Brian said they have crossed with the wolf, which accounts for their size.
5. English Dogs: I was involved in the dog world of breeding, training, showing, and judging for fifty years in both the United States and England. The English are world-renowned for their love of dogs and, for centuries, have bred them for specific work requirements. Well-documented in early records are the dogs on board ships to New England. The natives had a healthy respect for large breeds such as Great Danes and mastiffs. The natives were less likely to sneak on board ship during the night with the intent to do mischief if large dogs were on board.

---

529 Brian Wiggin of Center Conway, NH is a cousin, son of my father's brother

ROCKY SHORES[530]

[530] Photos by Joyce Elaine Wiggin-Robbins

PISCATAQUA PATENTS[531]

1. Laconia Company Patent: 27 November 1629, by patent of Plymouth Council to Sir Ferdinando Gorges and Captain John Mason, granted, including "lands lying and bordering upon the great lakes and rivers of the Iroquois and other nations adjoining."
2. The Hilton Patent: When in 1630 Edward Hilton obtained a patent from the Council of Plymouth of the land upon which he had settled he had been for some considerable time established thereon, so long that it had come to bear his name . . . "all that part of the river Piscataqua called or known by the name of Hilton's Point . . ." Livery &seisin[532] on 7 July 1631 to Edward Hilton: witness: Thomas Wiggin
3. Grant and Confirmation of Piscataway to Sr. Ferdinando Gorges and Captain Mason, John Cotton, Henry Gardner, George Griffith, Edwin Guy, Thomas Wannerton, Thomas and Eliza Eyer, 3 November 1631.

PISCATAQUA TIMELINE

Under the 1628 Charter of the Massachusetts Bay Colony, it had jurisdiction over the lands around Great Bay and the Piscataqua River. This was acknowledged by Captain Wiggin. In a letter dated 22 October 1631, Wiggin wrote Governor Winthrop of the murder of Walter Bagnall on Richmond's Isle by a native named Great Wat. By asking for Winthrop's assistance, Wiggin is acknowledging the authority of the MBC under their charter. This charter predates any other, and no land grants had yet been made about Great Bay.

This is where a timeline of events starts to get complicated, and it depends on which historian you place your trust in that will dictate what you believe in. William Hubbard says in 1632, Captain Wiggin and Captain Neale nearly came to sword points over jurisdiction of a piece of land now called Bloody Point. John S. Jenness says the encounter was in 1631, before any patents had been issued, and that Wiggin was acting under the 1628 MBC charter's jurisdiction. Jenness also states he believes Wiggin was a plant by Winthrop on the Piscataqua to watch out for the Puritans' best interests. Captain Wiggin's actions from 1632 to his death were always in the Puritan interest, but calling him a plant may be stretching the facts. He wasn't in Winthrop's employ, but the Bristol Merchant Venturers. His interests were not in Massachusetts, but on the upper Piscataqua River and bays. He wasn't looking toward the Puritans

---

531 The Avalon Project is an excellent search engine to find all early land transactions; Avalon Law at Yale Education.

532 Livery & seisin is a legal term for a ceremony of conveyance practiced in English common law. Specifically the conveyance of property.

for any sort of comfort and protection until he read their charter in 1630–31. At that point, he was quick thinking enough to decide posthaste to make good use of what the Puritans could provide him.

If Wiggin was a staunch Puritan, why did he get entangled with the Royalists in the very beginning? Men like Mason, Edward Hilton, and the Strawberry Bank and Laconia Company groups, along with the men at Casco Bay and Saco were all Royalists, and Wiggin was wading with ease through them all.

The Bristol Merchants had two very powerful men on the Maine coast, men Wiggin surely was acquainted with:

> In 1626 Robert Aldworth,[533] who had previously invested in Martin Pring's[534] 1602–03 and 1606 explorations of the New England coast and in the Newfoundland Company of 1610, bought Monhegan Island[535] from Captain Abraham Jennings[536] of Plymouth, another Newfoundland Company investor. In 1630–1631, Aldworth and his son-in-law Giles Elbridge acquired 12,000 acres on the Pemaquid Peninsula.[537] Thus, for Aldworth, perhaps the greatest Iberian and Mediterranean trader of his day, the hope for gain was much the same as it had been in Newfoundland.[538]

The Bristol Merchants are credited with sending Edward and William Hilton[539] to the Piscataqua, and the historian William Hubbard says they arrived in 1623 with David Thomson; however, it's a bit of a mix-up, to say the least. The Merchants may well have sent William Hilton to Piscataqua about 1625, but he arrived in Plymouth, Massachusetts, in 1623 on a relief mission to the Pilgrims. Also, at least one Hilton historian declares the Hiltons were

---

533 Aldworth and his son-in-law Elbridge were merchants of Bristol, but they seem to have been acting on their own behalf in their Maine adventures. Aldworth also owned several ships with Letters of Marque.

534 Pring (1580–1626) was an English explorer from Bristol, England.

535 Located off the Maine coast.

536 (200) ton ship, "Abraham" with Captain Abraham Jennings.

537 A point of land up the coastline from Portland, Maine.

538 Burrage, *Beginnings of Colonial Maine*, pp. 26, 142, 143, 143n, 180n, 271019. *The Widening Gate*, p. 50.

539 In 1621, William Hilton, a descendant of the Hiltons of Hylton Castle, from North Biddick Hall in the "original" Washington, England, sailed on the *Fortune* to rescue the Pilgrims at Plymouth. He stayed in America and became the founding father of what is today New Hampshire. His cousin Edward became one of the founding fathers of what is today the state of Maine. Source: http://www.ancestryuk.com/Helton-Hylton-Hilton.htm.

cousins, not brothers. Edward, the youngest, was admitted to the Fishmongers' Guild (London) in 1623, and William in 1616.

Another Royalist was Thomas Lake. He resided at Casco in a house often called "the house at Casco." Lake and Wiggin were good friends and held deeds together. Captain Richard Bonython and Captain Thomas Wiggin had a long history together, which I have covered in another chapter.

What I am getting at with all this is the "proof is in the pudding" and showing that Captain Thomas Wiggin was not a Puritan prior to his arrival on the Piscataqua. Nor did he become one—at least not for religious fulfillment. His association with the Puritans of Massachusetts was one of pure intentions regarding safety, in the beginning, and economics. It evolved into even more and came to encompass his leanings toward an orderly society under rules and regulations. If he was "staunch" about anything, it was his belief in law and order. He had no intention of allowing his newfound home to be overrun with disorderly people. He would eventually become a part of that system of law and order, and it was probably in that role he found his greatest satisfaction.

The Piscataqua River

Loving Cousin,
At our arrival at New Plymouth, in New England, we found all our friends and planters in good health, though they were left sick and weak, with very small means; the Indians round about us peaceable and friendly; the country very pleasant and temperate, yielding naturally, of itself, great store of fruits, as vines of divers sorts, in great abundance. There is likewise walnuts, chestnuts, small nuts and plums, with much variety of flowers, roots and herbs, no less pleasant than wholesome and profitable. No place hath more gooseberries and strawberries, nor better. Timber of all sorts you have in England doth cover the land, that affords beasts of divers sorts, and great flocks of turkeys, quails, pigeons and partridges; many great lakes abounding with fish, fowl, beavers, and otters. The sea affords us great plenty of all excellent sorts of sea-fish, as the rivers and isles doth variety of wild fowl of most useful sorts. Mines we find, to our thinking; but neither the goodness nor quality we know. Better grain cannot be than the Indian corn, if we will plant it upon as good ground as a man need desire. We are all freeholders; the rent-day doth not trouble us; and all those good blessings we have, of which and what we list in their seasons for taking. Our company are, for the most part, very religious, honest people; the word of God sincerely taught us ever Sabbath; so that I know not any thing a contented mind can here want. I desire your friendly care to send my wife and children to me, where I wish all the friends I have in England; and so I rest.
Your loving kinsman,
William Hilton (1621)[540]

[540] William Hilton arrived at New Plymouth, New England, on 9 Nov. 1621 on board the *Fortune*; From London; brother was Arthur of Northwich in 1612; fishmonger in London originally from Northwich, Counter Chester. Wife arrived with two children about 10 July 1623 and still in Plymouth in 1624. Printed in Captain John Smith, Works 1608-1631, Part 1, edited by Edward Arber, University of London, Westminster Archibald Constable and Co. 1895.

It would be letters like the above that would draw settlers to the Hilton Plantation by the later 1620s. Letters, books, and reports expounding the virtues of this wilderness were coming to the forefront of all the adverse publications previous to 1630. It was thought at that time that the Piscataqua River had its headwaters in the Great Lakes.

PHYSICAL DESCRIPTION: The Piscataqua River has the planet's third fastest current, with a rise and fall of six to eight feet with the tides. Sections of the river produce strong, swirling, and ever changing patterns of water flow, requiring skilled navigation. The channel opening from the Atlantic is wide and deep, but with rocky shores. Once past the island that guards the entrance of the Piscataqua, called Great Island, a masted ship reaches "the pool,"[541] an area of still, deep, safe harbor. It's a normal sight to see six or more masted ships anchored at the pool in the early 1600s. Fog is rare on this river that stretches sixteen miles northward to Salmon Falls. Sailing straight toward the Piscataqua from the Isle of Shoals, which lies eight miles out to sea, the river is well disguised by Great Island, which is located at its mouth, obscuring the large river behind it. Great Island is the reason the river wasn't documented by Englishmen until 1603. Seasonal fishermen may well have known of its existence for over two hundred years.

Charles H. Bell, the historian of Exeter, New Hampshire, described the River thus: " . . . represented as a man's left hand and wrist laid upon the table, back upwards and fingers wide apart. The thumb would stand for Oyster River, the third finger for Lamprey River, and the fourth finger for Exeter or Squamscott River; while the palm of the hand would represent Great Bay, into which most of the streams pour their waters, and the wrist the Piscataqua (sic) River."

Like the river, Great Bay contained about every kind of fish we could name. The Piscataqua abounded with seals, Canadian geese, fish, and other delectables. Early fishermen would string a net across narrow portions of the river and haul in salmon and process it for shipment back to England.

MARTIN PRING:[542] Early Explorer of the Piscataqua River

Martin Pring's 1603 voyage was sufficient for England to take note of the strategic and economic advantage of having control of the Piscataqua. Even

[541] Jeremy Belknap; History of New-Hampshire, III, pg. 198.

[542] Martin Pring, 1580–1626, from Bristol, England, at age 23 made expedition to North America to assess it for commercial potential. He explored what is now Maine, New Hampshire, and the Cape Cod area of Massachusetts. He was the first known European to sail up the Piscataqua River, New Hampshire.

so, it would take about a decade before activity on the river would begin to sharply rise.

Martin Pring of Bristol, on the ship *Speedwell,* accompanied by William Brown on *Discoverer,* spent some time exploring the river for at least eight miles northward.

Pring chose two huge mastiff dogs to go with them, as the natives were said to be more frightened of these dogs than of twenty men.[543] While they did not encounter Indians on this trip (it was summer and they were probably higher up the river, fishing) they saw signs of them on the river's banks and reported seeing, deer, bear, wolves, fox, and "doggies," which were probably coyotes as Pring says they "had pointed noses."[544]

Pring emphasizes the vast resources of the river, including a huge variety of birds and fish, and tall pines for ship masts. Ship masts are as important to the English Crown as cod and salmon. He was hoping to find sassafras trees, which were used in a variety of medicines.

There were more explorers who stumbled onto the river while looking for the Northwest Passage—and of course, fishermen. So there was no lack of literature on the river by the time Captain Wiggin went exploring.

THE HILTONS

I have covered the Hiltons elsewhere, so I won't reiterate more than is necessary.

In 1621, a man named William Hilton arrives in Plymouth Colony on a relief mission, bringing them food and supplies. He decides to stay and, two years later, brings his family to Massachusetts. The Hilton family moves to Pannaway,[545] a colony located at the mouth of the Piscataqua, following a man named David Thomson,[546] who founded the colony. David, a Scot by birth, is an agent and is supposed to remain at Pannaway for seven years. After five years, the settlers are to have title to the land they inhabit.[547] However, David leaves after two years and settles on an island[548] southward, where he dies two years later. His vacancy of the Pannaway settlement leaves it without leadership.

---

[543] *Ports of Piscataqua,* by William G. Saltonstall, 1941 by the President and Fellows of Harvard College; Harvard Press, pp. 8–9.

[544] Pring's ship was 50 tons, and Brown's only 20. They were backed by citizen merchants of West England.

[545] Pannaway was located at what is now Odiorne's Point on Little Harbor.

[546] David Thomson was the first white man to settle in New Hampshire, in 1621. He was born in Scotland, but was an agent for Captain John Mason.

[547] Colony, Province, State, 1623–1888: *History of New Hampshire;* John N. McClintock; pub 1889, B. B. Russell, Boston; pg. 29.

[548] Still called Thomson's Island.

1628

William Hilton[549] is successful in luring his brother/cousin,[550] Edward Hilton, to Pannaway. Together, with their families, they are determined to make a settlement on the Piscataqua. By 1628, they move eight miles northward, up the Piscataqua, to a point of land they name Hilton's Point.[551] In 1654, the General Court of Massachusetts Bay heard testimony from John Allen, Nicholas Shapleigh and Thomas Lake that Edward Hilton was possessed of the land about the year 1628.[552] This is also the year an assessment against Edward Hilton was levied for one pound as his share of passage to England for a person found guilty of selling arms to the natives. So if he was at the Point before 1628, there is no record of it. 1628 is also the year Hilton applied for, and was granted, his patent. It was also at this time that Hilton would have felt the pinch of new arrivals as the Laconia Company had sent over sixty settlers. Hilton would have wanted to secure his chosen property. His patent was granted in 1628 but didn't fall into his hands until 1631.

The Hiltons' combined skills of boat making, salt panning, fishing, and farming—as well as trading with the natives—stood them well.[553]

---

549 William Hilton was born about 1591, the son of William Hilton of Northwich, Cheshire; sailed to Plymouth Colony in 1621; had child bapt. there in 1624; died between June 28, 1655, and June 30, 1656, in Maine. Source: NEHGS; Robert c. Anderson, author. Data verified by an account of Captain John Smith, explorer. In 1621, *William Hilton*, a descendant of the Hiltons of Hylton Castle, from North Biddick Hall in the "Original" Washington, England, sailed on the *Fortune* to rescue the Pilgrims at Plymouth. Source: http://www.ancestryuk.com/Helton-Hylton-Hilton.htm.

550 Some historians claim the Hiltons are cousins, and others say they are brothers. For our purposes, it makes little difference.

551 Scales's map shows Hilton Hall located on the Fore River on the SE tip of Hilton's Point.

552 Notes on the first Planting of New Hampshire, Vol. 25, John S. Jenness; New Hampshire (Colony) Probate Court, Albert S. Batchellor, editor of State Papers, Concord, NH 1895.

553 The Hilton family had long been a seafaring family, many of them earning a living from the sea or in the salt-making industry that thrived on this part of England's coastline in Elizabethan times North-east. Salt making was then a monopoly controlled by a man called Casper Seeler, and over 400 people were employed making salt by evaporating seawater in salt pans using the easily accessible coal in the region. Cod was caught out in the North Sea, landed along the Northumberland coast and at both South Shields on the River Tyne and at Sunderland on the River Wear, where the fish was salted then shipped for sale at the salted *fish market* at Billingsgate in London, where *Edward Hilton, William's cousin*, was a fish merchant and a member of the Fishmongers' Guild of London. There was also a thriving coal industry in this region where "coals from Newcastle" were shipped to London to heat the homes in the rapidly expanding capital city. Source: William Hilton, Founding Father of New Hampshire; http://www.ancestryuk.com/HiltonWilliamFoundingFatherUSA.htm.

THE LACONIA COMPANY

While the Hiltons were establishing ownership over the point of land that bears their name and land on both sides of the Piscataqua River leading into Little Bay and Great Bay, another group of men were making their stance on the Maine side of the river. While the Hiltons were seeking to plant a colony from the beginning, the Laconia Company on the Maine side was seeking a connection to the Great Lakes of Canada and the fur trade. It was the belief at that time that the Piscataqua had its headwaters in the Great Lakes. After a few years of failure, the Laconia Company backers turned to the fishing and lumber trades.

BRISTOL MERCHANT VENTURERS

I have already covered this group extensively, so I will only write a paragraph or two here regarding them on the Piscataqua.

I sincerely doubt there was any way Captain Wiggin could have known of the coming Puritan influence over Great Bay and the Piscataqua when he set out to be the agent of the upper river for the Bristol Merchant Venturers. The BMV wanted to stop Mason's tying up the mouth of the river and stop his advancement into their interests in the upper river reaches. The BMV was all about profits, and they too wanted a way to get to the Great Lakes and bypass the French. Everyone, at that time, thought the river was the answer. The BMV sent a group of captains to New England, including Captain Bonython (who was a friend of Wiggin's) to Maine. The Wright brothers were the ramrods of the BMV when it came to exploring and establishing a settlement, but the rest of the merchants in the group had shares, as they always did in each other's ventures. It spread out the possibility of loss to work on shares. So when you read the BMV, think Wright brothers.

For those who aren't aware of it, the river has its origins at Mount Washington, New Hampshire.

Sails on Great Bay[554]

554 Photo by Perry Johnston of Stratham, NH, of a sailboat like the one Captain Thomas Wiggin would have used on Great Bay.

Captain Thomas Wiggin's Choices

The earliest map of Hilton's Point shows the Wiggin home (up to 1670) and is labeled "Thomas Wiggin and Thomas Wiggin Jr." So they maintained that home for a very long time. It would have been easier for Captain Wiggin to conduct his business from Hilton's Point than from his home on Great Bay, which was not navigable to large seagoing vessels. They could sail up to the Point without much trouble.

Captain Thomas Wiggin would feel right at home on a river that is so influenced by ocean tides and with a swift current. He was well versed on both the Thames and the Bristol Channel that are influenced by the tides. A ship navigated the Thames from its ocean outlet right to the Pool of London. The Bristol Channel from the sea to Bristol could be even trickier to navigate, where grounding a ship was all too common. The Piscataqua River of New England held the same traits.

The Piscataqua offered a natural defense against seagoing vessels with Great Island obstructing the view upriver from the ocean; it made an attack from the French in Canada and pirates more difficult. Once cannon were in place on the island, settlers upriver must have felt safer.

With tidal influences on Great Bay, which could nearly empty out during low tide, no one was going to sneak up on the Captain's family via water. Also, Quamscott House[555] offered him a direct view to the narrow passage from Great Bay into the Little Bay, and he would know if ships of any sort were coming. That was so important to him due to the lack of coastal patrols by England, whose ships were tied up with warfare against the French and Spanish at home. New England was not on the radar for the English navy.

With Great Isle and its cannon, and the blocking tidal influences on Great Bay, Wiggin had the perfect natural line of defenses in place.

---

555 His home was often called that.

Besides the natural defenses found in the character of this river, the fact that it did not freeze in the winter probably made Wiggin's business ventures a lot easier. He had seen the Thames frozen over in the winter, but this river's swift current would prevent freezing. Therefore, business never shut down due to weather.

Andrew's House [556]

556 Photo by Joyce ElaineWiggin-Robbins of Andrew's House painting owned by Florence Wiggin of Stratham, NH.

Squamscott House
The Farm

Since we are building the character of Captain Wiggin, we cannot neglect the character of the land he chose nor of the trappings of life that surrounded his family.

The shoreline of Great Bay, Little Bay, and the River Piscataqua can be very rocky and inhospitable. He did not choose them for that aspect; however, he did choose them for their safety aspects. He was building walls between himself and the outside world. He was making a home almost impenetrable by strangers and creating a safe haven for his family. Beyond that rocky shoreline and hidden behind a wall of trees were fields for planting and timber for milling. Both bays and river abound with fish for the taking, year round.

Seasoned boatmen that they were, Peter and Bruce Wiggin had to rock the boat free of the muddy bottom on our 2012 excursion on the river and the bays. Going upriver past the Wiggin farmland was very tricky, as the channel was noted for changing and was very narrow. Captain Wiggin would have been sailing a boat about the same size as Bruce's, and he would have encountered the same obstacles.

The land Captain Wiggin chose to farm is picturesque, even today. It is now owned and occupied by a dear lady named Florence Wiggin. Flo, as she is called, invited us into her home and so graciously showed us around. Captain Wiggin is thought to have died in this house, once owned by his son Andrew. Andrew's home is much as he left it, and Flo has taken great care to try and preserve what she can.

The Captain's house, called Squamscott House, is thought to have been on this same piece of land, close to Great Bay, but is long gone. A lot of archeological digging would need to take place if one were to try and find it—a very involved work to undertake and expensive.

Andrew's house is very typical in style akin to those found in England during the period: fireplaces in every room, wide board flooring, hand-carved staircase banisters, hand-carved moldings, stained glass windows, with a lot of small rooms.

The houses of the early Wiggin generations are still standing and occupied in Stratham. Artifacts dug up during the excavation of Thomas Junior's home at Sandy Point and the style of these homes tell us that even though Captain Wiggin chose to settle in the "howling wilderness," he still had a taste for the finer things in life. Silver buttons, china worthy of anyone's table, and so much more tell us Captain Wiggin and his sons had great pride in entertaining properly. How they dressed and what they ate off of mattered greatly. These were neither "wilderness" cabins nor primitive homesteads but very functional dwellings built to last these three-hundred-plus years. Yes, in the seventeenth century, men were judged in part by the houses they lived in.

The Captain was leaving England, a country that was struggling to feed its population. What people the plagues were not killing, starvation was. It mattered a great deal to him to choose a homestead that abounded with food for his family and that he could develop into a self-subsisting estate. He managed that with great style by choosing the land he did.

Taxes Paid: To show one's taxes had been paid, they were given this piece of ivory, which they inserted into the staircase banister.[557]

[557] Information from Florence Wiggin; photo by Joyce Elaine Wiggin-Robbins.

Natives[558]

[558] Native reenactor at Plymouth Colony; photo by Joyce Elaine Wiggin-Robbins.

Native Americans[559]

[559] Native reenactor at Plymouth Colony; photo by Joyce Elaine Wiggin-Robbins.

Native Americans on Great Bay and the Piscataqua River

There is every reason to believe that Captain Wiggin had wonderful relations with the natives of Great Bay. Even during times of great strife between the natives and the settlers of nearby Newfields and Dover, they never bothered the Wiggin clan of Stratham. The Captain had a trading relationship with them at Quamscott House and allowed them free access to the land below his property at Sandy Point. They came every summer to farm and fish that land. Even today, the "Indian cornfield" is evident.

From early on, relations between New England settlers and the Native Americans was strained, and the English built houses from Maine to Massachusetts to resemble forts as safe havens during attacks. There was one such house at Dover.

The fact that Captain Wiggin and his sons chose to build stylish homes on Great Bay and not this same fort type of structure speaks volumes of their trust in the native population and their relations with them.

Since Captain Wiggin's relationship with the natives of New England speaks more to his life after 1633 than before it, I will leave it to others to expound on. My purpose here is again to show Wiggin's character as reflected in the way he treated the natives he found on his new property on Great Bay. He acknowledged their rights to be there and did not rock the boat. Early historians believe he bought the rights to his lands from the natives, as was the custom of the day. He knew there was far more to be gained from contact with them than by alienating them through denial of their use of the land during the summer months, when they came to fish and farm.

Katherine Whiting

I am always telling genealogy buffs, "Don't overlook the wives." Men married "up" for many reasons (more wealth, more land, networking, and so forth) that came with a bride, and these were coveted incentives to marry someone you never knew. (Not that I'm insinuating Thomas Wiggin never knew Katherine.) It mattered little what the bride looked like—only what she could bring into the marriage. Her genes are just as important to the children of the union as his. One may also find the best genetic lines behind the bride, not the groom.

The fact that Katherine had not married until she was thirty-two certainly points to something lacking. No dowry could have been it, not very pretty maybe, illness in her youth—we can only guess. The one thing she did bring into the union was a solid tie to her brother and a lot of satisfied grins of the faces of the backers of both colonies.

I think when you know all there is possible to know about Captain Thomas Wiggin, you will see that Katherine Whiting Wiggin was a very strong and capable woman who would become his strongest ally. She probably also had a good dose of curiosity in her for embracing a move to the New England wilderness and confronting the native population.

The Captain was in the Boston area at least once a month. He also was making excursions up the coast of Maine and from the upper reaches of the Piscataqua River to the mouth of the river. As his responsibilities grew under the auspices of the Massachusetts Bay Colony, the demands on his time grew. He was also a very active agent for the backers of the Dover Patent.

Someone had to oversee the home, gardens, food-gathering, farm animals, and baby-raising. One guess on who was fulfilling that role! We often hear about the friendly relationship between the folks of Stratham area and the Native Americans. With her husband so often absent, Katherine was the one maintaining those close ties. It was she who would give medical aid, share food-storing and -raising techniques, and all those womanly things like knitting, sewing, quilting, and cooking with the women of the local tribe. Those are the things that build trust and admiration between the two cultures on the shores of Great Bay.

So apart from the Captain's trading activities with the natives, it was his wife, Katherine, who was building that strong bond—a bond that would prove valuable when the natives were attacking local settlements but never touching the folks of Stratham.

Native Hut[560]

560 Photo by Joyce Elaine Wiggin-Robbins.

The Fort Home[561]

561 Ibid: typical fort home built where Indians were a threat. Photo by Joyce Elaine Wiggin-Robbins.

1632 Letters

From the Calendar of State Papers, 1574–1628 at the National Archives, Kew, England. (Massachusetts Historical Society Collections, Series 3, Vol. VIII, p. 322)

August 31.

Bristol. 65. Thomas Wiggin to "Master Downing." Complains of the carriage of an unworthy person, Sir Christopher Gardiner, who has lately returned from New England, where he went more than two years ago. Isaac Allerton informed against him to the Governor. Would push some means to stop his mouth, having most scandalously and basely abused "that worthy Governor, Mar. Winthrop." Hopes one Lane, a merchant tailor, who has been in the West Indies, will talk with Mr. Humphreys concerning a certain staple commodity, which he desires to plant in New England. "Staple commodities are the things they want there." Need not declare the happy proceedings and welfare of New England. It is a wonder to see what they have done in so small a time. [Endorsed by Sec. Coke.][562]

November 19.

68. [Capt.] Tho. Wiggin to Sec. Coke. Having lately returned from New England, and visited the English plantations there, particularly the Massachusetts, "the largest, best, and most prospering in all that land," sends some observations of that country and plantation. The country well stored with timber, and will afford cordage, pitch, and tar. The English,

[562] From: "America and West Indies: August 1632," Calendar of State Papers Colonial, America and West Indies, Volume 1: 1574–1660 (1860), p. 155. Author's note: This letter is in the handwriting of someone other than Thomas Wiggin. It does not bear his signature either. He likely sanctioned this letter, but he did not write it or sign it. More likely, Coke or his secretary penned this letter.

numbering about 2,000, and generally most industrious, have done more in three years than others in seven times that space, and at a tenth of the expense. They are loved and respected by the Indians, who repair to the Governor for justice. He [John Winthrop] is a discreet and sober man, wearing plain apparel, assisting in any ordinary labour, and ruling with much mildness and justice. Is induced as an eyewitness to clear the reputation of the plantation from false rumours spread abroad by Sir Christ. Gardiner, Morton, and Ratcliffe, all discontented and scandalous characters; proofs of which are set forth. Upon their false information, Sir Ferd. Gorges is projecting how to deprive the plantation of the privileges granted by the King, and to subvert the Government, which will be the utter ruin of that hopeful colony. Has written this letter out of respect to the general good.[563]

Nov. 26.

Lord Chamberlain's House. Channel Row. Minutes of the Council for New England. Patents granted to Sir Christ Gardiner, Capt. Wiggin, and Mr. Delbordge [Delbridge] of Barnstaple. Delivery of the Great Seal. Examination of abuses in the plantations of New England referred to the Council on 29th May last, by the Lords of the Privy Council, to be speedily taken into consideration Capt. John Mason chosen Vice-President. [Colonial Corresp., 1631, Nov. 4, p. 18.][564]

After carrying copies of the transcriptions of the two 1632 letters around with me for at least two decades, I decided to hire a researcher to find the originals and copy them for me.[565] I supplied him with the source information as related by James Savage, but they are not there. Mike Day[566] found them in the following:

---

[563] From: "America and West Indies: November 1632," Calendar of State Papers Colonial, America and West Indies, Volume 1: 1574–1660 (1860), pp. 156–158. URL: http://www.british-history.ac.uk/report.aspx?compid=69097&strquery=Wiggin Date accessed: 15 June 2009.

[564] From: "America and West Indies: November 1632," Calendar of State Papers Colonial, America and West Indies, Volume 1: 1574–1660 (1860), pp. 156–158. URL: http://www.british-history.ac.uk/report.aspx?compid=69097&strquery=Wiggin Date accessed: 15 June 2009.

[565] Mayday Genealogy, Mike Day, Twickenham, England.

[566] Mayday Genealogy, Twickenham, England.

TNA REF	DATE	DESCRIPTION
CO 1/6 No. 65 Folios 174 and 175	31 Aug 1632	Letter to Master Downing
CO 1/6 No. 68 Folios 183 and 184	19 Nov 1632	Letter to Sir John Coke

James Savage[567] is credited with finding the two letters, in London, England, of which his transcribed copies are found in the Massachusetts Historical Society. I sought the input of the society regarding these transcriptions and received the following letter via e-mail on 21 May 2008:

> Dear Ms. Robbins:
>
> The transcriptions that were sent to you come from Collections of the Massachusetts Historical Society, Vol. VIII of the Third Series. They are part of a section written by James Savage, entitled *Gleanings for New England History.* The transcriptions and statements attached were written by James Savage.
>
> As for references, Savage credits Vol. X of Papers relating to Trade and Plantations fol. 22 and fol. 34. The letters are grouped under the heading Gatherings at her Majesty's State Paper Office, transcribed 9 September 1842.
>
> Sincerely,
> Caitlin Corless
> Library Assistant

The "statements" referenced above as penned by Savage are as follows:

> Ref: Letter dated XIXth daye of November 1632: "To the right hono'ble S'r John Cooke knt. Principall Secretary to hs Ma'tie and one of his highness most hono'ble privie councell: These dr."

Savage makes the comment that Thomas Wiggin's son must have written one of the two letters, as the handwritings are so obviously different on both letters. However, Thomas didn't have a son in 1632. A statement like that

567 Savage, James, antiquary, born in Boston, MA, 13 July 1784; died there 8 Mar 1873. Descended from Maj. Thomas Savage, who emigrated from England to MA in 1635. President of the Mass. Historical Soc. and author of numerous works on the genealogy and history of New England.

brings into focus just how much Wiggin was not researched and known by early historians.

Savage credits the writing of these two letters as happening in Bristol. There is nothing written on either of them indicating where they were penned. Both letters are credited to "Captain Wiggin of New England." "New England" appears on both letters with their dates more than once. If either letter was written while Thomas was in Bristol, it was the August letter to Downing. There are two statements contained within the letter to indicate he was not in London: "I determine to come and may bee to bee with you" and the tone of the reference to Mr. Lane's having been with him.

Another mistake James Savage makes is in his transcription of the August letter as follows: "There was an oulde acquaintance of mine, which was with me of late, on[e] LANCE, a merchant taylor . . ." The name should have been LANE. *Lane* is clearly written in the original letter.

One can only speculate why Savage would submit the wrong source location and the wrong surname for Lane.

Richard Lane[568]—born 1596 in Hereford, Herefordshire—resided in London from about the age of fourteen.[569] Richard was a merchant tailor, and his life story is well written and published in manuscript form by Frederick V. Schultz.[570] Richard Lane's life had many parallels to Thomas Wiggin's in that his father died about the time Richard entered apprenticeship in London, likewise Wiggin. Lane lived in the same London area and frequented the same shops Thomas did. After they parted ways in 1632, they likely never came in contact with each other again.

Richard Lane comes with his own bragging rights. He descends of Sir Ralph Lane, who married Maud Parr, first cousin of Katherine Parr, sixth wife of King Henry VIII. Sir Ralph Lane (son of Sir Ralph Lane),[571] sailed up the Chesapeake Bay in 1585 and is said to be the first Englishman to do so. Roger Lane, father of Richard, was an apothecary in Hereford, St. Peter's Church Parish. Richard Lane would have knowledge of medicine of the day from him. Captain John Lane (Richard's uncle) married the widow Elizabeth Saltonstall.

---

568 Slegel, A. Russell; "Major Samuel Lane (1628–1681) His Ancestry and Some American Descendants," *Maryland Historical Magazine*, Vol. 71, No. 4, Winter 1976. This manuscript is considered the "defining source of much Lane lore in America."

569 14 Dec. 1613, apprenticed to Nathaniel Thornhull of Burchin Lane, London, for seven years. Thornhull was a merchant taylor (sic) and Lane was admitted via his apprenticeship as a freeman of the Merchant Taylors company, age 24, on 26 Feb. 1620.

570 "A Reminiscence Sung 1559–1999," cc2000, Frederick V. Schultz, 1130 Fairway Drive, Waynesboro, VA 22980, dated 4 Jan. 2006.

571 Sir Ralph Lane, born about 1530 and died about 1603 was the son of Sir Ralph Lane who died in 1541.

Her first husband, Charles Saltonstall, is of the prominent family of London and Boston.

Wiggin states in his 1632 letter to Downing that Lane has made a discovery while on a voyage to the West Indies and desires to go to New England to plant it. Wiggin calls this discovery a "staple commodity" but does not tell us what it is. While Lane was sent to Providence Island to plant "his crop of madder," madder cannot be this "discovery" Wiggin speaks of, as madder was an ancient crop that had been grown in England and elsewhere for centuries. Madder's roots rendered the substance that would dye fabrics various shades of red. The hue was not the vibrant scarlet people wanted, nor would it hold its color, having a bad tendency to fade. It also cannot be cochineal[572] as that bug has to have cactus to feed on and become completely dried out before it can be used to render the scarlet red hue. There is a third possibility, the bark of a tree found on the islands that, when boiled, also rendered a scarlet hue. Lane's relative was already harvesting this product and selling it to the French and Spanish ships. The English would not allow its importation at that time.

After a lot of study, I came to the conclusion this crop had to be one that would stand cold winters, and the only answer was some variety of potato. I divulge the debacle of the discovery of the potato[573] elsewhere, and it was no wonder the lords of London rejected this idea totally, sending Lane back to the Caribbean to plant his madder. Lane, needing employment, was probably just as happy to get that assignment and didn't rock the boat.[574]

> *Nor do I say it is filthy to eat potatoes. I do not ridicule the using of them as a sauce. What I laugh at is, the idea of the use of them being a saving; of their going further than bread; of the cultivating of them in liew of wheat adding to the human sustenance of a country . . . As food for cattle, sheep or hots, this is the worst of all the green and root crops; but of this I have said enough before; and therefore, I now dismiss the Potato with the hope, that I shall never again have to write the word, or use the thing.*[575]

---

572 A bug that uses cactus as a host, and when it dries, the natives of Mexico would crush it and use it to dye fabric.

573 By Sir Walter Raleigh, British explorer, historian, first brought the potato into Ireland and then gifted it to Queen Elizabeth I, nearly killing her and her court when they ate the greens and not the root.

574 Gertrude Huens, Antinomianism in English History; London: The Cresset Prom, 1951; "October 1631, Examination of Richard Lane, taylor."

575 William Cobbett (1763–1835), British journalist and reformer. "The poor man's friend" is an apt description of William Cobbett. If you search his name, you will find fascinating biographies of this man, which makes for the most entertaining reading.

Madder was also used for medicinal purposes and the herbal of *Hildegard of Bingen's List* of plants.[576]

Another researcher suggested tobacco as being the crop. However, tobacco was not a new discovery in 1632 and was being grown in Virginia.

Wiggin, describing Lane as an "olde acquaintance," was probably correct. He was not necessarily an "old friend" but, rather, a business acquaintance in London between 1615 and 1627. Lane was married with children[577] by 1628. Wiggin's grandfather, Thomas Gybbes, and Lane's master were likely business acquaintances too.

Emmanuel Downing (1585–1658) and wife Lucy Winthrop, sister of John Winthrop, joined the Massachusetts Bay Colony in 1638. It's his son, Emmanuel Downing Jr., for whom Downing Street, London, the home of the prime ministers of England, is named.. Emmanuel Senior lived in London in 1632 and was recipient of one of the infamous 1632 letters credited to the pen of Captain Thomas Wiggin. After arriving in Salem in 1638, Emmanuel became a heavy investor in John Winthrop Jr.'s iron works on the Saugus.[578] The Downing family lived on Essex Street in Salem, also the home of Governor Simon Bradstreet from 1676 to 1697. Eventually, they would leave Massachusetts and go to Ireland. These families had political and economic ties that ran deep. In 1633, Downing penned a strong defense of the Massachusetts Puritans, saying they "emigrated for conscience's sake and to convert the heathen and were not contemplating secession."[579]

> *Bristoll last of August 1632*
> *Worthye Sir, Although I am not knowne unto you.*

These very first introductory words confirm to us that Thomas Wiggin did not at that time know Downing personally.

> *Yet I cannot but sertifie you of the carrage of an unworthy person, on[e]*
> *Sir Cristofor Gardner*

---

576 Hildegard of Bingen (1098–1179) used natural products for healing. She was a well-respected woman, consulted by kings and commoners alike.

577 Lane married Alice Carter in 1623, daughter of Humfrey Carter, ironmonger of London whose will dated 11 Apr. 1621 was pro 1 June 1621. They had more issue born in Providence Island.

578 Ironworks on the Saugus, E. N. Hartley, Norman, University of Oklahoma Press, ISBN 0-8061-0366, 1957.

579 Ibid, pg. 76.

Gardner was a thorn in the Puritan side. He was living with a mistress (" . . . in the Italian style"[580]), engaging in unacceptable associations with the Native Americans while supposedly an agent for Sir Ferdinando Gorges. He had left behind in England a dubious reputation and was doing nothing to further his cause while in the Colonies. He was eventually turned over to Governor Bradford by the Indians and returned to England as a prisoner.

> *Which is lately arrived here in Bristoll out of New England. He is a man I suppose you have herd of, for I am informed he hath in London two wives.*

To be fair here, one wife was never found, much less two.

> *About two years and some odd months he went from them both with a harlot into New England, where he remained some spasse of tyme, before they had intelligence what he was. But in the ende on[e] or both of his wives, this Gardner, understanding soe much, fearing he should be called in question, fled, thinking to hvegon to the Duc plantation, and soe to have freed himselfe from them, but they speedily making after him, by the helpe of the natives of the country apprehended him and brought him backe, and he remained with them some spasse of tyme. And then on[e[Purchess, a man who liveth in the estern part of New England, comminge to the Massatusets, there did he marrye with this Gardner's wench, and take her awaye and this Gardner both with him; which was done about 12 months since, where this Gardner remained ever since, til the 15th of August last he apeared here in Bristoll, where he doth most scandesle and baselye abuse that worthye Governor Master Winthrop with the Assistants and enhabitants who lyve under him, reporting that they are noelesse than traytors and rebels against his Majestye, with divers others most scandals and aproblous speeches, which on mye owne knolage is most falce, and sayth furthermore, that he was droven to swime for his lyfe, because he stoode for King's cause. But his truth is it was doutinge that they would have hanged him for his abigumle.*

Gardner claimed this "harlot" was his cousin. She was Mary Grove, and she married Thomas Purchase of Brunswick, Maine. Gardiner remained with the

[580] The Puritan Commonwealth, An Historical Review of the Puritan Government in MA; Peter Oliver, Riverside, Cambridge, H. O. Houghton & Co., 1856.

Purchase couple for the span of about a year before he returned to England.[581] However, because of his subversive activities in Massachusetts, he did spend some time "on the run" before he was captured by Native Americans, who had treated him so rough, he had swollen and bruised arms. The natives turned him over to the Massachusetts authorities.

Comparing the two 1632 letters with the last will and testament of Captain Thomas Wiggin, he clearly did not pen or sign one of the letters. It would be speculation as to who did write it, and even if Captain Wiggin knew of its writing, but I would so speculate someone close to Coke and Winthrop wrote that letter. One could spend some time comparing handwritings to find out just who wrote that letter—and we can also conclude that Captain Wiggin might have had another person aiding him in the writing of that letter, such as a secretary—but my question would be "why didn't Captain Wiggin sign it?"

And the debate goes on.

---

[581] Boston between 21 April 1631 and 30 August 1631; Mary Grove (Young's First Planters 333–35, MHSC 3:8:320). She died at Boston on 7 Jan 1655/56 [BVR 52]. In his letter to the Countess of Lincoln, Thomas Dudley wrote of Christopher Gardiner's companion: "This man [Gardiner] had in his family (and yet hath) a gentlewoman, whom he called his kinswoman, and whom one of his wives in her letter names as Mary Grove, affirming her to be a known harlot, whose sending [Gardiner] back into Old England she also desired . . ." One failed attempt to capture Gardiner did secure Mary Grove. . . . "This woman was brought unto us, and confessed her name, and that her mother dwells eight miles from Boirdly, in Salopshire . . . that both herself and Gardiner were Catholics till of late, but were now Protestants. The woman was impenitent and close confessing no more than was wrested from her by her own contradictions. So we have taken order to send her to the two wives in Old England, to search her further." Governor Bradford relates [Gardiner] brought over with him a servant or two and a comely young woman, whom he called his cousin, but it was suspected she (after the Italian manner) was his concubine" [Bradford 352]. Thomas Purchase prevented Mary from being transported back to England. "And then one Purchess, a man who liveth in the eastern part of New England, coming to the Massatusets, there did he marry with this Gardner's wench, and take her away and this Gardner both with him; which was done about twelve months since . . ." [MHSC 3:8:320]

Devon Colic

Devon colic was caused by lead poisoning. Symptoms included severe abdominal pains, which all too often proved fatal. Cider was a traditional drink of the early colonists to New England, and they too suffered from it. It wasn't until the 1760s that Dr. George Baker expounded on the idea that the poisoning was being caused by lead that was used in the cleaning of the cider presses. Once discovered, the elimination of lead saw the end of this malady. Autopsies of colonial skeletons have proven the lead content was high enough to cause death. Such an illness would have been building for years in its victims, and death would have been very painful in the coming. This could have very well been the cause of Captain Thomas Wiggin's death, but we will never know unless the corpse is found and tested.

Even young children were subjected to Devon colic through the drinking of apple juice. This could even have been one of the causes of early infant death.

The Author at Westminster[582]

[582] Photo by Arthur R. Mullis, the author contemplating shadows; Westminster, England.

Postscript

The Shadows Cast by Captain Thomas Wiggin do echo down through the generations; we just have to dig into them to discover what they tell us. He didn't make our job any easier by not leaving us ledgers, journals, or letters. (Or, at least, they haven't been discovered in some dark hiding place. He must have had a library, but what happened to that?)

Captain Wiggin kept his sons close to his side, settling Thomas at Sandy Point and Andrew near Squamscott House on the river, and he never did send them off to college or make use of an apprenticeship. This is significant as it speaks to the Captain's insecurities over losing so many family members early in his life. It's as if keeping his sons close to home guaranteed some sort of protection. It also speaks to the value he put on a college education: none. He felt the only education his sons needed was how to run his vast holdings. I also suspect that once his sons became old enough and trustworthy enough to run the farm, the Captain spent more time in his duties to the Massachusetts Bay Colony; holding court in several places certainly took up a great deal of his time.

If we only had records of "he says, she says," the job of compiling a character for Captain Thomas Wiggin would have been so much easier. However, as is so often quoted, "actions speak louder than words," and I think we have a very solid picture of who Captain Thomas Wiggin was through his actions and those of his associates.

Captain Thomas Wiggin had a mind-set equal to the picture he presented of a strong, upright, capable person determined to meet his life's goals. When you look back over this man's life, you view a very determined man who wanted nothing more than to succeed. Success in his world was measured in land and respect. He gained both.

Wiggin had the ability to adjust to any situation to benefit himself. He eagerly went with the flow of events and had the judgment to figure out which flow would suit his purposes. He moved with ease in any political situation and stayed neutral in religious scenarios.

The Honorable Captain and Governor Thomas Wiggin stood for all the traits we hold in high esteem, even today. One of the reasons this republic has stood the test of time so well is due to men like Wiggin. In his own world, Wiggin built a solid foundation for all that's valued in life that would echo down through the generations of his descendants. He is the trunk of the family tree from which we all descend and which we strive to honor. We take great pride in this man who smiles down at each of us through the ages, and we pray we have made him proud.

I cannot but think Captain Thomas Wiggin would have taken great pride in New Hampshire's motto: *Live free or die.*

Index

C

M

N

O

P

Q

R

S

T

U

V

W

Y

CPSIA information can be obtained
at www.ICGtesting.com
Printed in the USA
BVHW081556310720
585152BV00002B/110/J

9 781514 476987